Pastor Ross F. Norris

The Lord's Last Call

PUBLISHING GROUP

Published by
Hara Publishing
P.O. Box 19732
Seattle, WA 98109
(425) 775-7868

ISBN: 1-883697-19-0
Library of Congress Number: 98-073707

Manufactured in the United States
10 9 8 7 6 5 4 3 2

Cover Design: Scott Carnz
Desktop Publishing: Scott & Shirley Fisher

Table Of Contents

IMPORTANT NOTE:

UNLESS OTHERWISE STATED, **ALL SCRIPTURE REFERENCES ARE FROM THE AUTHORIZED KING JAMES BIBLE.** (Including spelling & pronunciation of words.) **NOT** The *New* King James Version.

Forward

As I perused this manuscript, the following bit of verse came to mind:

"This book is the soul of Ross Norris laid bare. Let the timid, the skeptic, the traditionalists beware. But to the bold and believing, there's great power and joy, as they walk in the truth which nothing can destroy."

One cannot get very far into this book before realising that the author is a champion for the Pentecostal experience of the Baptism of the Holy Ghost with speaking in other tongues.

Many readers will no doubt find some of the conclusions in this book controversial, but the author is a flame with passion to see the Church of Jesus Christ appropriate all that Calvary has provided - that they may live a power filled, victorious life in Christ.

With confidence and authority, the author reaffirms again and again, the fact that every believer should be baptized with the Holy Ghost. This is a needful, and often sadly neglected message in the Church of Jesus Christ today.

Love in Jesus
Pastor Kirk Duncan
Bible Fellowship, Surrey, British Columbia, Canada

About The Author

With joy and thankfulness on behalf of the many many people in this country, and those around the world, whose lives have been touched through the Ministry of Pastor Ross Norris, I share these things.

In the early days of his life in Christ, the Lord spake to him through the laying on of hands in 1958 at the Bible Camp in Ocean Park, Crescent Beach, British Columbia, attended by many ministries, including Pastor Reg Layzell, Pastor Schoch and Pastor Broker who was used of the Lord in Prophecy saying:

"Ross Norris, the Lord has called thee and as Paul thou shalt go from city to city, nation to nation, and thou shalt never be still. Thou shalt have the strength of Samson. Mountains of darkness shall stand before thee and much troubles in many areas. But hear this saith the Lord, that I am in charge, and thou shalt overcome them all. For I have set before thee stepping stones, a place for thee to walk in My way, even My Holy Way, saith the Lord. For I have spoken it saith the Lord."

In those days of a glorious revival and outpouring still through the revival in North Battleford, Saskatchewan, I'm sure Pastor Ross did not yet know the hardships, suffering and heartbreak that was ahead. He heard and obeyed the Word of the Lord and with faith was sent out to many places to build and found many works of the Lord, and these local churches remain today.

In 1968, he travelled with Pastor Reg Layzell to Uganda and Kenya, East Africa. Every one that was there recalls how when Pastor Ross ministered to the thousands of Africans and the anointing and glory of the Lord was so strong and so evident that his complete body was lifted up. His toes barely touched the ground as his face shone white with the Shakina Glory of God.

Just recently in 1997, again we saw the anointing of the Lord upon his ministry. As he walked through the streets and alleys of Madras, India. People came out of their homes and children converged on him just to touch him and be near. At that time he laid hands on them and the deaf heard, the dumb spake. Health was restored to those who came and many were baptized in the Holy Ghost.

Another important prophecy was later to come to Pastor Ross in 1981, through Dr. Robert Mueller. The Lord said:

"Brother Norris, you've been a blessing to many, and you've been an encouragement to many and where your ministry has gone, many people have been helped. I'd like you to receive even as you have given, and as you withdraw with Me and let My Spirit minister to you, you are going to get a deeper revelation and a stronger understanding of the Scriptures and they are going to come alive to you and you are going to speak them out with purity and righteousness. You just rest in Me and know that I have ordained you and put you forth and I am the source of your power and I am your strength. For I want you to know Me as your friend."

In the early 1980's, Pastor Ross and Shirley Norris, by the leading of the Holy Ghost founded the North Shore Christian Centre, in North Vancouver, British Columbia. With prayer warriors and pillars like Sister Jean Winczura, they forged ahead and as always, ministered the truth unwavering while the Church grew daily and I might say, that 99 percent of the church is baptized in the Holy Ghost and speaks in other tongues with the love of God shed abroad in their hearts by the Holy Ghost. As a Father in the Church Pastor Ross' vision was always to guide, teach and raise up young Pastors to preach the truth, not with just words, but in demonstration and power by the HOLY GHOST and FIRE, and to send them out to the nations of the world.

Pastor Ross, always fearing and reverencing the timing of the moving of the Holy Spirit, obeyed the moving of the Holy Spirit one night, which became the most precious memory of my life.

I was eight years old when we were driving on the highway at night, and as I laid on the back seat of the family vehicle, I remember feeling this warmth and presence of the Lord which I did not understand. As I was looking up at the stars in the night sky, I began to cry. With urgency I tapped my dad on the shoulder and said, "Daddy!" When he turned around and saw that I was crying he said, "What's wrong?" I replied, "I want Jesus in my heart right now!" Most parents would have said, "That's wonderful honey, but we're on the freeway, and we'll be there soon and we'll pray together then." But Pastor Ross fearing the moving and timing of the Lord's calling, immediately pulled over to the side of the highway. As he knelt on the concrete of the highway with cars whizzing by, I knelt on the floor of the back seat, and there I accepted personally the Lord Jesus into my heart. There was nothing too small or too insignificant about a child hearing the call of the Lord Jesus.

Years later, with that same reverence to the Father's timing and obedience to His word and in the truth unwavering, Pastor Ross, the voice of one crying in the wilderness, answered the call and wrote this book, "THE LORD'S LAST CALL".

Deborah Smith

Dedication

I dedicate this book to the Glory of God and His Kingdom and especially to the young men and women, who have caught the same vision that is written herein. They are an encouragement to me in my ministry to know that I have not ministered in vain.

A very special word to my wife Shirley, a good soldier of Jesus Christ who through her ministry in the Word of Knowledge that she received as a Spiritual Gift from the Holy Ghost, has encouraged so many of the sheep in her counseling. She is my friend and encouragement standing always beside me knowing the truth of the Word of God for herself. We have together, dedicated our lives in sacrifice for the Kingdom of God.

Through much heartache, crying and tears, my dear wife Shirley and I agree together with our love for the Church of Jesus Christ, to write to you all the truth of the baptism of the Holy Ghost no matter what the cost.

Pastor Ross F. Norris

Acknowledgments

I would like to thank Joan Styles for her love, and work in helping put together the final stages of the book.

Also, I thank my dear sister Lori Donnelly who laboured unceasingly in helping me put this book together. The Lord bless her for her labour of love.

A very, very special thanks to Jim Collins, my brother, and servant of the Lord, a renowned Canadian artist, who did the artwork for the cover of this book.

I would also like to thank my dear sister, Dr. E. Charlotte Baker for her input which I appreciate so very much, whom I have known for 38 years and appreciated her in the ministry of praise and worship for she has had a great effect on my ministry.

I would like to acknowledge Pastor Reg Layzell Pastor of Glad Tidings Temple, who was my mentor, and taught me the way of truth and to search the scriptures for myself. He also administered to me the discipline that was required in my early days.

Brother Earle Hewitt who established me in the faith when I was young in the Lord, especially instilled in my heart, God's love for me, and my calling in the Kingdom of God.

Both Pastor Layzell and Brother Hewitt have finished their work here on earth, and have gone to be with the Lord, and to us they throw the torch, that the fire from the alter of God shall ever be burning as we wait for the coming of our Great Shepherd, The Lord Jesus Christ.

I thank also Jean Winczura our special friend and sister who laboured with us in our ministry, who was always there when we needed her.

And a very special mention to my daughter Debbie, who laboured with me in putting this book together, whom I thank very much for her encouragement in completing this book.

Because I love the brethren who are presently labouring with me as servants of Jesus Christ, Pastor Rob Tarnowski, and my dear son Pastor David Norris and to all our Pastors who labour in our branch works. The Lord Jesus anoint you with his presence to the revelation and vision of his plan he has given us to reach the world in our generation.

Pastor Ross F. Norris

Author's Preface

Even as I write this message to all the pastors and teachers, and the children of the Lord, let it be known unto you that I also am challenged by the message on the Baptism of the Holy Ghost.

I know for a surety in my old age, the Lord has committed unto me without reservation in these end times, the wake up call to the Church.

THERE ARE FOUR SCRIPTURES WHICH SPIRITUALLY CHALLENGE THE PRESENT DAY TEACHING, THAT REJECTS THE BAPTISM OF THE HOLY GHOST

THE FIRST SCRIPTURE:

JESUS OUR LORD IS THE HOLY GHOST

1 John 5:7 **"There are THREE that BEAR RECORD IN HEAVEN, THE FATHER, THE WORD *(SON)* AND THE HOLY GHOST: "AND THESE THREE ARE ONE".**

So many in their spiritual blindness, resist the baptism of the Holy Ghost AND THE SPEAKING IN OTHER TONGUES! AS THE FATHER, THE SON AND THE HOLY GHOST **"ARE ONE"**, THEN WHEN WE RESIST THE HOLY GHOST, WE RESIST ALL THREE, BECAUSE THEY ARE ONE! Also, we then RESIST OUR LORD JESUS WHO IS THE HOLY GHOST, AND THE BAPTIZER WITH THE HOLY GHOST.

Matt 3:11 **"I indeed baptize you with WATER unto REPENTANCE: But HE that cometh after me is mightier than I, whose shoes I am not worthy to bear: HE *(JESUS)* SHALL BAPTIZE YOU WITH THE HOLY GHOST, AND WITH FIRE."**

| John 1:33 | "And I knew him not: but He that sent me to baptize with water, the same said unto me, Upon whom thou shalt see the Spirit descending, and remaining on him, the same is HE WHICH BAPTIZETH WITH THE HOLY GHOST." |

THE SECOND SCRIPTURE:
THE LORD IS THE ONE THAT SPEAKS IN TONGUES

| Isaiah 28:11-12 | "FOR WITH STAMMERING LIPS AND ANOTHER TONGUE, WILL HE SPEAK TO THIS PEOPLE. To whom He said, This is the rest wherewith ye may cause the weary to rest; and this is the refreshing: YET THEY WOULD NOT HEAR." |

| 1 Corinth 14:21 | Paul mentions the above scripture, "IN THE LAW IT IS WRITTEN, WITH MEN OF OTHER TONGUES AND OTHER LIPS WILL I SPEAK unto this people; AND YET FOR ALL THAT THEY WILL NOT HEAR ME, SAITH THE LORD!" |

How much clearer can the Lord reveal the truth, that it is the **LORD HIMSELF** THAT SPEAKS IN TONGUES out of a human body, which is HIS TEMPLE THAT WAS CREATED FOR HIM in Genesis 1:26 - Genesis 2:7.

| Genesis 1:26 | "And God said, Let us make man in our image, after our likeness: and let them have dominion over the fish of the sea, and over the fowl of the air, and over the cattle, and over all the earth, and over every creeping thing that creepeth upon the earth." |

| Genesis 2:7 | "And the LORD God formed man of the dust of the ground, and breathed into his nostrils the breath of life; and man became a living soul." |

Note: If we resist the BAPTISM OF THE HOLY GHOST and the SPEAKING IN OTHER TONGUES, we are RESISTING THE LORD, WHO WAS CRUCIFIED FOR OUR SINS, AND IS SPEAKING IN OTHER TONGUES. Care to argue with THE LORD?

THE THIRD SCRIPTURE:
JESUS IS THE BAPTIZER WITH THE HOLY GHOST

Matt 3:11   "I indeed baptize you with WATER unto
               REPENTANCE: But HE that cometh after me
               is mightier than I, whose shoes I am not worthy
               to bear:

HE *(JESUS)* **SHALL BAPTIZE YOU WITH THE HOLY GHOST, AND WITH FIRE."**

I say, WAKE UP CHURCH TO THE SPIRITUAL TRUTH OF THE BAPTISM OF THE HOLY GHOST. WE CANNOT CALL JESUS OUR LORD AND THEN RESIST HIM WHEN HE **IS** THE BAPTIZER WITH THE HOLY GHOST!!

THE FOURTH SCRIPTURE:

THE SPIRIT THAT WE ARE BORN AGAIN OF
GAVE THE UTTERANCE OF TONGUES

Acts 2:4   "And they were ALL FILLED WITH THE
               HOLY GHOST, and began to SPEAK WITH
               OTHER TONGUES, AS THE SPIRIT GAVE
               THEM UTTERANCE."

I would say, dear children of the Lord, that if we are born again of the spirit of God, how can we resist the Holy Ghost baptism when **the SPIRIT** THAT WE ARE BORN OF **GAVE THE UTTERANCE** OF SPEAKING IN OTHER TONGUES ON THE DAY OF PENTECOST?!

REMEMBER: THE PROPHET SAID, "TO THE LAW AND TO
                  THE TESTIMONY:
Isaiah 8:20   IF THEY SPEAK NOT ACCORDING TO
                  THIS WORD, IT IS BECAUSE THERE IS
                  NO LIGHT IN THEM." (For the Spirit and the
                  Word agree!)

If we reject the word that is written herein, there is something wrong with the way we have been taught, for Jesus IS the Word!

Introduction

To my dear pastors and brethren in the faith, grace and peace be unto you from God the Father and our Lord Jesus Christ!

After forty years in the ministry of the Gospel of our Lord Jesus Christ and now a father in the church, yet not known, but well known, the Lord has laid upon me THE LORD'S LAST CALL to His church of which I am a member.

HISTORY IS REPEATING ITSELF. When our precious Lord Jesus came the first time and was presented to the religious leaders of that day, they rejected Him, calling Him many names because His word upset their traditions. And, if the religious leaders had had their way, we would have no Saviour and no salvation and still be in our sins.

Today, many religious leaders are rejecting Him once more by rejecting the baptism of the HOLY GHOST when Jesus IS the baptizer with the Holy Ghost!

MATTHEW 3:11 reads, "I INDEED BAPTIZE YOU WITH WATER UNTO REPENTANCE: BUT HE THAT COMETH AFTER ME IS MIGHTIER THAN I, WHOSE SHOES I AM NOT WORTHY TO BEAR: **HE** SHALL BAPTIZE YOU WITH THE HOLY GHOST AND WITH FIRE."

As I proceed the Lord will reveal that He is not only the baptizer with the Holy Ghost but that He IS the Holy Ghost. He IS also the one that speaks in tongues out of His temple, which is our human body. Also, the Spirit we are born of spoke in tongues on the day of Pentecost. I shall reveal by the Word of the Lord, following this introduction, the scriptures that substantiate the above.

By now you may ask yourself this question, "HOW CAN I RECEIVE JESUS AS MY LORD AND SAVIOUR AND REJECT THE BAPTISM OF THE HOLY GHOST, WHEN JESUS IS THE BAPTIZER WITH THE HOLY GHOST?"

It is a sad hour to find that many pastors have built their denominations around the born again experience and have rejected the baptism of the Holy Ghost because of the spiritual blindness of their hearts.

Dear children of the Lord, though I may speak from time to time in this writing with great boldness, please bear with me for it is with much love and for your ministry and the church that the truth of the baptism of the Holy Ghost be revealed in this writing.

I SAY ONCE MORE that there is only one church, the many membered body of Christ. The rejection by many leaders regarding the baptism of the Holy Ghost and the speaking in other tongues has divided the church when the word of God so plainly reveals that the baptism of the Holy Ghost is for every child of God in this hour!

Finally, I know that all the ministry will stand before the Lord in that day to give an account of what we have done in our ministry. I sincerely do not want to be known as one that divided the church through the rejection of the baptism of the Holy Ghost or any other word that the Lord has spoken!

I AM SURE, DEAR CHILDREN OF THE LORD, *AFTER* YOU HAVE READ WITH AN OPEN HEART, THIS WRITING ON THE BAPTISM OF THE HOLY GHOST, you will not cause a division in THE PRECIOUS CHURCH OF JESUS, but preach it from the house tops that we may be ONE and have power in our ministries!

Chapter One

Signs
Of
The
Last Days

SIGNS IN THE WORLD

The signs of the last days and the return of our Lord Jesus can take place at any time!

Matt 24:44   **"Therefore be ye also ready: for in such an hour as ye THINK NOT the Son of man cometh."**

Again, I say, IT IS THE LAST CALL from the Lord, and the SIGNS OF HIS COMING are everywhere and many are sleeping, saying in their heart, "HE DELAYETH HIS COMING" by the way they live for Christ!

Matt 24:3   **READ:**
                                  The most important question for this hour,...
                                  "...WHAT SHALL BE THE SIGN OF THY COMING AND OF THE END OF THE WORLD?"

Matt 24:4-5   "And Jesus answered and said unto them, **TAKE HEED THAT NO MAN DECEIVE YOU. FOR MANY SHALL COME IN MY NAME, SAYING, I AM CHRIST; AND SHALL DECEIVE MANY."**

To all the children of the Lord. Deception is everywhere, as Satan goes **"all out"** through his subtlety to deceive and destroy the child of God by diminishing the Word! If ever there was a time for the children of the Lord to search the Word of God for themselves, it is now! **"For your faith should not stand in the wisdom of man's preaching, but in the DEMONSTRATION and POWER of the HOLY GHOST."**

THE DECEPTIONS THE CHURCH FACES TODAY

Matt 24:   ...**"What shall be THE SIGN OF THY COMING AND OF THE END of THE world?"**

To this question, THE LORD REPLIED, **"Take heed that no man deceive you. For many shall come in my name saying I am CHRIST and shall deceive many."**

That deception is in the land today, while they say HE IS Christ, they deny THE WORD which IS CHRIST. They honour ME with their lips, but their heart is far from ME, denying the Lord that bought them.

At a glance we can see the corruption in other Bibles out there. The three versions in particular are: The New International Version; The American Standard Version, and; The Living Bible. They are written as though Satan wrote them himself.

Lk 8:12   Jesus said, **"... then cometh the devil, and taketh away the Word.."**

These people who changed the Word of God, have no fear of the consequence in adding or taking away from the Word.

Rev 22:18   **"For I testify unto every man that heareth the words of the prophecy of this book, If any man shall add unto these things, God shall add unto him the plagues that are written in this book:"**

Deut 4:1-2   **"Now therefore hearken, O Israel, unto the statutes and unto the judgments, which I teach you, for to do them, that ye may live, and go in and possess the land which the LORD God of your fathers giveth you."**

Example: N.I.V. says in Acts 19:2 "Did you receive the Holy Spirit when you believed?"
The Authorized King James Bible states: **Acts 19:2 "He said unto them, Have ye received the Holy Ghost since ye believed? And they said unto him, We have not so much as heard whether there be any Holy Ghost."**

These same people did away with the virgin birth in the N.I.V. and the N.A.S. when they referred to Joseph as the father of Jesus in Luke 2:33. The entire N.I.V. also completely omitted "THE GODHEAD" where ALL truth originated. And last of all I shall mention that the N.I.V. omitted the "BLOOD" in many places in particular:

Colossians 1:14 where it reads: "In whom we have redemption, the forgiveness of sins."

The Authorized King James Bible states: **Colossians 1:14 - "In whom we have redemption THROUGH HIS BLOOD, even the forgiveness of sins:"**

What else can I say? The lies in these new versions are too numerous to mention.

Note: The same people that changed the Word and added to it in Acts 19:2, **"He said unto them, Have ye received the Holy Ghost SINCE ye believed? And they said unto him, We have not so much as heard whether there be any Holy Ghost."**

All three versions mentioned say, "Did you receive the Holy Spirit WHEN you believed?" The people that corrupted the Word are the same people that have corrupted the Word in all these three Bibles. Something to think about!

Matt 24:6-7   SIGNS IN THE NATIONS OF THE WORLD, **"AND YE SHALL HEAR OF WARS AND RUMORS OF WARS: ...FOR NATION SHALL RISE AGAINST NATION, AND KINGDOM AGAINST KINGDOM: AND THERE SHALL BE FAMINES, AND PESTILENCES, AND EARTHQUAKES, IN DIVERS PLACES. ALL THESE ARE THE BEGINNING OF SORROWS."**

The coming of our Lord is fast approaching, and these signs are being revealed all around us today as we read the news headlines, and see it before our very eyes.

THE GREATEST SIGN OF HIS COMING IS TAKING PLACE TODAY!

THE DAYS OF LOT

Lk 17:28-30   **"LIKEWISE ALSO AS IT WAS IN THE DAYS OF LOT; THEY DID EAT, THEY DRANK, THEY BOUGHT, THEY SOLD, THEY**

PLANTED, THEY BUILDED; BUT THE
SAME DAY THAT LOT WENT OUT OF
SODOM IT RAINED FIRE AND
BRIMSTONE FROM HEAVEN, AND
DESTROYED THEM ALL. Even thus shall it
be in the day when the son of man is revealed."

WE ARE FAST APPROACHING THE COMING OF OUR LORD

Due to the INCREASE OF HOMOSEXUALITY all over the WORLD, WE
MUST NOT LOSE sight that HOMOSEXUALITY IS ONE OF THE
GREATEST SIGNS OF THE END OF THIS AGE, AND THE COMING OF
OUR LORD! Homosexuality destroys our moral values and discredits the
creation of God - man and woman as Christ and the Church.

Recently, when "THE GAY COMMUNITY" took over the streets of Vancouver,
thousands paraded OPENLY. They made THIS PROCLAMATION,
"THE GAY COMMUNITY IS OUT OF THE CLOSET AT LAST AND
MAY OPENLY DECLARE THEIR HOMOSEXUALITY!"

THE PROPHETS FORETOLD OF THESE DAYS IN WHICH WE LIVE

Is 3:9   **"THE SHEW OF THEIR COUNTENANCE,
                                  DOTH WITNESS AGAINST THEM; THEY
                                  DECLARE THEIR SIN AS SODOM, THEY
                                  HIDE IT NOT. WOE UNTO THEIR SOUL!
                                  FOR THEY HAVE REWARDED EVIL UNTO
                                  THEMSELVES."**

Many so-called churches have even ORDAINED some of them into THE
MINISTRY OF THE GOSPEL. WHAT WILL SATAN DO NEXT to TRY TO
DESTROY THE TRUE CHURCH OF JESUS CHRIST?

THE FIRST ACT OF SODOMY BY HAM

Gen 9:20-25   **READ:**
                                  **"And Noah awoke from his wine, and knew what
                                  his younger son had done unto him."**

THE MEN OF SODOM AS HOMOSEXUALS TODAY

Gen 13:12-13   READ:
                        "BUT THE MEN OF SODOM WERE
                        WICKED AND SINNERS BEFORE THE
                        LORD EXCEEDINGLY."

THE ANGELS OF THE LORD VISIT SODOM

Gen 19:1-28   READ:

                        The husbands of LOT'S two daughters, refuse
                        to leave the HOMOSEXUAL LIFESTYLE!

THERE IS STILL HOPE FOR THE HOMOSEXUAL IF THEY WILL LEAVE
THEIR HOMOSEXUAL LIFESTYLE AND TURN TO CHRIST.

Jude Verses 7-8   SODOM IS SET FORTH AS AN EXAMPLE:
                        "Even as Sodom and Gomorrha, and the cities
                        about them in like manner, giving themselves
                        over to fornication, and going after strange flesh,
                        are set forth FOR AN EXAMPLE, SUFFERING
                        THE VENGEANCE OF ETERNAL FIRE.
                        Likewise also these *filthy* dreamers defile the
                        flesh, DESPISE DOMINION, AND SPEAK
                        EVIL OF DIGNITIES."

A STRONG MESSAGE TO HOMOSEXUALS AND LESBIANS

Rom 1:24-32   "Wherefore GOD also GAVE THEM UP TO
                        UNCLEANNESS through the LUSTS of THEIR
                        OWN HEARTS, to DISHONOUR their own
                        BODIES BETWEEN THEMSELVES:

                        Who changed the TRUTH OF GOD INTO A
                        LIE, and worshipped and served the creature
                        more than the CREATOR, who is blessed for
                        ever. Amen.

FOR THIS CAUSE GOD GAVE THEM UP UNTO VILE AFFECTIONS: for even their women did change the natural use into that which is AGAINST NATURE: (Women with women).

And likewise ALSO THE MEN, LEAVING THE NATURAL USE of the WOMAN, BURNED IN THEIR LUST ONE TOWARD ANOTHER; MEN WITH MEN WORKING that which is UNSEEMLY, AND RECEIVING IN THEMSELVES THAT RECOMPENCE OF THEIR ERROR WHICH WAS MEET.

And even as THEY DID NOT LIKE TO RETAIN GOD IN *THEIR* KNOWLEDGE, GOD gave them over to a REPROBATE MIND, to do those things which are not convenient;

Being FILLED with ALL unrighteousness, fornication, wickedness, covetousness, maliciousness; full of envy, murder, debate, deceit, malignity; whispers, - (Revealing what the Lord thinks of homosexuals today.)

Backbiters, haters of God, despiteful, proud, boasters, inventors of evil things, disobedient to parents,

Without understanding, covenant breakers, without natural affection, implacable, unmerciful:

Who <u>KNOWING THE JUDGMENT OF GOD,</u> that THEY WHICH COMMIT SUCH THINGS ARE WORTHY OF DEATH, *NOT <u>ONLY DO</u> THE SAME, BUT HAVE <u>PLEASURE IN THEM</u> THAT DO THEM.*"

Peter gives another example: **THE SINS AND
JUDGMENT OF SODOM AND GOMORRHA
ARE GIVEN AS AN EXAMPLE UNTO
THOSE WHO AFTERWARDS SHOULD
LIVE UNGODLY.**

2 Pet 2:4-6   **"For if God spared not the angels that sinned,
but cast them down to hell, and delivered them
into chains of darkness, to be reserved
unto judgment;**

**And spared not the old world, but saved Noah
the eighth person, a preacher of righteousness,
bringing in the flood upon the world of
the ungodly;**

**And turning the cities of Sodom and Gomorrha
into ashes condemned them with an overthrow,
making them an example unto those that after
should live ungodly;"**

Gen 2:18-25   God's plan for man and woman, (shadow of the
church). **"And the rib which the LORD GOD
had taken from man, MADE HE A WOMAN..."**
(NOT A MAN).

Gen 1:28   **"...Be fruitful and multiply and REPLENISH
THE EARTH**..." This cannot be fulfilled with
same sex partners.

THERE IS DELIVERANCE FOR HOMOSEXUALS AND LESBIANS IF
THEY LEAVE their wicked lifestyles as LOT did.

2 Pet 2:7-8   **"AND DELIVERED JUST LOT, VEXED
WITH THE FILTHY CONVERSATION OF
THE WICKED:**

(For that righteous man dwelling AMONG
THEM, in SEEING AND HEARING, VEXED
HIS RIGHTEOUS SOUL FROM DAY TO DAY
with their unlawful deeds;)"

The Christians, as Lot, are seeing and hearing about them, vexing their
righteous souls from day to day, especially as some are made teachers of our
children at school!

SIGNS IN THE CHURCH

THE LORD REVEALS HOW DECEPTION WILL COME IN THE CHURCH

Lk 12:45-47	The "...SERVANT says in HIS HEART, THE LORD DELAYETH HIS COMING..." (Causing many to be lukewarm as they are today.)
Rev 3:15-16	"I know thy works, that thou art neither cold nor hot: I would thou wert cold or hot. So then because thou art lukewarm, and neither cold nor hot, I will spue thee out of my mouth." (Something to think about.)
2 Thes 2:3	"Let no man deceive you by any means: for THAT DAY shall not come, EXCEPT THERE COME A FALLING AWAY FIRST,..."

Again, as we know many are preaching, "There is going to be a great revival
in the Church;" however, the scriptures teach the opposite. Did you know
that you and I can still attend church on Sunday and have already fallen away
from our relationship with the Lord?

2 Thes 2:7	"For the MYSTERY OF INIQUITY doth already work: ONLY HE WHO NOW LETTETH WILL LET, until be he TAKEN OUT OF THE WAY."

This scripture, again, reveals it is not enough to say, "I am a Christian" or, "I am saved" for the mystery of iniquity is working and our salvation is in our own hands. There is a possibility we could be taken out of THE WAY if we will let it.

2 Tim 3:1-5   **READ:**
                          "...Lovers of PLEASURE more than lovers of GOD.

                          HAVING A FORM OF GODLINESS, but DENYING THE POWER thereof, FROM SUCH TURN AWAY."

Many say that they are Christians, and act like Christians but at the same time reject the POWER of the Holy Ghost, that will lead them into further TRUTH.

2 Tim 3:7   **"EVER LEARNING, and NEVER ABLE TO COME TO THE KNOWLEDGE OF THE TRUTH."** (The Holy Ghost)

Here again is THE SPIRIT OF TRUTH, that is revealed in the BAPTISM OF THE HOLY GHOST.

2 TIM 4:3   **"The time will come when they will not endure SOUND DOCTRINE; But after their own LUSTS, shall they heap to themselves TEACHERS, having itching EARS;"**

Hebrews 6:1 reveals the doctrines of the Church including the baptism of the Holy Ghost. Many, rejecting the Holy Ghost baptism and speaking in other tongues, find a local church that does not believe and have "itching ears" to hear what that church says against the Holy Ghost, or, eliminate THE HOLY GHOST altogether!

2 Tim 4:4   **"AND THEY SHALL TURN AWAY THEIR EARS FROM THE TRUTH, AND SHALL BE TURNED UNTO FABLES."**

Again, Jesus said, **"I am the way, <u>THE TRUTH</u> and the LIFE."** Many today are turning their ears from the TRUTH which is the Holy Ghost and our Lord Jesus. We cannot by-pass the TRUTH to arrive at the LIFE.

Titus 1:16   **"THEY PROFESS THAT THEY KNOW GOD; BUT IN WORKS THEY DENY HIM, BEING ABOMINABLE, AND DISOBEDIENT, AND UNTO EVERY GOOD WORK REPROBATE."**

Again, the TRUTH **IS** Jesus or the Holy Ghost. How often have I heard on television Church leaders, through their SPIRITUAL BLINDNESS, speak evil of tongues and the baptism of the Holy Ghost which is the Spirit of TRUTH, when JESUS **IS** THE BAPTIZER WITH THE HOLY GHOST, revealed in the following scriptures.

Matt 3:11   **"I INDEED BAPTIZE YOU WITH WATER UNTO REPENTANCE: BUT HE THAT COMETH AFTER ME IS MIGHTIER THAN I, WHOSE SHOES I AM NOT WORTHY TO BEAR: HE SHALL BAPTIZE YOU WITH THE HOLY GHOST, AND *WITH* FIRE:"**

Jn 1:33   **"AND I KNEW HIM NOT: BUT HE THAT SENT ME TO BAPTIZE WITH WATER, THE SAME SAID UNTO ME, UPON WHOM THOU SHALT SEE THE SPIRIT DESCENDING, AND REMAINING ON HIM, THE SAME IS HE WHICH BAPTIZETH WITH THE HOLY GHOST."**

2 Pet 2:2-3   **"AND MANY SHALL FOLLOW THEIR PERNICIOUS WAYS; BY REASON OF WHOM THE WAY OF TRUTH SHALL BE EVIL SPOKEN OF.** (The HOLY GHOST BAPTISM) **AND THROUGH COVETOUSNESS SHALL THEY WITH FEIGNED WORDS MAKE MERCHANDISE OF YOU: WHOSE**

JUDGMENT NOW OF A LONG TIME LINGERETH NOT, AND THEIR DAMNATION SLUMBERETH NOT."

This scripture is revealed mostly on television where false teachers ask for your tithes and offerings. This practice will weaken the local Church. The Lord says, **"Bring all your tithes into the storehouse that there may be meat in my house."** Then these false teachers through their covetousness cannot **"make merchandise of you."**

1 Tim 4:1   **"NOW THE SPIRIT SPEAKETH EXPRESSLY, THAT IN THE LATTER TIMES SOME SHALL DEPART FROM THE FAITH, GIVING HEED TO SEDUCING SPIRITS, AND DOCTRINES OF DEVILS;"**

We still say we are Christians and go to Church, but we've departed from the faith.

Jude 18   **"HOW THAT THEY TOLD YOU THERE SHOULD BE MOCKERS IN THE LAST TIME, WHO SHOULD WALK AFTER THEIR OWN UNGODLY LUSTS."**

The above scripture speaks of those that profess they are Christians, "Lovers of pleasure more than lovers of God," who cannot cease from sin and put Jesus to an open shame.

Jude 19   **"These be they who SEPARATE themselves, SENSUAL, having NOT THE SPIRIT."**

Many separate themselves from churches that preach the baptism of the Holy Ghost. It is not the Spirit leading them but their sensual desires to escape THE TRUTH and the conviction of THE HOLY GHOST, because of the anointing.

Lk 21:28   **"And when THESE THINGS begin to COME TO PASS, LOOK UP, and lift up your heads; FOR YOUR REDEMPTION DRAWETH NIGH."**

Chapter Two

Satan's Deception

THERE ARE THREE EVENTS IN THE BIBLE WHERE SATAN HAS
ATTACKED THE WORD OF GOD THROUGH HIS SUBTLETY.

THE REASON FOR WRITING THIS BOOK is to:

1.   EXPOSE SATAN'S DECEPTIVE WAYS IN THE BEGINNING,
2.   REVEAL HOW THAT MANY CHRISTIANS ARE DECEIVED
      REGARDING THEIR SPIRIT BIRTH,
3.   REVEAL THEIR REJECTION OF THE BAPTISM OF THE
      HOLY GHOST.

Many Christians are deceived today by Satan's voice as he transforms
himself into a "minister of righteousness," rejecting the truth, altering the
Word, diminishing from the Word and adding to it.

THE <u>EVIDENCE</u> OF SATAN'S INFLUENCE on the Church today is seen
in the division of the Church, which is His body, when Jesus prayed that we
be ONE.

THE FIRST ATTACK ON OUR OBEDIENCE TO THE WORD OF GOD

THE LORD SPAKE AND GAVE THE CONDITIONS:

Gen 2:16:   "...Of every tree of the garden thou mayest freely eat."

Gen 2:17:   "But the tree of knowledge of good and evil, thou shalt not
                eat of it: for the day that thou eatest thereof **THOU SHALT
                SURELY DIE."** Satan knew the Word of the Lord, and the
                conditions the Lord gave.

Adam had beautiful fellowship with God in the garden and Satan set about to
destroy that fellowship by his subtlety.

SATAN SPEAKS TO CHALLENGE THE WORD:

Gen 3:1   "Now the serpent was more subtle than any beast of the
                field which the LORD God had made. And he said unto
                the woman,..."

"YEA, HATH GOD SAID, YE SHALL NOT EAT OF <u>EVERY TREE</u> OF THE GARDEN?"

"Yea hath God said": Satan sows doubt and the attack begins. Satan through his subtlety adds "EVERY TREE". This would include the tree of knowledge of good and evil, that would cause Adam and Eve to die.

Gen 3:2-3 **READ:**
      The woman knows and repeats to Satan what the LORD really said. Many know what the Lord said regarding the baptism of the Holy Ghost, but would rather listen to Satan's deceptive voice, than the voice of the Lord of Glory that died for their sins and rose again.

Acts 19:2 **READ:**
      Is a good example of how the new versions of the Bible written by man were changed to say: "Did you receive the Holy Spirit **<u>WHEN</u>** you believed?" (Quoted from The Living Bible) Satan again sows the doubt, when he knows that we receive the Holy Ghost baptism **<u>AFTER</u>** we believe!

Gen 3:4   "And the serpent said unto the woman, **YE SHALL NOT SURELY DIE!"**

The deceptive voice of Satan speaks to every child of God today, causing them to profess they are Christians while they live like the world. They are "dreaming" to think that they cannot lose their salvation. It is quite evident today that Satan is a liar; because the soul that sinneth, **it shall die.**

Because of the subtlety of Satan and **<u>DISOBEDIENCE</u>** to the Word of God, sin came upon the human race! Through obedience to the Word of God <u>sin shall be removed from the human race</u>!

SATAN WAS VICTORIOUS IN THE FIRST ATTACK!

THE SECOND ATTACK

OUR SPIRITUAL BIRTH INTO THE KINGDOM OF GOD

If Satan is unable to stop our spiritual birth into the Kingdom of God, he will by subtlety hinder our walk in the Kingdom by attacking our salvation so that we remain as babes, saying, "I AM SAVED" when we are on a JOURNEY unto life eternal and are BEING SAVED.

How many times have we heard from many Christians these words: "**I AM SAVED**" or "**WHEN I WAS SAVED**" and also "**ARE YOU SAVED?**" This is a deceptive snare of Satan to lull us into a false security that all Christians are saved and are going to heaven, when the Word teaches that "WE ARE BEING SAVED," IF we are obedient to the Word and meet the **conditions to be saved!**

First, we must understand - the Spirit birth is ONLY THE BEGINNING of our life in Christ; we are on a JOURNEY in God's Holy Word, as Israel was on a JOURNEY TO THE PROMISED LAND!

If we say, "I AM SAVED," we are being deceived and will not go beyond the Spirit birth to receive the end of our salvation.

After reading the following scriptures, I am sure we will say, "I am being saved IF I meet the conditions to be saved."

A FEW CONDITIONS TO BE SAVED:

Rom 10:9   "**That if thou shalt CONFESS WITH THY MOUTH THE LORD JESUS, and shalt BELIEVE IN THINE HEART that GOD HAS RAISED HIM FROM THE DEAD, THOU "SHALT BE SAVED"** (This reveals the future IF we are obedient to HIS WORD.)

1 Cor 10:11 "**Now all these things happened unto them (ISRAEL** on their journey) **for ensamples: and they are written for our ADMONITION, upon whom the ENDS OF THE WORLD are come.**"

THE SECOND ATTACK(cont.)

1 Cor 10:12   "Wherefore LET HIM THAT THINKETH HE STANDETH (is saved?) TAKE HEED LEST HE FALL."

Matt 7:15-23   READ:
"Not everyone that saith, LORD, LORD, (or "I AM SAVED") shall enter THE KINGDOM OF HEAVEN; but he that DOETH THE WILL OF MY FATHER WHICH IS IN HEAVEN."

Jms 1:22   "BE YE DOERS OF THE WORD and not HEARERS ONLY, deceiving your own selves."

Heb 3:14   "For we are made PARTAKERS OF CHRIST, IF we hold the beginning of our CONFIDENCE STEADFAST UNTO THE END."

Heb 4:1   "LET US THEREFORE FEAR, lest a PROMISE (the Holy Ghost) being left us of ENTERING INTO HIS REST, any of you should seem to come SHORT of it."

Rom 11:19-22   READ:

Rom 11:22   "...IF THOU CONTINUE IN HIS GOODNESS: OTHERWISE THOU ALSO SHALT BE CUT OFF."

Jude 5   "I WILL THEREFORE PUT YOU IN REMEMBRANCE, THOUGH YE ONCE KNEW THIS, HOW THAT THE LORD, HAVING SAVED THE PEOPLE OUT OF THE LAND OF EGYPT, AFTERWARD DESTROYED THEM THAT BELIEVED NOT."

"The people" were all Jews and were all "**SAVED**" out of Egypt, but many failed because they would not take THE JOURNEY to the promised land, as it is with many local churches in this hour!

THE SECOND ATTACK(cont.)

"TODAY IF YOU WILL HEAR HIS VOICE"

Heb 3:6-19   "But Christ as a son over his own house; whose house are we, if we hold fast the confidence and the rejoicing of the hope firm unto the end.

Wherefore (as the Holy Ghost saith, TO DAY IF YE WILL HEAR HIS VOICE,

Harden not your hearts, as in the provocation, in the day of temptation in the wilderness:

When your fathers tempted me, proved me, and saw my works forty years.

Wherefore I was grieved with that generation, and said, <u>They do alway err in *their* heart; and they have not known my ways.</u>

So I sware in my wrath, They shall not enter into my rest.)

Take heed, brethren, lest there be in any of you an evil heart of unbelief, in departing from the living God.

But exhort one another daily, while it is called To day; lest any of you be hardened through the deceitfulness of sin.

For we are made partakers of Christ, <u>if</u> we hold the beginning of our confidence stedfast unto the end;

While it is said, TO DAY IF YE WILL HEAR HIS VOICE, harden not your hearts, as in the provocation.

For some, when they had heard, did provoke: howbeit not all that came out of Egypt by Moses.

THE SECOND ATTACK(cont.)

> But with whom was he grieved forty years? *Was it* not with them that had sinned, whose carcases fell in the wilderness?
>
> And to whom sware he that they should not enter into his rest, but to them that believed not?
>
> So we see that they could not enter in because of unbelief."

Can we now say "WE ARE SAVED" when considering the above scriptures?

SAVED? A FEW SCRIPTURAL WARNINGS

Satan's voice says, "Once saved, always saved" which means we can walk any way we please. If we believe this lie, we can see that the ONLY DIFFERENCE between a CHRISTIAN and the LOST is that we go to CHURCH and say we are saved. WE CAN LOSE OUR SALVATION!

Rom 11:19-22   "THOU WILT SAY THEN, THE BRANCHES WERE BROKEN OFF, THAT I MIGHT BE GRAFTED IN. WELL; BECAUSE OF UNBELIEF THEY WERE BROKEN OFF, AND THOU STANDEST BY FAITH. BE NOT HIGHMINDED, BUT FEAR: FOR IF GOD SPARED NOT THE NATURAL BRANCHES, TAKE HEED LEST HE ALSO SPARE NOT THEE.

BEHOLD THEREFORE THE GOODNESS AND THE SEVERITY OF GOD: ON THEM WHICH FELL SEVERITY; BUT TOWARD THEE, GOODNESS, IF THOU CONTINUE IN HIS GOODNESS. OTHERWISE, THOU ALSO SHALL BE CUT OFF."

Lk 12:45-46   "But and if that SERVANT say in his heart, MY LORD DELAYETH HIS COMING; And shall begin to beat the menservants and maidens, and to eat and drink and be drunken.

THE SECOND ATTACK(cont.)

THE LORD OF THAT SERVANT will come in a day when he looketh not for HIM, AND AT AN HOUR WHEN HE IS NOT AWARE, AND WILL CUT HIM IN SUNDER, AND WILL APPOINT HIM HIS PORTION WITH THE UNBELIEVERS."

1 Pet 4:18, 19   "And if THE RIGHTEOUS SCARCELY BE SAVED, WHERE SHALL THE UNGODLY AND THE SINNER APPEAR? WHEREFORE LET THEM THAT SUFFER ACCORDING TO THE WILL OF GOD COMMIT THE KEEPING OF THEIR SOULS TO HIM IN WELL DOING, AS UNTO A FAITHFUL CREATOR."

ARE YOU LUKEWARM?

Rev 3:15-16   READ:
"So then, because thou art LUKEWARM, and neither COLD nor HOT, I WILL SPUE THEE OUT OF MY MOUTH."

We may not care for the above scriptures, but they are written to ADMONISH us and to warn us NOT TO TAKE OUR SALVATION FOR GRANTED! THE SCRIPTURE SAYS, **"THE FEAR OF THE LORD IS THE BEGINNING OF WISDOM."**

Heb 2:1-3   "Therefore we ought to give the MORE EARNEST HEED TO THE THINGS WHICH WE HAVE HEARD, LEST AT ANY TIME we should let *THEM* SLIP.

For if the WORD spoken by angels was steadfast, and EVERY transgression and disobedience received a just recompense of reward;

HOW SHALL WE ESCAPE, IF WE NEGLECT SO GREAT SALVATION; which at the first began to be spoken by the LORD, and was confirmed unto us by them that heard *HIM*;"

TO THOSE THAT SAY TO THE LOST "GOD LOVES YOU"
THE SECOND ATTACK(cont.)

This is a DECEPTIVE SNARE OF SATAN to **DESTROY** THE LOST, NOT **SAVE** THEM!

Every SINNER MUST START their Christian life at CALVARY, where "GOD SO LOVE**D**" (past tense) HE GAVE HIS ONLY BEGOTTEN SON" for their sins if they would BELIEVE! Let me clarify that the child of God who lost faith, the Father's love through His Son Jesus, will be calling him to come home again. For we are **ALL** sinners saved by grace, **IF** we continue in His grace.

How many times have we heard on television and in THE CHURCH many preachers of THE GOSPEL say, "GOD LOVES YOU" when ministering to LOST SOULS. We very seldom hear them GIVE THE **CONDITIONS** FOR THE LOST TO ENTER IN TO "HIS LOVE".

To say that "GOD LOVES YOU" to THE LOST is a <u>half truth</u> and a grave mistake. This statement does away with the WORK OF THE HOLY GHOST to convict the lost of sins in their lives.

Furthermore, they will remain IN THEIR SINS, with a FALSE COMFORT saying, "GOD LOVES ME" and, "I will go to heaven anyway when I die" when OUR LORD JESUS gave the **CONDITIONS** ON CALVARY TO ABIDE IN HIS LOVE!

A FEW OF THOSE CONDITIONS:

Jn 3:18   **"He that believeth on HIM is NOT CONDEMNED: BUT HE THAT BELIEVETH NOT <u>IS</u> CONDEMNED ALREADY, because he hath not believed IN THE NAME of the only begotten SON OF GOD."**

Mk 16:16   **"He that believeth and is baptized <u>SHALL BE</u> saved; BUT HE THAT BELIEVETH NOT SHALL BE DAMNED."**

Jn 3:36   **"He that believeth on the SON hath everlasting life: and he that believeth <u>NOT</u> the SON SHALL <u>NOT</u> SEE LIFE; BUT THE WRATH OF GOD ABIDETH ON HIM."**

THE SECOND ATTACK(cont.)

QUESTION:

Do the above scriptures qualify us to say to THE LOST that "GOD LOVES YOU" when THE SCRIPTURES TEACH that the unbeliever is CONDEMNED ALREADY and that the WRATH OF GOD ABIDETH ON HIM?

I believe THE SUBTLETY OF SATAN is at work here, discrediting GOD'S LOVE!

THE THIRD ATTACK

First, it is strange that there are at least twenty-four published Bibles today that have deleted or added to the HOLY WORD OF GOD by man's opinions, and have attacked THE AUTHORIZED KING JAMES BIBLE that holds <u>ALL</u> THE TRUTH for the child of GOD. The Authorized King James Bible has endured SATAN'S ATTACK on THE WORD which <u>IS</u> OUR LORD JESUS CHRIST for hundreds of years!

As I proceed, I WILL CHALLENGE THE SUBTLETY OF SATAN **BY** THE HOLY WORD OF GOD. Certain men, deceived by Satan, crept in unawares to CHANGE THE WORD OF GOD through the BLINDNESS OF THEIR HEART. The most important message from THE LORD in this hour <u>IS</u> THE BAPTISM OF THE HOLY GHOST!

THE FOLLOWING SCRIPTURES REVEAL THE SUBTLETY OF SATAN AND THE REASON FOR THIS WRITING - TO WAKE UP THE CHURCH.

Acts 19:1   **"And it came to pass, that Apollos was at Corinth, Paul having passed through the upper coasts came to Ephesus: and FINDING CERTAIN DISCIPLES,"** (who were Christian believers).

Acts 19:2   "And Paul said, unto these Christian believers, **"...HAVE YE RECEIVED THE HOLY GHOST <u>SINCE</u> YE BELIEVED?..."**

THE THIRD ATTACK (cont.)

The above scripture reveals that THE HOLY GHOST BAPTISM IS A SEPARATE EXPERIENCE that **follows** the BORN AGAIN experience.

THE HOLY WORD OF GOD WAS CHANGED TO READ:

"The Living Bible" states in Acts 19:2, "DID YOU RECEIVE THE HOLY SPIRIT, **<u>WHEN</u>** YOU BELIEVED." It was changed by individuals who crept in unawares and who, through the BLINDNESS of their HEARTS, resist THE HOLY WORD OF GOD regarding THE BAPTISM OF THE HOLY GHOST, when CHRIST **IS** THE HOLY GHOST, **<u>AS THE FATHER</u>** - **THE SON** and **THE HOLY GHOST** are **ONE**. AND ALSO THAT JESUS IS THE ONE THAT BAPTIZES WITH THE HOLY GHOST.

Matt 3:11   **"I INDEED BAPTIZE YOU WITH WATER UNTO REPENTANCE: BUT HE THAT COMETH AFTER ME IS MIGHTIER THAN I, WHOSE SHOES I AM NOT WORTHY TO BEAR: HE SHALL BAPTIZE YOU WITH THE HOLY GHOST AND WITH FIRE."**

Jn 1:33   **"AND I KNEW HIM NOT: BUT HE THAT SENT ME TO BAPTIZE WITH WATER, THE SAME SAID UNTO ME, UPON WHOM THOU SHALT SEE THE SPIRIT DESCENDING, AND REMAINING ON HIM, THE SAME IS HE WHICH BAPTIZETH WITH THE HOLY GHOST."**

I say, **WAKE UP CHURCH** to the TRUTH OF GOD'S WORD and be not blinded by man's traditions and opinions that are attempting to divide and destroy THE CHURCH - when JESUS prayed that we may BE ONE!

Moreover, Jesus said, "MY SHEEP HEAR MY VOICE, I KNOW THEM, THEY FOLLOW ME."

THE THIRD ATTACK (cont.)

My dear children of THE LORD, if there was ever a time to listen to HIS VOICE in these last days before HIS COMING, it is today, for HIS VOICE WILL NEVER DECEIVE YOU!

THE GREATEST QUESTION THAT IS ASKED TODAY

Matt 24:3-5   This question was asked by HIS disciples, **"...WHAT SHALL BE THE SIGN OF THY COMING AND OF THE END OF THE WORLD?"**

AND JESUS ANSWERED AND SAID UNTO THEM, TAKE HEED THAT NO MAN DECEIVE YOU.

FOR MANY SHALL COME IN MY NAME, SAYING, I AM CHRIST; AND SHALL DECEIVE MANY."

2 Peter 2:1   **"But there were false prophets also among the people, even as there shall be false teachers among you, who privily shall bring in damnable heresies, even denying the Lord that bought them, and bring upon themselves swift destruction."**

2 Cor 11:14   **"And no marvel; for Satan himself is TRANSFORMED INTO AN ANGEL OF LIGHT."**

Therefore it is no great thing if his ministers also be transformed as the ministers of RIGHTEOUSNESS; who's end shall be according to their works.

There is no greater way to DECEIVE the CHRISTIAN CHURCH in this hour than to CHANGE THE HOLY WORD OF GOD, in which we trust, and to print new Bibles in an attempt to do away with THE BAPTISM OF THE HOLY GHOST!!

Satan in the beginning, through his subtlety by adding and changing the Word, caused Adam through DISOBEDIENCE to THE WORD, to lose his fellowship with the Lord and caused SIN to come on the human race, BECAUSE HE LISTENED TO THE WRONG VOICE!!

THE THIRD ATTACK (cont.)

That same voice, through subtlety is speaking today as he goes about like a roaring lion, seeking whom he may devour or destroy, and many Christians once more are listening to his voice as he CHALLENGES THE HOLY WORD OF GOD by distorting THE TRUTH and ADDING and TAKING AWAY FROM THE WORD OF GOD. By CHANGING the WORD, and printing many NEW BIBLES he subverts THE PRECIOUS CHURCH OF JESUS CHRIST. The irony of it all, is that he found many who call themselves Christians to carry out his PLAN OF DECEPTION to DIVIDE THE CHURCH, when Jesus said take heed that no man (Christian) deceive you, as we can see today, when there is ONLY ONE CHURCH, and JESUS prayed to THE FATHER that we be ONE AS THEY ARE ONE.

THE PURPOSE OF THIS WRITING is to expose THE ERRORS written in "THESE **DIFFERENT** BIBLES", once and FOR ALL, and it will amaze you how they have attempted to DISTORT and remove THE PRECIOUS TRUTHS that our HEAVENLY FATHER gave us in THE AUTHORIZED KING JAMES BIBLE, which has endured its critics for hundreds of years!

WE MUST ASK OURSELVES THIS QUESTION:

Why should these individuals CHANGE THE WORD OF GOD and print NEW BIBLES, when, THE AUTHORIZED KING JAMES BIBLE reveals the POWER AND THE ANOINTING, that has been operating through THE BAPTISM OF THE HOLY GHOST, by great men of GOD, like C.T. STUD, DAVID LIVINGSTON and many others as they healed the sick, opened the deaf ears and made the lame to walk and THE BLIND to see?

"YE SHALL KNOW THE TRUTH AND THE TRUTH SHALL SET YOU FREE."

I'd like to mention in particular two versions of the Bible, "The New International Version and The New American Standard Version."

One might ask, "What is their purpose for being written in the first place?"

1)   To do away with the Baptism of the Holy Ghost.

THE THIRD ATTACK (cont.)

2)   To change the Godhead where all understanding begins.
3)   To distort the truth and give a fleshly interpretation by adding to the Word and taking away from the Word the commandments of the Lord, that the children of the Lord become confused, and ask themselves, "Is it the Word of man?" or "Is it the Word of God, whose commandments we must obey?"

They do this, knowing the judgement of God for committing such ungodly acts in changing the Word and adding to it, when the Lord warned,

Deut 4:1-2   "NOW THEREFORE HEARKEN, O ISRAEL, UNTO THE STATUTES AND UNTO THE JUDGMENTS, WHICH I TEACH YOU, FOR TO DO *THEM*, THAT YE MAY LIVE, AND GO IN AND POSSESS THE LAND WHICH THE LORD GOD OF YOUR FATHERS GIVETH YOU.

YE SHALL NOT ADD UNTO THE WORD WHICH I COMMAND YOU, NEITHER SHALL YE DIMINISH *OUGHT* FROM IT, THAT YE MAY KEEP THE COMMANDMENTS OF THE LORD YOUR GOD WHICH I COMMAND YOU."

Rev 22:18-19   "FOR I TESTIFY UNTO EVERY MAN THAT HEARETH THE WORDS OF THE PROPHECY OF THIS BOOK, IF ANY MAN SHALL ADD UNTO THESE THINGS, GOD SHALL ADD UNTO HIM THE PLAGUES THAT ARE WRITTEN IN THIS BOOK:

AND IF ANY MAN SHALL TAKE AWAY FROM THE WORDS OF THE BOOK OF THIS PROPHECY, GOD SHALL TAKE AWAY HIS PART OUT OF THE BOOK OF LIFE, AND OUT OF THE HOLY CITY, AND *FROM* THE THINGS WHICH ARE WRITTEN IN THIS BOOK."

THE THIRD ATTACK (cont.)

We should ask ouselves this question as Christians, **"DOES THE LORD DIVIDE HIS CHURCH THROUGH HIS HOLY WORD THAT HE HAS WRITTEN, WHEN THE SPIRIT AND THE WORD AGREE?** When each Christian is born of that Spirit?

Did the Lord in these last days change his mind and bring confusion into the body of Christ? When He said, **"I AM THE LORD AND I CHANGE NOT!"**

Will the changes in these Bibles regarding the Holy Word give you **POWER** over all the works of the enemy?

In the deceitfulness of their act to introduce their ungodly thoughts, they mixed the True Word of God, with their spirit of error.

As we proceed, I will endeavor to reveal to those with a true heart, the truth by exposing the falseness of their interpretation of the Word and their "speaking against it," When our Lord said, **"TO THE LAW AND THE TESTIMONY IF ANY MAN SHALL SPEAK AGAINST THIS WORD, IT IS BECAUSE THERE IS NO LIGHT IN THEM."**

As I proceed you will well understand what I meant when I said, "Put your trust in the Authorized King James Bible, for their are no ungodly lies in its pages."

THE BLOOD:

THE TRUTH:

THE AUTHORIZED KING JAMES BIBLE states in Colossians 1:14: "In whom we have redemption through His blood, even the forgiveness of sins."

THE NEW VERSIONS DO AWAY WITH THE BLOOD

THE LIE:

THE THIRD ATTACK (cont.)

The New American Standard version reads and I quote Colossians 1:14:
- "In whom we have redemption _____(THE BLOOD OMITTED!) the forgiveness of sins.

The New International version reads and I quote Colossians 1:14:
- "In whom we have redemption _____(THE BLOOD OMITTED!) the forgiveness of sins.

Comment:	My dear brothers and sisters in Christ, the subtlety of taking away from the Word, the most precious of all; **THE BLOOD OF JESUS CHRIST GOD'S HOLY SON,** takes away our salvation for without the shedding of blood revealed in the Father's writings, that **ALL LIFE OF THE FLESH IS IN THE BLOOD,**
Lev 17:11	**"For the life of the flesh *is* in THE BLOOD: and I have given it to you upon the altar to make an atonement for your souls: for it *is* THE BLOOD *that* maketh an atonement for the soul."**

For where there is no **SHEDDING OF BLOOD**, there shall be **NO** forgiveness of sins. If we delete from the Word, the PRECIOUS BLOOD OF CHRIST, we have done away with the crucifixion of OUR LAMB, and we are still in our sins.

THE VIRGIN BIRTH

THE TRUTH:

THE AUTHORIZED KING JAMES BIBLE states in Luke 2:33: "And Joseph and his mother marvelled at those things which were spoken of him."

THE NEW VERSIONS DO AWAY WITH THE VIRGIN BIRTH

THE LIE:

The New American Standard version reads and I quote Luke 2:33:
- "And his **FATHER AND MOTHER** were amazed at the things that were being said about him."

THE THIRD ATTACK (cont.)

The New International Version reads and I quote Luke 2:33:

• "The CHILD'S FATHER AND MOTHER marvelled at what was said about him."

Comment: Let us concentrate for the present time on **FATHER AND MOTHER.**

JESUS was child of the **HOLY GHOST** and Joseph was **NOT HIS FATHER!**

If they say that Joseph is his father, then they have done away with the sinless virgin birth and we have no hope.

Remember that we have only revealed two of the most important truths, that are really, the foundation of our faith.

THE VIRGIN BIRTH and the PRECIOUS BLOOD OF CHRIST. I don't think it is important to reveal all the other lies, that are written in these books, for they are too numerous to mention. For if they say there is no VIRGIN BIRTH, and omit the BLOOD OF CHRIST, we are still in our sins. As a brother and a father in Christ, I exhort you to get rid of these new Bibles mentioned, before they vex your righteous souls.

QUESTION: Where are THE FATHERS and PILLARS of THE CHURCH, that they have not cried out against THE CHANGING OF THE WORD in **Acts 19:2**? Are they DECEIVED BY SATAN as well? Are they in darkness that they cannot see where they are leading THE CHURCH OF JESUS CHRIST?

Is 8:20   The Prophet said, **"To the law and to the testimony: If they speak not according to this word, it is because THERE IS NO LIGHT IN THEM."**

CHALLENGING SCRIPTURES REGARDING CHANGE

Gen 2:7   **"And the Lord God formed man of the dust of the ground, and breathed into his nostrils the breath of life; and man became a living soul."**

THE THIRD ATTACK (cont.)

Shall THE SOUL that was CREATED BY THE WORD, now CHANGE THE WORD that created him?

One might ask, "WHAT PORTION OF THE HOLY WORD OF GOD WILL THESE MEN ATTEMPT TO CHANGE NEXT?" When our Lord Jesus <u>IS</u> the WORD.

Mal 3:6   *When THE LORD SAID:*
                "FOR I AM THE LORD, (THE WORD) **I CHANGE NOT;..."**

                TO CHANGE THE WORD IS TO CHANGE JESUS WHO <u>IS</u> THE WORD!

I see the subtlety of Satan at work here!

Chapter Three

The Lord's Message To Us Without Words

As I proceed I will reveal THE WORK OF OUR HEAVENLY FATHER, as HE reveals THE SHADOWS of GOOD THINGS TO COME. I will also show you THE FOUNDATIONS OF TRUTH for all generations, that can never be changed!

SPECIAL ATTENTION will be given to THE JOURNEY OF THE CHURCH and THE HOLY GHOST, THE THIRD PERSON OF THE GODHEAD.

THE LORD'S MESSAGE TO US WITHOUT WORDS:

As we begin to reveal THE SHADOWS (Hebrews 10:1 "FOR THE LAW HAVING A SHADOW OF GOOD THINGS TO COME") and THE FOUNDATIONS OF TRUTH written in THE WORD OF OUR HEAVENLY FATHER, WE MUST FIRST UNDERSTAND THAT ALL THINGS THAT WERE MADE IN HEAVEN AND ON EARTH REVEAL A MESSAGE TO US WITHOUT WORDS.

Children of the Lord, many do not UNDERSTAND the WORK OF THE FATHER in the OLD TESTAMENT. To make the OLD TESTAMENT exciting for you, please look for FOUNDATION TRUTHS AND THE SHADOWS TO COME, beginning in Genesis, THE LAW OF MOSES, THE PSALMS, THE PROPHETS. You will find that at the time of this writing, much has been fulfilled, except a few scriptures in THE PSALMS regarding WORSHIP, and also in THE PROPHETS regarding THE END OF THIS AGE. Most important of all, THE BAPTISM OF THE HOLY GHOST, mentioned in Isaiah 28:11 ("FOR WITH STAMMERING LIPS AND ANOTHER TONGUE WILL HE SPEAK TO THIS PEOPLE.") This experience, though rejected by many, SHALL BE FULFILLED beyond what it is today, no matter what man's opinions are and the traditions of his local church!

Let us now look at a few examples in HEAVEN and on EARTH, that THE LORD has made, that speak to us WITHOUT WORDS.

Ps 19:1-3   **"THE HEAVENS DECLARE THE GLORY OF GOD; AND THE FIRMAMENT SHEWETH HIS HANDY WORK. DAY UNTO DAY UTTERETH SPEECH, AND NIGHT UNTO NIGHT SHEWETH KNOWLEDGE. THERE IS NO SPEECH NOR LANGUAGE, WHERE THEIR VOICE IS NOT HEARD."**

LET US EXAMINE THE HEAVENS FOR AN EXAMPLE:

Gen 1:16   **"...GOD (HE) MADE TWO GREAT LIGHTS;..." "...HE MADE THE STARS ALSO."**

These THREE lights (sun, moon and stars) reveal THE GODHEAD without WORDS. They show THE FATHER, THE SON and THE HOLY GHOST CHURCH, that in THEIR WORKS, will reveal all THE TRUTH in the HOLY SCRIPTURES.

THE SUN, THE FATHER - THE MOON, OUR LORD JESUS - THE STARS, THE MANY MEMBERED BODY OF CHRIST, THE CHURCH.

1 Jn 5:7   The apostle JOHN received the above revelation when he wrote, **"...THERE ARE THREE THAT BEAR RECORD IN HEAVEN, THE FATHER, THE WORD, AND THE HOLY GHOST: AND THESE THREE ARE ONE."**

THE SUN - A GOOD EXAMPLE:

Ps 50:1-6   **READ:**
                      HE HAS CALLED THE EARTH, FROM THE RISING OF THE SUN, TO THE GOING DOWN OF THE SAME.

Every day, as the SUN rises in THE EAST, THE LORD is calling, men and women from all over the world to repent of their sins and receive salvation through HIS SON, OUR LORD JESUS CHRIST!

And as we observe THE GOING DOWN OF THE SUN, we often see a CRIMSON GLOW IN THE SKY, while the Lord is SPEAKING TO US WITHOUT WORDS OF THE SACRIFICE OF HIS SON ON THE CROSS FOR OUR SINS.

THE ELEMENTS--THE WIND, THE DARK CLOUDS, THE STORMS IN THE HEAVENS AND THE RAIN-- speak to us without words of the trials of our faith that we must endure until THE SUN rises again!

Rom 1:20	Paul the apostle makes it very plain: **"FOR THE INVISIBLE THINGS OF HIM FROM THE CREATION OF THE WORLD ARE CLEARLY SEEN, BEING UNDERSTOOD BY THE THINGS THAT ARE MADE, EVEN HIS ETERNAL POWER AND GODHEAD; so that we are without excuse."**

THINGS ON EARTH FOR EXAMPLES:

TREES   •   JESUS IS THE TREE OF LIFE.
            •   JESUS BORE OUR SINS ON A TREE.
            •   TREES ARE OUR GREATEST RESOURCE, THEY ARE CUT DOWN OR KILLED, as our LORD JESUS was, CUT INTO LUMBER AND TRANSPORTED ALL OVER THE WORLD. AS MEMBERS OF "THE TREE" ARE EVIDENT IN EVERY COUNTRY OF THE WORLD.

SHEEP   •   Reveal CHRISTIANS, AND JESUS IS THE GREAT SHEPHERD OF THE SHEEP. IF WE WANT TO KNOW MORE ABOUT SHEEP, WE MUST STUDY OURSELVES TO FIND THE ANSWER, FOR THE LORD SEES US AS A DEFENCELESS CROWD AND THE SHEEP OF HIS PASTURE.

VINEYARD   John 15:1-12   **READ:**
                                          "I AM THE TRUE VINE, AND MY FATHER IS THE HUSBANDMAN."

The TRUE MEANING OF THE VINEYARD is revealed in John's writing. Every Christian should understand that this scripture reveals OUR CALLING, OBEDIENCE, AND THE LORD'S COMMANDMENT TO LOVE ONE ANOTHER. There are many more scriptures that I am sure you will find that reveal THE GOSPEL WITHOUT WORDS.

THE LIVING CREATION

Ps 50:11	**"I KNOW ALL THE FOWLS OF THE MOUNTAINS: AND THE WILD BEASTS OF THE FIELD ARE MINE."** (saith THE LORD.)

LIONS   •   Study the lives of THE LIONS for they will reveal THE LORD, WHO IS "THE LION OF THE TRIBE OF JUDAH."

FOWL   •   I often ponder the MIGRATION OF GEESE and other types of fowl. I know they are THE LORD'S because HE leads them by HIS SPIRIT in their migrations to save their lives as HE does with all the wild beasts of the field.

As we, HIS SHEEP who are born with our own wills to choose, THE LORD DESIRES THAT WE TOO BE LED BY HIS SPIRIT as THE FOWLS and the WILD BEASTS OF THE FIELD, FOR THEY HAVE NO OPPOSITION TO HIS SPIRIT FOR THEY ARE ALREADY HIS!

If we consider every living creature that THE LORD has made, and their characteristics, we will find a MESSAGE FROM THE LORD, WITHOUT WORDS.

Chapter Four

The Revelation Of The Godhead

THEIR WORK FROM GENESIS 1, TO THE DAY OF PENTECOST

IN THE BEGINNING

Again, without our UNDERSTANDING of the GODHEAD, we will never understand the VISION of their plan for our Christian lives.

Let us concentrate just on the GODHEAD, beginning at Genesis to THE DAY OF PENTECOST, when the Father and the Son came down from heaven, who **ARE** the Holy Ghost to fill the stars, or the Church with power to be workers together with them, to the end of this age.

Gen 1:16   "AND GOD MADE TWO GREAT LIGHTS;" "...HE MADE THE STARS ALSO."

1 Jn 5:7   John confirms the meaning "FOR THERE ARE THREE THAT BEAR RECORD IN HEAVEN, THE FATHER, THE WORD AND THE HOLY GHOST: **AND THESE THREE ARE ONE**."

These THREE are the SPIRITUAL REVELATION and the beginning of our UNDERSTANDING of the HOLY SCRIPTURES that are written to us.

THE GODHEAD MAKES THEIR FUTURE TEMPLE

Gen 1:26   **"...LET US MAKE MAN IN OUR IMAGE, AFTER OUR LIKENESS:..."**

Gen 2:7   MAN IS MADE A LIVING SOUL. **"And the Lord God formed man of the dust of the ground, and breathed into his nostrils the breath of life; and man became a living soul."**

Man is THE TEMPLE, and by man's invitation, THE GODHEAD would come and live in it on THE DAY OF PENTECOST, through the BAPTISM OF THE HOLY GHOST.

THE FATHER SEEKS A BRIDE FOR JESUS HIS SON

Gen 24: READ: This chapter is a SHADOW OF THE FATHER on THE DAY OF PENTECOST seeking a BRIDE FOR JESUS through the BAPTISM OF THE HOLY GHOST.

THE GODHEAD ANNOUNCES THE REJECTION
OF THE BAPTISM OF THE HOLY GHOST

Is 28:11, 12
Cross ref. 1 Cor 14:21   **"FOR WITH STAMMERING LIPS AND AN OTHER TONGUE WILL HE SPEAK TO THIS PEOPLE. TO WHOM HE SAID, THIS IS THE REST WHEREWITH YE MAY CAUSE THE WEARY TO REST; AND THIS IS THE REFRESHING: YET THEY WOULD NOT HEAR."**

Paul refers to Isaiah 28:11-12 in 1 Corinthians 14:21: **IN THE LAW IT IS WRITTEN, WITH MEN OF OTHER TONGUES AND OTHER LIPS WILL I SPEAK UNTO THIS PEOPLE AND YET FOR ALL THAT WILL THEY NOT HEAR ME, SAITH THE LORD."**

THE REVELATION OF THE GODHEAD IN MOSES' TABERNACLE

Revealing SALVATION TO TRANSLATION for every Christian.
- Beginning at the FOUR PILLARS OF THE GATE, or THE FOUR GOSPELS.
- The first thing we see is THE BRAZEN ALTAR or THE CROSS OF CALVARY.
- Next, we see THE <u>OUTER COURT</u> where many take their place, saying, "I AM SAVED."
- Many go to THE LAVER ("WASHING OF WATER BY THE WORD") and make a DECISION to go forward and see that there is more for them than just standing in the OUTER COURT, or the Born Again experience.
- Next, we enter THE HOLY PLACE or ROOM OF SERVICE, wherein is THE CANDLESTICK and THE TABLE OF SHEWBREAD, revealing JESUS, THE LIGHT OF THE WORLD and THE BREAD

OF LIFE, where we began our beautiful BORN AGAIN EXPERIENCE! So wonderful is THE HOLY PLACE, that many never left that room, not understanding that a GREATER EXPERIENCE was waiting for them beyond THE VEIL in the next room, called THE HOLY OF HOLIES, which IS the **BAPTISM OF THE HOLY GHOST.**

•   If we proceed beyond THE BORN AGAIN EXPERIENCE through THE HOLY PLACE, we enter into THE HOLY OF HOLIES where the Cherubims of Glory overshadow the mercy seat and where the ANOINTING OF HIS PRESENCE fills the room; it is HOLY GROUND!

The main piece of furniture in the room is THE ARK OF THE COVENANT, which contains THE SHADOWS OF THE FATHER, SON AND HOLY GHOST (THE GODHEAD).

THE CONTENTS OF THE ARK REVEAL THE GODHEAD

1)   TABLES OF STONE - Representing - **THE FATHER**

Ex 31:18   **"AND HE GAVE UNTO MOSES, when HE had made an end of communing with him on MOUNT SINAI, TWO TABLES OF TESTIMONY, TABLES OF STONE, WRITTEN WITH THE FINGER OF GOD."**

2)   THE GOLDEN POT THAT HAD MANNA - Revealing - **THE SON**

Jn 6:26-35 READ:
    "...I AM THE BREAD OF LIFE..."

3)   AARON'S ROD THAT BUDDED - Revealing - THE POWER OF **THE HOLY GHOST**
AARON'S ROD was alive with POWER and was used to deliver Israel out of Egypt.

Num 17:1-10 READ:
    AARON'S ROD or MINISTRY was challenged by other rods that had no POWER.

- AARON'S ROD THAT BUDDED is a SHADOW OF THE **HOLY GHOST FILLED** MINISTRY TODAY.
- AARON'S ROD can be likened to a person's MINISTRY when it is ANOINTED WITH POWER.
- ISRAEL was challenging Aaron's ministry and THE LORD put them to the test, as HE puts every ROD or MINISTRY to the test in these final hours.
- It is one thing to have a ROD or MINISTRY but what good IS THE ROD without POWER?

NOTE:　　**THE CHURCH BEGAN TO BUD ON THE DAY OF PENTECOST**, many RODS REJECTED THE BAPTISM OF THE HOLY GHOST and their ministry did not BUD and BLOOM as the Lord intended.

As we can now agree, THE CONTENTS OF THE ARK are a SHADOW OF THE GODHEAD, FATHER, SON AND HOLY GHOST, the beginning and the end of this message.

NATURAL ISRAEL (a shadow of the Church) through their BLINDNESS OF HEART, are still searching for THE ARK today on THE TEMPLE MOUNT in JERUSALEM.　What a blessing we have, when we have the spiritual revelation of THE CONTENTS OF THE ARK before us for understanding and that AARON'S ROD is a SHADOW OF THE HOLY GHOST BAPTISM that will give THE CHURCH POWER **IF** they will receive it!

Jn 5:17　　JESUS SAID, "...MY FATHER WORKETH HITHERTO AND I WORK."

Col 2:9　　"FOR IN HIM DWELLETH THE FULLNESS OF THE GODHEAD BODILY."

JESUS IS THE FATHER, THE SON AND THE HOLY GHOST.

- **THE FATHER** - that laid all THE FOUNDATIONS OF TRUTH.
- **THE SON** - sent by THE FATHER to deliver us from SIN through HIS BLOOD because HE now would live in HIS TEMPLE.
- **THE HOLY GHOST** - to give us POWER to be workers together with HIM.

THE FATHER AND THE SON, WHO ARE THE HOLY GHOST, ANNOUNCE THEIR COMING

Jn 14:18 "...<u>I WILL COME TO YOU</u>"

Jn 14:20 The Godhead revealed, **"AT THAT DAY** (THE DAY OF PENTECOST) **YE SHALL KNOW THAT I AM IN MY FATHER, AND YE IN ME AND I IN YOU."**

THIS REVEALS THE FINAL PLAN FROM THE BEGINNING.

Jn 14:23 THE GODHEAD SPEAKS AGAIN, **"...IF A MAN LOVE ME, HE WILL KEEP MY WORDS: AND MY FATHER WILL LOVE HIM, AND <u>WE</u> WILL COME TO HIM, AND MAKE <u>OUR</u> ABODE WITH HIM:"** REVEALING AGAIN THAT THE FATHER AND THE SON <u>ARE</u> THE HOLY GHOST

Jn 14:28 **"Ye have heard how I said unto you, I GO AWAY, AND COME AGAIN UNTO YOU. If ye loved me, ye would rejoice, because I said, I go unto the Father: for my Father is greater than I."** Jesus reveals that He <u>IS</u> the HOLY GHOST.

Jn 14:29 **"AND NOW I HAVE TOLD YOU BEFORE IT COME TO PASS, (DAY OF PENTECOST) THAT WHEN IT IS COME TO PASS,** (THE BAPTISM OF THE HOLY GHOST) **YE MIGHT BELIEVE."** These are the words of our Lord Jesus, before the outpouring of the Holy Ghost. How can you still not believe when it <u>IS</u> already come to pass?

THE GODHEAD REVEALED IN THE PERSON OF THE HOLY GHOST, COMES DOWN ON THE DAY OF PENTECOST

Acts 2:1-4 READ:
"AND THEY WERE ALL FILLED WITH THE HOLY GHOST (The Godhead) **AND BEGAN TO SPEAK WITH OTHER TONGUES, AS THE SPIRIT GAVE THEM**

UTTERANCE." As we are born of the Spirit into the Kingdom of God, this verse of scripture reveals the Holy Ghost, tongues, and the Spirit we are born of.
Something to think about.

Read - 2 Cor 6:1-10 NOW THE GODHEAD, accomplished THEIR WORK to live in their TEMPLE they created in the beginning. Through our obedience to THEIR voice, we will be WORKERS TOGETHER with them, with POWER to finish THEIR WORK!

AMEN!

THE GODHEAD REVEALED IN THE HEAVENS

Gen 1:14-16   **"And God said, Let there be lights in the firmament of the heaven to divide the day from the night; and let them be for signs, and for seasons, and for days, and years: And let them be for lights in the firmament of the heaven to give light upon the earth: and it was so. AND GOD MADE TWO GREAT LIGHTS; the greater light to rule the day, and the lesser light to rule the night: HE MADE THE STARS ALSO."**

To the natural mind, THESE THREE lights are just the SUN, MOON and STARS that we can see every day and night when there are no clouds. To the spiritual mind, THESE THREE REVEAL THE GODHEAD--THE FATHER, THE SON, AND THE HOLY GHOST CHURCH--and the beginning of our understanding of the Holy Scriptures and THE LORD'S plan for our Christian lives.

As we know THERE IS ONLY **ONE** GOD, **ONE** SPIRIT and **ONE** CHURCH. Though THE GODHEAD IS ONE SPIRIT, the LORD chose to reveal them as THREE PERSONS, THE FATHER, THE WORD AND THE HOLY GHOST, and through their ministry, all THE TRUTH in THE HOLY SCRIPTURES shall be revealed as we continue.

THE SUN   - OUR HEAVENLY FATHER
THE MOON   - THE SON OF GOD
THE STARS   - THE MANY MEMBERED BODY OF CHRIST, "THE CHURCH"

1 Jn 5:7   The apostle John confirms again the above revelation, **"FOR THERE ARE THREE (not two) THAT BEAR RECORD IN HEAVEN, THE FATHER, THE WORD, AND THE HOLY GHOST, AND <u>THESE THREE ARE ONE</u>."**

The division in THE PRECIOUS CHURCH OF JESUS CHRIST, through the rejection of THE BAPTISM OF THE HOLY GHOST, began with the LACK OF SPIRITUAL UNDERSTANDING by the Church, of the HOLY GHOST, which IS the THIRD PERSON OF THE GODHEAD.

Col 2:9   **"FOR IN HIM (JESUS) DWELLETH THE FULLNESS OF THE GODHEAD BODILY."**

1 Jn 5:7   **"...AND THESE THREE ARE ONE."**

These two scriptures alone, reveal that our LORD JESUS **IS** THE HOLY GHOST. If we reject THE BAPTISM OF THE HOLY GHOST, as many have done, we reject THE FATHER AND THE SON also "BECAUSE THESE THREE ARE ONE".

Many Christians should ask themselves this question, "HOW CAN I RECEIVE JESUS AS MY LORD AND SAVIOUR, AND THEN REJECT HIM AS THE HOLY GHOST, WHEN HE IS THE BAPTIZER WITH THE HOLY GHOST, revealed in the following scriptures?"

Matt 3:11   **"I indeed baptize you with water unto repentance: but he that cometh after me is mightier than I, whose shoes I am not worthy to bear: HE SHALL BAPTIZE YOU WITH THE HOLY GHOST, AND WITH FIRE."**

Jn 1:33   **"And I knew him not: but he that sent me to baptize with water, the same said unto me, UPON WHOM THOU SHALT SEE THE SPIRIT DESCENDING, AND REMAINING ON HIM, THE SAME IS HE WHICH BAPTIZETH WITH THE HOLY GHOST."**

Let us now look at the SUN and how it speaks to us from heaven, revealing many TRUTHS, for an example:

THE SUN

Is 45:5-7   "I AM THE LORD, AND THERE IS NONE ELSE, there is no God beside me: I girded thee, though thou hast not known me: THAT THEY MAY KNOW FROM THE RISING OF THE SUN, and from the west, that there is none beside me. I AM THE LORD, AND THERE IS NONE ELSE. I form the light, and create darkness: I make peace, and create evil: I the Lord do all these things."

This is a direct statement from THE LORD that HE has a message for us, revealed in the RISING OF THE SUN!

Ps 50:1-6   (A Psalm of Asaph.) "The mighty God, even THE LORD, HATH SPOKEN, AND CALLED THE EARTH FROM THE RISING OF THE SUN UNTO THE GOING DOWN THEREOF. Out of Zion, the perfection of beauty, God hath shined. Our God shall come, and shall not keep silence: a fire shall devour before him, and it shall be very tempestuous round about him. He shall call to the heavens from above, and to the earth, that he may judge his people. Gather my saints together unto me; those that have made a covenant with me by sacrifice. And the heavens shall declare his righteousness: for God is judge himself. Selah."

The WORD of the LORD has spoken and gone out to all the earth revealing the SIGNS from the RISING OF THE SUN, calling everyone to come and be SAVED.

And in the going down of the SUN, we see the CRIMSON RED in the sky, reminding the world of THE CRUCIFIXION OF HIS SON JESUS, our LORD and SAVIOUR who shed His blood for our sins.

Matt 5:45   Jesus said, "...**For he maketh his sun to rise on the evil and on the good, and sendeth rain on the just and on the unjust.**"

Many take THE SUN for granted, when THE SUN rises on THE TARES and THE WHEAT, JUST AND UNJUST, EVIL AND GOOD, until THE HARVEST of the LORD, when HE WILL GATHER THE WHEAT (children of the Lord) from among the tares. **NOW** is the accepted time to come to Him as He calls us from THE RISING OF THE SUN to the GOING DOWN of the same. For the day will come, when THE SUN will be turned into DARKNESS and HIS SPIRIT will not strive with man anymore to come unto HIM.

Eccles12:1,2   (TO YOUNG MEN AND WOMEN THE LORD HAS A MESSAGE,) **"REMEMBER NOW THY CREATOR IN THE DAYS OF THY YOUTH..." "...WHILE THE SUN, OR THE LIGHT, OR THE MOON, OR THE STARS, BE NOT DARKENED..."**

This is a CALL FROM THE LORD to young men and women to work with HIM now while it is DAY, for the NIGHT cometh when no man can work, for darkness will cover the earth and gross darkness the people.

Eph 4:26   THE SUN HAS SOMETHING TO DO WITH OUR ANGER, **"...LET NOT THE SUN GO DOWN UPON YOUR WRATH:"**

Ps 113:3   **"FROM THE RISING OF THE SUN UNTO THE GOING DOWN OF THE SAME THE LORD'S NAME IS TO BE PRAISED."**

The reason to PRAISE THE LORD, as we see HIM calling us from THE RISING OF THE SUN, and reminding us of HIS CRUCIFIXION as THE SUN IS GOING DOWN.

Lk 23:44-45   THE SUN withdrew her shining at the crucifixion. **"AND IT WAS ABOUT THE SIXTH HOUR, AND THERE WAS A DARKNESS OVER ALL THE EARTH UNTIL THE NINTH HOUR. AND THE SUN WAS DARKENED, AND THE VEIL OF THE TEMPLE WAS RENT IN THE MIDST."**

For three hours THE SUN was darkened, as THE FATHER (THE SUN) turned His face and could not look on HIS SON while HE bore the sins, past, present and future of all mankind.

Remember, in the darkness of the three hours, there was a LONELY, MYSTERIOUS CRY, "MY GOD, MY GOD, WHY HAST THOU FORSAKEN ME?"

This is an example that everything in the HEAVEN and the EARTH that was created by our heavenly Father, has a message for us in HIS WORD.

Rom 1:20   **"FOR THE INVISIBLE THINGS OF HIM FROM THE CREATION OF THE WORLD ARE CLEARLY SEEN, BEING UNDERSTOOD BY THE THINGS THAT ARE MADE, EVEN HIS ETERNAL POWER AND GODHEAD; SO THAT THEY ARE WITHOUT EXCUSE."**

THE GODHEAD MAKE THEIR FUTURE DWELLING PLACE

Gen 1:26,27   **"AND GOD SAID, LET US** (The Godhead) **MAKE MAN IN OUR IMAGE, AFTER OUR LIKENESS:..."**

One might ask,   "Why did THE GODHEAD make man in their own IMAGE and LIKENESS?"
The answer: "Man would be THEIR TEMPLE or DWELLING PLACE on THE DAY OF PENTECOST.

Jn 14:23   JESUS SAID, **"...IF A MAN LOVE ME, HE WILL KEEP MY WORDS: AND MY FATHER WILL LOVE HIM, AND WE WILL COME UNTO HIM AND MAKE OUR ABODE WITH HIM."**

THESE WORDS were spoken by OUR LORD JESUS before THE DAY OF PENTECOST, that the GODHEAD would live in us through THE BAPTISM OF THE HOLY GHOST.

2 Corinth 6:16-18	Paul again said, "And what agreement hath the temple of God with idols? for **YE ARE THE TEMPLE OF THE LIVING GOD; AS GOD HATH SAID, I WILL DWELL IN THEM, AND WALK IN THEM; AND I WILL BE THEIR GOD, AND THEY SHALL BE MY PEOPLE**. Wherefore come out from among them, and be ye separate, saith the Lord, and touch not the unclean thing; and I will receive you, And will be a Father unto you, and ye shall be my sons and daughters, saith the Lord Almighty."
1 Corinth 6:19	Paul said, **"WHAT? KNOW YE NOT, THAT YOUR BODY IS THE TEMPLE OF THE HOLY GHOST..."**
Is 66:1	**"Thus saith the LORD, The heaven is my throne, and the earth is my footstool: where is the house that ye build unto me? and where is the place of my rest?"**

THE GOD OF GLORY, came down and visited MOSES in THE TABERNACLE, and visited Solomon in THE TEMPLE, saying what HOUSE WILL YE BUILD ME? I will not live in TEMPLES made with man's hands!

Now in these last days, through THE BAPTISM OF THE HOLY GHOST, we can understand that the GODHEAD desires to live in THEIR TEMPLE, THAT THEY HAD MADE SO LONG AGO IN THEIR IMAGE AND LIKENESS, and this began to take place on THE DAY OF PENTECOST, through THE BAPTISM OF THE HOLY GHOST.

Haggai 2:9	Revealing the above, **"THE GLORY OF THE LATTER HOUSE** (or temple) **SHALL BE GREATER THAN THE FORMER..."** **(HOUSE).**

THE CREATION OF THE LIVING SOUL

Gen 2:7	**"And THE LORD GOD, formed man of the dust of the ground, AND BREATHED INTO HIS NOSTRILS THE BREATH OF LIFE; AND MAN BECAME A LIVING SOUL."**

First we MUST UNDERSTAND that we are that living soul, and that GOD has a plan for each one of us if we are obedient to HIS VOICE. We are created in HIS IMAGE, with our OWN WILL to choose LIFE or DEATH, because our SOUL is in our own hands.
Psalm 119:109, My soul is continually in my hand:

AS THE PROPHET said, "Many, many are in THE VALLEY OF DECISION, choose ye this day whom you will serve!"

GOD is a SPIRIT and the WORD IS HIS VOICE, and the LORD needs a human body (HIS TEMPLE) to speak and express HIMSELF in. As the CHILDREN OF GOD are BORN OF HIS SPIRIT, they must now learn to be led by THE SPIRIT to become the children of GOD!

What a beautiful GOD! HE could **make** us serve HIM, as we breathe HIS BREATH to stay alive! There are many other things, too numerous to mention! But HE GAVE us our OWN WILL and SPIRIT that we may choose to be HIS FRIEND and come to HIM in FAITH and ENTER into HIS LOVE and be saved from HIS WRATH to come.

On the other hand, because HE made us with OUR OWN WILL to CHOOSE to obey HIS voice or reject HIS voice, HE will JUDGE us in the last day, regarding our response.

The STATE of OUR SOUL is revealed on our faces as we WALK and have a good relationship with HIM, purifying OUR SOULS in obedience to HIS WORD unto the end.

SHADOW OF THE CHURCH BEING FORMED

Gen 2:21-23   **"AND THE LORD CAUSED A DEEP SLEEP
                         TO FALL UPON ADAM, and he slept: AND HE
                         TOOK ONE OF HIS RIBS AND CLOSED UP
                         THE FLESH INSTEAD THEREOF.
                         AND THE RIB, WHICH THE LORD HAD
                         TAKEN FROM MAN, MADE HE A WOMAN**
                         (The Church)**, AND BROUGHT HER UNTO
                         THE MAN"** (JESUS).

This is a PERFECT SHADOW of OUR LORD JESUS injured or crucified,
and returned to HIS FATHER IN HEAVEN, "THE DEEP SLEEP" while the
CHURCH or HIS BRIDE IS being gathered together in "ONE" from all over
the earth and is MAKING HERSELF READY, TO BE PRESENTED TO (the
man) OUR LORD JESUS ON HIS RETURN from HEAVEN.

Gen 2:23   **"And ADAM said, THIS IS NOW BONE OF
                      MY BONES, AND FLESH of my FLESH: SHE
                      SHALL BE CALLED WOMAN** (The Church)**,
                      because she was taken out of man"** (our
                      LORD JESUS).

THE SPIRITUAL REVELATION FOR ALL THE CHILDREN OF GOD, is
that we are MEMBERS OF HIS BODY, HIS FLESH AND HIS BONES,
THE CHURCH, and HE IS LIVING IN THAT BODY OF BELIEVERS BY
HIS SPIRIT TODAY!

PAUL THE APOSTLE CONFIRMS THE REVELATION

Eph 5:30   **"FOR WE ARE MEMBERS OF HIS BODY,
                      HIS FLESH, AND OF HIS BONES."**

We can now confirm that the IMPORTANT TRUTHS IN THE NEW
TESTAMENT are hidden in the SHADOWS OF THE OLD TESTAMENT,
ONLY TO BE REVEALED BY HIS SPIRIT!

Rev 19:7-13

"LET US BE GLAD AND REJOICE, AND GIVE HONOUR TO HIM FOR THE MARRIAGE OF THE LAMB IS COME, AND HIS WIFE (The Church) HATH MADE HERSELF READY.

And to her was granted that she should be arrayed in fine linen, clean and white: for the fine linen is the righteousness of saints.

And he saith unto me, Write, Blessed *are* they which are called unto the marriage supper of the Lamb. And he saith unto me, These are the true sayings of God.

And I fell at his feet to worship him. And he said unto me, See *thou do it* not: I am thy fellowservant, and of thy brethren that have the testimony of Jesus: worship God: for the testimony of Jesus is the spirit of prophecy.

And I saw heaven opened, and behold a white horse; and he that sat upon him *was* called Faithful and True, and in righteousness he doth judge and make war.

His eyes *were* as a flame of fire, and on his head *were* many crowns; and he had a name written, that no man knew, but he himself.

And he *was* clothed with a vesture dipped in blood: and his name is called THE WORD OF GOD."

ISRAEL, SHADOW OF THE CHURCH'S DELIVERANCE, OUR EXAMPLE:

1 Corinth 10:11

"Now all these things happened unto them for ensamples (or types): and they are written for

OUR ADMONITION, upon whom the ends of
the world are come."

1 Corinth 10:12   "WHEREFORE LET HIM THAT THINKETH
HE STANDETH TAKE HEED LEST
HE FALL."

Ex 12:3-13   READ:
Reveals THE ACCOUNT of Israel's deliverance
from Egypt, also for the CHURCH. The account
is self explanatory, so I will not have to proceed
verse by verse.

THE LAMB   THE PREPARATION FOR DELIVERANCE
A SHADOW OF OUR LORD JESUS

Ex 12:3   "...Take to them, every man A LAMB..."
Ex 12:5   "Your LAMB shall be without blemish, a male
of the first year:..."
Ex 12:6   "...And the whole assembly of THE
CONGREGATION OF ISRAEL, shall kill it in
the EVENING."

THE BLOOD

Ex 12:7   "And they shall take of THE BLOOD, and
strike it on the two side posts and the upper door
posts of the houses, where they shall eat it."
Ex 12:13   "And THE BLOOD shall be to you for a token
upon the houses where ye are: AND WHEN I
SEE THE BLOOD, I WILL PASS OVER
YOU, and the plague shall not be upon you to
destroy you, when I smite the land of Egypt."

THIS IS THE LORD'S PASSOVER OR FEAST OF UNLEAVENED
BREAD, written as a SHADOW OF THE CRUCIFIXION OF THE LAMB
OF GOD, WHO SHED HIS BLOOD AS THE EVENING SACRIFICE FOR
OUR SINS.

| Lk 22:7-16 | **READ:**
"Then came THE DAY OF UNLEAVENED BREAD, WHEN THE PASSOVER MUST BE KILLED." |

The Lord's supper as we partake of it today, is THE LORD'S PASSOVER, through HIS BLOOD, and remember through our generations and teach our children, that THE LORD has done this for us that we might live!

Israel, as THE CHURCH, was now free from Egypt. WAS THE PASSOVER LAMB AND THE SHEDDING OF HIS PRECIOUS BLOOD THE END OF OUR SALVATION?

Though many today celebrate the deliverance through the SPIRIT BIRTH, saying "I AM SAVED", not understanding that it is ONLY THE BEGINNING. Israel is an example to THE CHURCH, that after their DELIVERANCE from EGYPT, they were to take THEIR JOURNEY TO THE PROMISED LAND.

THE JOURNEY OF ISRAEL AND THE CHURCH

As Israel was delivered out of Egypt, there was a JOURNEY they were to make to reach "THE PROMISED LAND".

So with THE CHURCH, as we are delivered from the darkness and bondage of this world by THE BLOOD OF THE LAMB and THE SPIRIT BIRTH, it is not sufficient to declare, "I AM SAVED", when we are on a JOURNEY as ISRAEL, to our PROMISED LAND and shall be SAVED when we reach the END OF THE JOURNEY!

Prov 29:18 **"Where there is NO VISION, the people perish:..."**

If we have no VISION, we will not take our JOURNEY UNTO LIFE, and will remain in THE TRUTH of THE BORN AGAIN EXPERIENCE which is ONLY THE BEGINNING OF THE JOURNEY.

The Lord explained to ISRAEL, one of the reasons for the JOURNEY, was to **(Deuteronomy 8:2) "...PROVE THEE, TO KNOW WHAT *WAS* IN THINE HEART, WHETHER THOU WOULDEST KEEP HIS COMMANDMENTS, OR NO."**

Jn 16:13   Jesus spake of a JOURNEY, "**...WHEN HE, THE SPIRIT OF TRUTH** (THE HOLY GHOST) **IS COME, HE WILL GUIDE YOU INTO ALL TRUTH:...**"

In the beginning, all THE TRUTH we have is THE BORN AGAIN EXPERIENCE, and many don't want to JOURNEY beyond THAT TRUTH, into THE TRUTH OF THE BAPTISM OF THE HOLY GHOST.

2 Pet 1:12   Peter speaks of a JOURNEY IN TRUTH, "**...THOUGH YE KNOW THEM, AND BE ESTABLISHED IN THE PRESENT TRUTH.**"

Revealing there is "PAST TRUTH" - "PRESENT TRUTH" and "FUTURE TRUTH" that we must be led into by THE SPIRIT OF TRUTH.

One might ask themselves, "WHAT TRUTH AM I ESTABLISHED IN?"

Jn 14:6   JESUS again speaks of a JOURNEY, "**...I AM THE WAY, THE TRUTH, and THE LIFE:...**"

Revealing "THE WAY" IS THE SPIRIT BIRTH. "THE TRUTH" IS THE JOURNEY. "THE LIFE" IS THE END.

Heb 6:1   Paul reveals THE JOURNEY, "**Therefore leaving the principles of the DOCTRINE OF CHRIST,** (THE SPIRIT BIRTH) **Let US GO ON TO PERFECTION;...**"

Gen 5:24   ENOCH gave the example, "**AND ENOCH WALKED WITH GOD: AND WAS NOT; FOR GOD TOOK HIM.**"

Question: Do you still want to stay where you are, or JOURNEY ON IN FURTHER TRUTH?

Chapter Five

The
Baptism
Of
The Holy Ghost

THE PROPHET SPEAKS OF THE HOLY GHOST TO COME

Lk 24:44-45	"...ALL THINGS MUST BE FULFILLED WHICH ARE WRITTEN IN, THE LAW, THE PSALMS <u>AND THE PROPHETS</u> CONCERNING ME. <u>THEN</u> OPENED HE THEIR UNDERSTANDING TO UNDERSTAND THE SCRIPTURES."
Is 28:9	"WHOM SHALL THE LORD TEACH KNOWLEDGE? AND WHOM SHALL HE MAKE TO UNDERSTAND DOCTRINE?" THEM THAT ARE WEANED FROM THE MILK, AND DRAWN FROM THE BREASTS."

The Lord is speaking of our SPIRIT BIRTH into THE KINGDOM OF GOD, where at that time we are BABES in CHRIST and are fed the sincere MILK OF THE WORD, as is taught in many local churches today!

But as I have written before, THE SPIRIT BIRTH is only the beginning of our life in CHRIST, and THE LORD wants us to be WEANED FROM THE MILK of the WORD, and DRAWN FROM THE BREAST and grow up in CHRIST!

Heb 5:13	Paul reveals the TRUTH, **"FOR EVERYONE THAT USES MILK, IS UNSKILLFUL IN THE WORD OF RIGHTEOUSNESS, FOR HE IS A BABE."**
Heb 6:1	Paul again says, **"THEREFORE LEAVING "THE PRINCIPLES" OF THE DOCTRINE OF CHRIST** (Born again experience) **LET US GO ON TO PERFECTION;..."**

If we do not journey in TRUTH beyond THE SPIRIT BIRTH, and be weaned from THE MILK, it is automatic that we will REJECT further TRUTH, THE BAPTISM OF THE HOLY GHOST and the EVIDENCE OF SPEAKING IN OTHER TONGUES as the SPIRIT GIVES THE UTTERANCE (Acts 2:4).

Now, why does THE LORD want us WEANED FROM THE MILK and DRAWN FROM THE BREAST? Because HE wants to reveal THE BAPTISM OF THE HOLY GHOST to come.

Is 28:11,12   Again, **"FOR WITH STAMMERING LIPS AND ANOTHER TONGUE, WILL HE SPEAK TO THIS PEOPLE, YET THEY WOULD NOT HEAR."**

REVEALING, that as our bodies are HIS TEMPLE, THE LORD HIMSELF is going to SPEAK WITH STAMMERING LIPS AND ANOTHER TONGUE OUT OF HIS TEMPLE, which many are rejecting today, when THE PROPHET said before hand, "YET THEY WOULD NOT HEAR".

1 Corinth 14:21   Paul refers to the above scripture, **"WITH MEN OF OTHER TONGUES AND OTHER LIPS WILL I SPEAK UNTO THIS PEOPLE, AND YET FOR ALL THAT, WILL THEY NOT HEAR ME, SAITH THE LORD!"**

JESUS IS THE BAPTIZER WITH THE HOLY GHOST

John the Baptist speaks, (the forerunner of Christ).

Jn 1:33   **"And I knew HIM not: but HE that sent me to baptize with WATER, the same said unto me, UPON WHOM THOU SHALT SEE THE SPIRIT DESCENDING, AND REMAINING ON HIM, THE SAME IS HE WHICH BAPTIZETH WITH THE HOLY GHOST."**

Matt 3:11   **"I indeed baptize you with water unto REPENTANCE: but HE that cometh after me is mightier than I, whose shoes I am not worthy to bear: HE SHALL BAPTIZE YOU WITH THE HOLY GHOST, AND WITH FIRE."**

This is the voice of the last of the OLD TESTAMENT PROPHETS who said, **"I AM THE VOICE OF ONE CRYING IN THE WILDERNESS,"** and THAT VOICE is crying again,

Heb 3:7-19

"Wherefore (as the Holy Ghost saith, To day if ye will hear his voice,

Harden not your hearts, as in the provocation, in the day of temptation in the wilderness:

When your fathers tempted me, proved me, and saw my works forty years.

Wherefore I was grieved with that generation, and said, They do alway err in *their* heart; and they have not known my ways.

So I sware in my wrath, They shall not enter into my rest.)

Take heed, brethren, lest there be in any of you an evil heart of unbelief, in departing from the living God.

But exhort one another daily, while it is called To day; lest any of you be hardened through the deceitfulness of sin.

For we are made partakers of Christ, if we hold the beginning of our confidence stedfast unto the end;

While it is said, To day if ye will hear his voice, harden not your hearts, as in the provocation.

For some, when they had heard, did provoke: howbeit not all that came out of Egypt by Moses.

THE PROPHET SPEAKS OF THE HOLY GHOST TO COME (cont.)

> **But with whom was he grieved forty years? was it not with them that had sinned, whose carcases fell in the wilderness?**
>
> **And to whom sware he that they should not enter into his rest, but to them that believed not?**
>
> **So we see that they could not enter in because of unbelief."**

In these pages, OUR HEAVENLY FATHER gave THE FOUNDATIONS and SHADOWS of THE HOLY GHOST to be fulfilled by our LORD JESUS, HIS SON.

OUR HEAVENLY FATHER spake to the fathers of old, by THE PROPHETS, and today HE SPEAKS TO US BY HIS SON.

Jn 5:17   JESUS SAID, **"MY FATHER WORKETH HITHERTO, AND I WORK."**

Let us explore THE WORK OF THE SON regarding THE BAPTISM OF THE HOLY GHOST.

SHADOWS OF THE HOLY GHOST SEEKING A BRIDE FOR JESUS

Acts 2:1-4:   **"And when the day of Pentecost was fully come, they were all with one accord in one place.**

> **And suddenly there came a sound from heaven as of a rushing mighty wind, and it filled all the house where they were sitting.**
>
> **And there appeared unto them cloven tongues like as of fire, and it sat upon each of them."**

SHADOWS OF THE HOLY GHOST SEEKING A BRIDE FOR JESUS (cont.)

AND THEY WERE ALL FILLED WITH THE HOLY GHOST, AND BEGAN TO SPEAK WITH OTHER TONGUES, AS THE SPIRIT GAVE THE UTTERANCE."

As I mentioned earlier, ALL THE FOUNDATIONS and SHADOWS written in THE OLD TESTAMENT, must be FULFILLED in THE NEW TESTAMENT.

This is A SHADOW of THE DAY OF PENTECOST, when THE HOLY GHOST was sent down from heaven, TO SEEK A BRIDE FOR JESUS, and the HOLY GHOST is STILL seeking for that BRIDE through THE BAPTISM OF THE HOLY GHOST!

LET US BEGIN TO REVEAL THE SHADOW:

ABRAHAM	-	As our HEAVENLY FATHER
THE SERVANT	-	AS THE HOLY GHOST
REBEKAH	-	AS THE BRIDE
ISAAC	-	AS OUR LORD JESUS
CAMELS	-	One for THE BRIDE, NINE to carry the NINE GIFTS to be presented to THE BRIDE

Gen 24:3	"...Thou shalt not take A WIFE unto MY SON, of the daughters of the Canaanites (unbelievers)..."
Gen 24:4	"But thou shalt go unto my country, and to my kindred, (Born again) and take a WIFE unto MY SON, ISAAC."
Gen 24:5-8	"What if "...the woman will not be WILLING TO FOLLOW ME..."

There are so many today, that have rejected the HOLY GHOST, and will not follow!

Gen 24:10 READ:	And THE SERVANT the Holy Ghost took TEN CAMELS... one for THE BRIDE, NINE for the NINE GIFTS, of the Spirit... for ALL the goods of his MASTER WERE IN HIS HAND.

Gen 24:11 READ:	Stops at a well in the evening, where women come to draw water from the well.
Gen 24:14 READ:	The Servant asks for a sign, (one that gives drink to others, then shall I know).
Gen 24:15-21 READ:	The sign was given, as Rebekah appears, the test of the water was made by THE SERVANT, and REBEKAH fulfilled all that THE SERVANT required.
Gen 24:22 READ:	The FIRST GIFTS given were for HER EARS and HER HANDS. Note: Her ears that would hear the Master's voice and her hands that would reach out with compassion to others.
Gen 24:24-25 READ:	Who's daughter art thou? (Are you a Christian?) Is there room in THY FATHER'S HOUSE for US (the Holy Ghost) to dwell in? The final test, confession of who's daughter she was (who she belonged to) and accepted the SERVANT into her house.
Gen 24:27-31 READ:	The excitement began to grow as REBEKAH RAN to her father's house to witness to all her house, the things that THE SERVANT asked of her. (This is the result after we are baptized in the Holy Ghost.)
Gen 24:34 READ:	THE SERVANT reveals HIMSELF, "I AM ABRAHAM'S SERVANT, And I have come to find a BRIDE for MY MASTER'S SON, ISAAC." Acts 2:4 **"AND THEY WERE ALL FILLED WITH THE HOLY GHOST, AND BEGAN TO SPEAK WITH OTHER TONGUES, AS THE SPIRIT GAVE THEM UTTERANCE."**
Gen 24:53 READ:	The GIFTS OF THE HOLY GHOST are given. **1 Corinthians 12:7-10 "BUT THE MANIFESTATION OF THE SPIRIT IS GIVEN TO EVERY MAN TO PROFIT WITHAL. FOR TO ONE IS GIVEN BY THE SPIRIT THE WORD OF WISDOM; TO ANOTHER THE WORD OF KNOWLEDGE BY THE SAME SPIRIT; TO ANOTHER**

SHADOWS OF THE HOLY GHOST SEEKING A BRIDE FOR JESUS (cont.)

	FAITH BY THE SAME SPIRIT; TO ANOTHER THE GIFTS OF HEALING BY THE SAME SPIRIT; TO ANOTHER THE WORKING OF MIRACLES; TO ANOTHER PROPHECY; TO ANOTHER DISCERNING OF SPIRITS; TO ANOTHER DIVERS KINDS OF TONGUES; TO ANOTHER THE INTERPRETATION OF TONGUES:"
Gen 24:54 READ:	Great rejoicing followed the giving of the GIFTS. Note: These are only given by the Holy Ghost, when we are baptized in the Holy Ghost.
Gen 24:55 READ:	Resistance began with REBEKAH'S mother and brother, not understanding the importance of the SERVANT'S coming in the first place. (As is happening in many churches today.)
Gen 24:56 READ:	THE SERVANT SAID, "HINDER ME NOT!" Though many in this hour hinder THE HOLY GHOST, and prevent those that would come.
Gen 24:57 READ:	DECISION TIME, we will call REBEKAH and let HER MAKE THE DECISION. Note: Rebekah is the church and each local church must make their decision on the Baptism of the Holy Ghost. **Joel 3:14 "MULTITUDES, MULTITUDES IN THE VALLEY OF DECISION: FOR THE DAY OF THE LORD IS NEAR IN THE VALLEY OF DECISION."**
Gen 24: 58 READ:	"WILT THOU GO WITH THE SERVANT?" REBEKAH ANSWERED, "**I WILL GO!**" What wonderful joy when we hear of the church that says, "Yes Lord," to the baptism of the Holy Ghost.
Gen 24: 60 READ:	THE CALLING OF THE BRIDE, "BE THOU THE MOTHER OF THOUSANDS OF MILLIONS, AND LET THY SEED POSSESS THE GATE OF THOSE WHICH HATE THEM."
Gen 24:61 READ:	THE JOURNEY OF THE BRIDE TO MEET ISAAC BEGINS. SHE FOLLOWED THE

SERVANT, AND THE SERVANT LED HER IN HIS WAY. **John 16:13** **"HOWBEIT WHEN HE, THE SPIRIT OF TRUTH, IS COME, HE WILL GUIDE YOU INTO ALL TRUTH: FOR HE SHALL NOT SPEAK OF HIMSELF; BUT WHATSOEVER HE SHALL HEAR, THAT SHALL HE SPEAK: AND HE WILL SHEW YOU THINGS TO COME."**

Gen 24:62 READ: AND ISAAC CAME FROM THE WAY OF "THE WELL".

Gen 24:63 READ: In the EVENING, (as the sun is setting, the Bride is presented to her husband who is waiting for her), ISAAC saw "THE CAMELS WERE COMING," as HE LIFTED UP HIS EYES.

Gen 24:64 READ: AND REBEKAH LIFTED UP HER EYES, and when she SAW ISAAC, SHE jumped off the camel. **Jeremiah 33:11** **"THE VOICE OF JOY, AND THE VOICE OF GLADNESS, THE VOICE OF THE BRIDEGROOM, AND THE VOICE OF THE BRIDE, THE VOICE OF THEM THAT SHALL SAY, PRAISE THE LORD OF HOSTS: FOR THE LORD IS GOOD; FOR HIS MERCY ENDURETH FOR EVER: AND OF THEM THAT SHALL BRING THE SACRIFICE OF PRAISE INTO THE HOUSE OF THE LORD. FOR I WILL CAUSE TO RETURN THE CAPTIVITY OF THE LAND, AS AT THE FIRST, SAITH THE LORD."**

Gen 24:65 READ: REBEKAH SAID, "WHAT MAN IS THIS, THAT WALKETH IN THE FIELD TO MEET US?" The SERVANT SAID, "IT IS MY MASTER." REBEKAH TOOK A VEIL and covered herself in preparation for the wedding.

We may not understand the completeness of THE SHADOW that shall be fulfilled, but THE CHURCH has an opportunity NOW, to make herself ready to meet OUR LORD through THE BAPTISM OF THE HOLY GHOST that came, calling you and I on THE DAY OF PENTECOST!

AARON'S ROD THAT BUDDED

**THIS IS A SHADOW OF THE CHALLENGE TO
THE POWER OF THE HOLY GHOST MINISTRY TODAY**

Is 11:1   JESUS IS THE ROD, **"AND THERE SHALL
                            COME FORTH A ROD OUT OF THE STEM
                            OF JESSE, AND A BRANCH SHALL GROW
                            OUT OF HIS ROOTS:"**

The CHURCH IS THE BRANCH that grew out of HIS ROOTS. Shall we not
have a ROD and POWER also, as THE ROD (JESUS) dwells in us in THE
POWER OF THE HOLY GHOST?

Aaron's ROD THAT BUDDED, is a SHADOW of the HOLY GHOST FILLED
CHURCH today on their way to THE PROMISED LAND in TOTAL
VICTORY!

Aaron's ROD can be likened to a person's ministry, ANOINTED AND
WITH POWER!

Israel, as many in the CHURCH, are CHALLENGING THE ROD, or the
ANOINTED MINISTRY today over THE BAPTISM OF THE HOLY GHOST,
when JESUS, "THE ANOINTED ONE", **IS** THE BAPTIZER WITH THE
HOLY GHOST!

Matt 3:11   **"I INDEED BAPTIZE YOU WITH WATER
                            UNTO REPENTANCE: BUT HE THAT
                            COMETH AFTER ME IS MIGHTIER THAN
                            I, WHOSE SHOES I AM NOT WORTHY TO
                            BEAR: HE SHALL BAPTIZE YOU WITH
                            THE HOLY GHOST, AND WITH FIRE:"**

AS THE LEADERS of the tribes of Israel were put to the TEST, so the LORD
is putting every ROD or MINISTRY to THE TEST in these final hours, over
THE BAPTISM OF THE HOLY GHOST that will cause our ROD or ministry
to begin BUDDING with POWER, which I believe is the cry of all our hearts.

1 Corinth 4:19   Paul said, **"But I will come to you shortly, if the LORD WILL, AND I WILL KNOW, NOT THE SPEECH OF THEM WHICH ARE PUFFED UP, BUT THE POWER."** (of the Holy Ghost)

Acts 1:8   **"But ye shall receive power, after that the Holy Ghost is come upon you: and ye shall be witnesses unto me both in Jerusalem, and in Judaea, and in Samaria, and unto the uttermost part of the earth."**

THE CHURCH began to BUD on the DAY OF PENTECOST, and there has been much opposition from other RODS or MINISTRIES ever since, over THE BAPTISM OF THE HOLY GHOST.

Every ROD or MINISTRY should ask, "IS MY ROD or MINISTRY BUDDING, DO I HAVE THE POWER IN MY MINISTRY or am I just ANOTHER ROD?"

THE TRUE CHURCH WILL BLOSSOM AND BRING FORTH FRUIT IN THE FINAL HOUR. THE PROPHET SAID,

Haggai 2:9   **"THE GLORY OF THIS LATTER HOUSE SHALL BE GREATER THAN OF THE FORMER, SAITH THE LORD OF HOSTS: AND IN THIS PLACE WILL I GIVE PEACE, SAITH THE LORD OF HOSTS."**

Rom 14:17   **"For the Kingdom of God is not meat and drink; but righteousness, and peace, and joy in the Holy Ghost."**

AND THE MINISTRY ARE RESPONSIBLE BEFORE THE LORD TO SEE THAT THE LATTER HOUSE **IS** GREATER THAN THE FORMER HOUSE, BY RECEIVING THE POWER, THROUGH THE BAPTISM OF THE HOLY GHOST!

Many will be challenged as Aaron was, by the brethren who have RODS that are not BUDDING.

As with ISRAEL, so with us today, THE LORD SETTLES THE ROD PROBLEM.

Num 17:2	**"...TAKE EVERYONE OF THEM (THE LEADERS) <u>A ROD</u>..." "...WRITE EVERY MAN'S NAME UPON HIS ROD."**
Num 17:5	**"AND IT SHALL COME TO PASS, THAT THE MAN'S ROD, WHOM I SHALL CHOOSE, SHALL BLOSSOM."**
Num 17:7	**"AND MOSES LAID UP THE RODS BEFORE THE LORD, IN THE TABERNACLE OF WITNESS."**
Num 17:8	**"AND, BEHOLD, THE ROD OF AARON..." "...BROUGHT FORTH BUDS, AND BLOOMED BLOSSOMS, AND YIELDED ALMONDS."**

Dear children of the Lord, as we preach THE GOSPEL of the KINGDOM, our ROD or ministry is beginning to BUD, but we must go beyond THE ROD BUDDING, and let it BLOSSOM with THE POWER OF THE HOLY GHOST and bring forth in your ministry (FOR THE WORD IS WITH POWER!)

So important is THE ROD, that it appears again in THE ARK OF THE COVENANT as THE HOLY GHOST!

As THE GODHEAD, FATHER, SON AND HOLY GHOST, were revealed in the beginning, THEY NOW APPEAR AS THE CONTENTS OF THE ARK.

cross reference:

Heb 9:4	**"Which had the golden censer, and the ark of the covenant overlaid round about with gold, wherein was the GOLDEN POT THAT HAD MANNA, and AARON'S ROD THAT BUDDED, and the TABLES OF THE COVENANT;"**

AARON'S ROD THAT BUDDED (cont.)

Ex 31:18 READ: THE FATHER - Two tables of testimony, tables of stone, written with the finger of GOD.

Heb 9:4 READ: THE SON - THE GOLDEN POT THAT HAD MANNA, THE BREAD OF LIFE.

Heb 9:4 READ: THE HOLY GHOST - AARON'S ROD THAT BUDDED.

Finally,
1 Jn 5:7   **"THERE ARE THREE THAT BEAR RECORD IN HEAVEN, THE FATHER, THE WORD, (or SON) and THE HOLY GHOST: AND THESE THREE ARE ONE."**

The contents of THE ARK then is CHRIST OUR LORD, because these three are ONE!

Col 2:9   To confirm **"FOR IN HIM DWELLETH ALL THE FULLNESS OF THE GODHEAD BODILY."**

The Church will come into its fullness very soon.

To have the CONTENTS OF THE ARK complete in us, EVERY WORD OF GOD FROM THE PAST AND PRESENT will be required, to have THE FIRE OF THE HOLY GHOST BAPTISM burning within us, to bring back our KING!

Chapter Six

The Anointing Of His Presence

JESUS CHRIST, "THE ANOINTED ONE"

Just a few scriptures to reveal the POWER of the ANOINTING OF HIS PRESENCE. For what purpose is a vessel of THE LORD, if we have no POWER to finish HIS WORK which is revealed through the Baptism of the Holy Ghost.

The mystery of the ANOINTING OF HIS PRESENCE, is not understood by many in THE MINISTRY today. For we can minister THE WORD by knowledge, without the ANOINTING, or we can have a relationship with THE WORD and minister THE WORD with the ANOINTING and POWER!

1 Corinth 4:19-20   Paul said, "BUT I WILL COME TO YOU SHORTLY, IF THE LORD WILL, AND WILL KNOW, NOT THE SPEECH OF THEM WHICH ARE PUFFED UP, BUT THE POWER."

                          "FOR THE KINGDOM OF GOD *IS* NOT IN WORD, BUT IN POWER."

1 Corinth 2:5   "THAT YOUR FAITH SHOULD NOT STAND IN THE WISDOM OF MEN, BUT IN THE POWER OF GOD."

THE POWER OF THE ANOINTING

Is 10:27   "...THE YOKE SHALL BE DESTROYED BECAUSE OF THE ANOINTING..."

Is 61:1-3   "THE SPIRIT OF THE LORD GOD *IS* UPON ME;
                        BECAUSE THE LORD HATH ANOINTED ME TO PREACH GOOD TIDINGS UNTO THE MEEK; HE HATH SENT ME TO BIND UP THE BROKENHEARTED, TO PROCLAIM LIBERTY TO THE CAPTIVES, AND THE OPENING OF THE PRISON TO *THEM THAT ARE* BOUND;"

Bondage, sickness, fear, etc., shall be destroyed by THE ANOINTING!

2 Kings 13:21   **"...WHEN THE MAN WAS LET DOWN, AND TOUCHED THE BONES OF ELISHA, HE REVIVED, AND STOOD UP ON HIS FEET."**

Even after the death of his body, ELISHA contained the ANOINTING in his bones.

A FEW EXPERIENCES I have had in my life with the anointing

My personal experiences IN THE ANOINTING, stir my heart into a closer relationship with THE LORD than ever before, that I might please HIM.

About eleven years ago, I was dying, there was none to help, as my heart was failing. The whole assembly of the CHURCH witnessed one Sunday Morning as I practically crawled to the pulpit to minister THE WORD. As I approached the pulpit, THE ANOINTING came on me, and in a few seconds, I was leaping, and so strong, I could have leaped over a wall! PRAISE GOD FOR THE POWER OF HIS ANOINTING!

With my faith now standing on THE POWER OF HIS ANOINTING, I found that Satan did not fear THE PREACHING OF THE WORD, but he was afraid of the ANOINTING that should accompany the WORD.

The devil also knows who GOD'S ANOINTED are. We found this taking place as my wife and I stopped in a Cafe in New Orleans. A well dressed business man with a brief case, was seated two tables from us. As we set our eyes on him, he threw all his food on the floor and began barking like a dog and departed quickly from the Cafe.

THE UGANDA EAST AFRICA EXPERIENCE

While ministering THE KINGDOM OF GOD to about three thousand natives, the PRESENCE OF THE LORD AND THE ANOINTING was so powerful, that I could not stand on my feet, and my face and hands were white as snow. What an experience!

THE INDIA EXPERIENCE

In India where the people are very poor, I came to preach THE GOSPEL OF THE KINGDOM unto them. I knew then, as the people brought forth the sick and the dumb into the streets to be healed, that the preaching of the WORD was not sufficient, but that I must have THE POWER OF THE ANOINTING present to heal. In a few seconds THE ANOINTING was present and the LORD healed them all.

THE GOSPEL IS NOT IN WORD ONLY, BUT WITH POWER! I say all this to encourage all to seek the Lord with all their heart, that they may accomplish these things mentioned, in their ministry. Also, that our Lord Jesus Christ through the baptism of the Holy Ghost, may be glorified.

MOSES KNEW THE IMPORTANCE OF HIS PRESENCE

Ex 33:14   **"...MY PRESENCE SHALL GO WITH THEE, AND I WILL GIVE THEE REST."**

How wonderful for us to have a GOD that we have never SEEN, give us HIS WRITTEN WORD for us to believe and act upon it.

But how much more wonderful, for HIM to give us THE ANOINTING OF HIS PRESENCE to encourage our hearts that HE is with us, even if we cannot see HIM!

THE SKIN OF MOSES' FACE SHONE BECAUSE OF THE ANOINTING

Ex 34:29-35 READ: **Moses didn't know that HIS FACE SHONE while he talked with the LORD.**

THE ANOINTING REQUIRED TO BE IN THE RAPTURE

Matt 25:1-13 READ: **Five were wise and had the ANOINTING.**
                      Five were foolish and had no ANOINTING.

PERSECUTION BECAUSE OF THE ANOINTING

Ps 105:15   **"Saying, TOUCH NOT MINE ANOINTED, and do my prophets no harm."**

This is a direct commandment from THE LORD. One might ask, "Why is the LORD so concerned about HIS ANOINTED?"

Because, THE ANOINTING in them will convict men of the way they are serving HIM, and of SIN in their lives!

The ANOINTED VESSEL is THE LORD HIMSELF living in a human body and is the closest we will be to THE LORD, until the JUDGMENT DAY.

If we do not want to be persecuted for THE KINGDOM OF GOD'S sake, all I can say is, "Don't have THE ANOINTING OF HIS PRESENCE!"

THE ANOINTING OF HIS PRESENCE

FINALLY:

Acts 1:8   **"Ye shall receive POWER (or ANOINTING) after that THE HOLY GHOST is come upon you:..."**

The POWER OF THE ANOINTING was transferred from HEAVEN TO EARTH on the DAY OF PENTECOST, which is why many are persecuted that are BAPTIZED in THE HOLY GHOST, for this is the first experience of THE ANOINTING in our lives!

The anointing is not something the Lord gives for blessing, but for delivering **power** to break **every** yoke! It is not given to just anyone, but through His great wisdom, knowing the heart of the individual and his obedience to His Word, and that the individual will first be of this mind, and be prepared to sacrifice their lives for the Kingdom.

For when the Lord said, "TOUCH NOT MINE ANOINTED," He knew that all the forces of darkness would come against that individual, for the enemy knows that **only** the anointing of His Holy presence will break **every** yoke that Satan puts upon God's people.

The anointing of the Lord, reveals God's stamp of approval. After being tried and proven, now through their love for the Saviour, the people will know that God is surely manifested in this person's life through sacrifice.

AMEN!

Chapter Seven

The Father, Son And Holy Ghost Are One

IF WE UNDERSTAND THE GODHEAD IN THE BEGINNING, WE WILL UNDERSTAND THE GODHEAD IN THE END AND THE DAY OF PENTECOST.

1 Jn 5:7	**"For There are THREE THAT BEAR RECORD in HEAVEN;**

    1) **THE FATHER,**
    2) **THE WORD, and**
    3) **THE HOLY GHOST: <u>AND THESE THREE ARE ONE</u>."**

The above scripture reveals to us, that JESUS IS the FATHER - SON and HOLY GHOST **"<u>BECAUSE THESE THREE ARE ONE</u>."**

CONFIRMATION

Col 2:8	**"Beware lest any man spoil you through philosophy and vain deceit, after the tradition of men, after the rudiments of the world, and not after Christ."** (who is the Holy Ghost)
Col 2:9	**"<u>FOR IN HIM DWELLETH ALL THE FULLNESS OF THE GODHEAD BODILY</u>."**

Again it is REVEALED, that JESUS IS THE HOLY GHOST, if you can receive it, ALL THREE CAME DOWN ON THE "DAY OF PENTECOST" IN THE PERSON OF THE HOLY GHOST.

TO RESIST THE HOLY GHOST BAPTISM, WE RESIST JESUS WHO IS THE HOLY GHOST, AND THE BAPTIZER WITH THE HOLY GHOST!

THE ABOVE IS THE REASON FOR THIS WARNING ABOUT THE HOLY GHOST

Matt 12:31-32	**"Wherefore I say unto you, ALL MANNER OF SIN and BLASPHEMY shall be forgiven unto men: But the BLASPHEMY against THE HOLY GHOST SHALL NOT BE FORGIVEN UNTO MEN."**

Speaking against the HOLY GHOST BAPTISM is speaking against THE GODHEAD.

> **"And WHOSOEVER SPEAKETH A WORD AGAINST THE SON OF MAN, it shall be forgiven him: but WHOSOEVER SPEAKETH AGAINST THE HOLY GHOST, it shall NOT be forgiven him, NEITHER in this WORLD, or the WORLD TO COME."**

Matt 12:30   **"HE THAT IS NOT WITH ME IS AGAINST ME: and he that GATHERETH NOT WITH ME scattereth abroad."**

I believe that many of us should examine ourselves whether we be in THE FAITH, regarding the BAPTISM OF THE HOLY GHOST, if THE LORD will not FORGIVE US IF WE SPEAK AGAINST IT!

To those that SPEAK AGAINST and RESIST THE HOLY GHOST, they should take special care in what they are doing and saying, for the HOLY GHOST IS THE FATHER and THE SON also, and **ALL THREE** came down ON THE DAY OF PENTECOST in the PERSON of THE HOLY GHOST to LIVE IN HIS TEMPLE, our human bodies, that we would be workers together with HIM and FINISH HIS WORK WITH POWER, to bring about the RETURN of our LORD JESUS. Please don't be one that HINDERS HIS WORK!

Jn 10:30   **"I and MY FATHER are ONE."**

Jn 14:9   **"...He that hath seen ME, has seen THE FATHER;..."**

JESUS REVEALS THAT HE IS THE HOLY GHOST

Jn 14:28   **"Ye have heard how I said unto you, I GO AWAY, AND COME *AGAIN* UNTO YOU. If ye loved me, ye would rejoice, because I said, I go unto the Father: for my Father is greater than I."**

Again, revealed by OUR LORD JESUS, that HE WOULD COME AGAIN TO US on the DAY OF PENTECOST, as the PERSON OF THE HOLY GHOST!

Jn 14:18   **"I WILL NOT LEAVE YOU COMFORTLESS; _I_ WILL COME TO YOU."**

"JESUS REVEALS, **_HE_** IS THE COMFORTER, THE HOLY GHOST," and <u>will</u> come again.

**THE GODHEAD WILL LIVE IN HIS TEMPLE
THAT THEY *(THE GODHEAD)* CREATED in Genesis 1:26-27**

Gen 1:26   **"...Let US make man in OUR image, after OUR LIKENESS:..."**
Gen 1:27   **"So God created man in HIS own image, in the image of God created HE him; male and female created HE them."**

Jn 14:23   **"...WE [I AND THE FATHER** (who are the Holy Ghost)] **WILL COME AND MAKE OUR ABODE WITH YOU."**

Revealing, THE FATHER and THE SON came down from HEAVEN on the DAY of PENTECOST to live in THEIR DISCIPLES, by the BAPTISM OF THE HOLY GHOST, the THIRD PERSON OF THE GODHEAD! AND JESUS IS THE BAPTIZER WITH THE HOLY GHOST.

Matt 3:11   **"I indeed baptize you with water unto repentance: but He that cometh after me is mightier than I, whose shoes I am not worthy to bear: he shall baptize you with the Holy Ghost, and with fire:"**

FINALLY:

THEREFORE any person or Church, that REJECTS or RESISTS the BAPTISM OF THE HOLY GHOST, REJECTS THE GODHEAD AND JESUS, who <u>IS</u> THE HOLY GHOST because these <u>THREE ARE ONE</u>!

**PAUL GIVES THE GREATEST TRUTHS
FOR OUR UNDERSTANDING!**

Col 2:8-10   **"Beware lest any man spoil you through
                              philosophy and VAIN DECEIT, after the
                              TRADITIONS of MEN, after the rudiments of
                              the WORLD and not after CHRIST."** (WHO is
                              the Holy Ghost!)

WE MUST UNDERSTAND

                              **"FOR IN HIM DWELLETH <u>ALL</u> THE
                              FULLNESS OF THE GODHEAD BODILY."**

This scripture reveals the ONENESS OF THE GODHEAD, and that JESUS
IS THE HOLY GHOST as well as the FATHER.

                              **"AND WE ARE COMPLETE IN HIM, which
                              is THE HEAD of ALL PRINCIPALITY
                              and POWER."**

1)   Paul warns, beware of the TRADITIONS of MEN, their
       PHILOSOPHY and VAIN DECEIT.

2)   That JESUS <u>IS</u> also THE HOLY GHOST, THIRD PERSON OF
       THE GODHEAD.

3)   That JESUS is THE HEAD OF <u>ALL</u> PRINCIPALITY AND POWER,
       and returned to earth on the DAY OF PENTECOST to dwell in us
       (HIS TEMPLE), to give us POWER through the HOLY GHOST
       (THE GODHEAD) to be workers together with HIM, in
       PREACHING the <u>GOSPEL with POWER</u> in all the world, until
       the END!

REVEALING THE GODHEAD AS ONE IN WATER BAPTISM

Matt 28:19-20   **"GO ye therefore, and TEACH ALL NATIONS, BAPTIZING THEM IN THE NAME OF THE FATHER, THE NAME OF THE SON, AND THE NAME OF THE HOLY GHOST:"** (The Godhead)

You will observe, many Pastors baptize in THE NAME OF THE FATHER, THE NAME OF THE SON, AND THE NAME OF THE HOLY GHOST - THESE THREE ARE ONE.

QUESTION: One might ask: "What is the NAME OF - THE FATHER - THE SON and THE HOLY GHOST, that we are to BAPTIZE IN, FOR THESE THREE ARE ONE?"

ANSWER: THE NAME IS JESUS. "FOR IN HIM DWELLETH THE FULNESS OF THE GODHEAD BODILY."

AND THE ANSWER IS REVEALED IN THE FOLLOWING SCRIPTURES

Acts 8:14-17   **"Now when the APOSTLES which were at JERUSALEM, heard that SAMARIA had**
1)   **Received THE WORD OF GOD,** (Born Again of the SPIRIT) **they sent unto them, PETER and JOHN:**

2)   **(For as yet, _HE_ was fallen upon none of them: ONLY THEY WERE <u>BAPTIZED IN THE NAME OF THE LORD JESUS</u>)** (WATER BAPTISM)

                      Then laid they their hands on them, and they

3)   **RECEIVED THE HOLY GHOST."**

1)   This scripture reveals that JESUS IS THE NAME TO BAPTIZE IN. THE NAME OF THE FATHER - THE NAME OF THE SON - THE NAME OF THE HOLY GHOST, <u>AND THESE THREE ARE ONE</u>.

2)   REVEALING ALSO:

        1)   THE SPIRIT BIRTH;
        2)   WATER BAPTISM;
        3)   HOLY GHOST BAPTISM.

AGAIN THE NAME TO BAPTIZE IN IS JESUS

"What shall we do?"

THE ANSWER FOR EVERY BELIEVER TODAY!

For many baptize in THE NAME of the FATHER - SON & HOLY GHOST but never mention "THE NAME"!

Acts:2:38   **"Then Peter said unto them, Repent and be**

    1)   **BAPTIZED every one of you <u>IN THE NAME OF JESUS CHRIST</u> for the remission of sins,**
    2)   **And ye shall RECEIVE THE GIFT OF THE HOLY GHOST."** (Not Holy Spirit)

This scripture reveals again, that <u>JESUS IS</u> THE NAME TO BAPTIZE IN. Revealing also, THAT THE BAPTISM OF THE HOLY GHOST came <u>after</u> WATER BAPTISM.
That JESUS <u>IS</u> the: FATHER, SON AND HOLY GHOST!

REVEALING AGAIN: 1)   **THE SPIRIT BIRTH;**
                         2)   **WATER BAPTISM;**
                         3)   **HOLY GHOST BAPTISM.**

REVEALED IN THIS PORTION OF GOD'S HOLY WORD

Acts 19:1-6   **"...Paul having passed through the upper coasts came to Ephesus:**

1)   And finding CERTAIN <u>DISCIPLES,</u> (Born Again of the SPIRIT).

"HE said unto them, HAVE YE RECEIVED THE HOLY GHOST *SINCE* YE BELIEVED? And they said unto him, we have not so much as heard, whether there be any HOLY GHOST.

Unto what then were ye BAPTIZED? They said, unto John's BAPTISM.

Then said Paul; John verily BAPTIZED with the BAPTISM OF REPENTANCE, saying unto the people, that they should BELIEVE ON HIM, which should come after him, that is, on CHRIST JESUS.

2)   When they heard this THEY WERE BAPTIZED IN THE NAME OF THE LORD JESUS. *(WATER BAPTISM)*

3)   And when Paul laid his hands on them, <u>THE HOLY GHOST came</u> on them and they <u>SPAKE WITH TONGUES AND PROPHESIED!"</u>

REVEALING: 1) THE SPIRIT BIRTH;
              2) WATER BAPTISM;
              3) HOLY GHOST BAPTISM.

How can we believe if we reject the WORD OF GOD written above?

Chapter Eight

Different Names That Refer To The Holy Ghost

1) **THE HOLY GHOST** - *The Third Person of the GODHEAD.*

THE PICTURE: JESUS IS PREPARING HIS DISCIPLES FOR HIS RETURN TO OUR HEAVENLY FATHER.

Jn 14:26   "But the <u>COMFORTER</u>, which <u>IS</u> the <u>HOLY GHOST</u>, whom the FATHER will send in <u>MY NAME</u>, *HE* <u>SHALL TEACH YOU ALL THINGS</u>, and bring ALL THINGS to your remembrance, whatsoever I have said unto you."

2) THE COMFORTER

Jn 14:16   "And I will pray the FATHER, and HE shall give you another COMFORTER, (THE HOLY GHOST) that HE may abide with you forever."

1)   THE FATHER WILL SEND THE COMFORTER. (THE HOLY GHOST.)

2)   ANOTHER COMFORTER THAT WOULD GIVE US POWER TO FINISH HIS WORK.

Jn 15:26   "But when the COMFORTER is come, whom I will send unto you from the FATHER, (SPEAKING OF THE HOLY GHOST) even the SPIRIT OF TRUTH, which proceedeth from the FATHER, <u>HE</u> shall testify of ME:"

THE COMFORTER IS THE SPIRIT OF TRUTH.

Jn 16:7   "...It is expedient for you that I go away: for if I go not away, the COMFORTER will not come unto you; (or THE HOLY GHOST) But if I depart, I will send HIM unto you." (on the day of Pentecost)."

JESUS WAS LEAVING IN **ONE HUMAN BODY**, TO **RETURN** AS THE HOLY GHOST ON THE DAY OF PENTECOST TO BAPTIZE IN THE HOLY GHOST A **MANY MEMBERED BODY**, HIS **CHURCH** TO FINISH THE WORK, THOUGH MANY REFUSE THE HOLY GHOST POWER.

3) THE SPIRIT OF TRUTH

Jn 14:16-17

"And I will pray the FATHER, and **HE** shall give you another COMFORTER, that **HE** may abide with you forever;
Even the **SPIRIT OF TRUTH**; (THE HOLY GHOST) whom the world cannot receive, because it seeth **HIM** not, neither knoweth **HIM**; for **HE** dwelleth with you, and shall be IN YOU."

REVEALING - THE **PERSON** OF THE HOLY GHOST AS THE **SPIRIT OF TRUTH**.

THE SPIRIT OF TRUTH IS THE COMFORTER

Jn 15:26

"But when the COMFORTER is come, whom **I will** send unto you from the FATHER, even the **SPIRIT OF TRUTH,** (WHO IS THE HOLY GHOST) which proceedeth from the FATHER, **HE** shall testify of ME:"

THE SPIRIT OF TRUTH

Jn 16:13

"Howbeit when *HE,* the **SPIRIT OF TRUTH**, is come, *HE* will guide you into ALL TRUTH: for *HE* shall not speak of *HIMSELF*; but whatsoever *HE* shall hear, that shall *HE* speak: and *HE* will shew you things to come."

Speaking again of THE HOLY GHOST, THE SPIRIT OF TRUTH, THE PERSON.

1)   HE WILL GUIDE YOU INTO <u>ALL</u> TRUTH. (Not just some
        TRUTH)

2)   HE WILL SHEW YOU THINGS TO COME.

4) THE SPIRIT OF PROMISE

Acts 1:4   **"And, (JESUS) being assembled together with
                                them, commanded them that they should not
                                depart from Jerusalem, but wait for the
                                <u>PROMISE of the FATHER</u>, which, *saith HE*,
                                ye have heard of ME."**

                                - THE HOLY GHOST, THE PROMISE OF
                                THE FATHER.

JESUS GIVES HIS FINAL INSTRUCTIONS BEFORE HE LEFT:

1)   DO NOT DEPART FROM JERUSALEM.

2)   WAIT FOR THE **<u>PROMISE</u>** OF THE FATHER THAT I TOLD
        YOU ABOUT. Today, we can see that the FATHER kept His Word.
        The SPIRIT OF PROMISE **<u>HAS</u>** COME.

THE HOLY SPIRIT OF PROMISE

Eph 1:13-14 READ: **(We are) "...ye were sealed with that <u>HOLY
                        SPIRIT OF PROMISE</u>."**

                        <u>Which IS THE HOLY GHOST.</u>

                        In whom ye also *trusted*, after that ye heard the
                        word of truth, the gospel of your salvation: in whom
                        also <u>AFTER THAT YE BELIEVED</u>, YE WERE
                        SEALED WITH THAT HOLY <u>SPIRIT OF
                        PROMISE</u>, (which <u>IS</u> the Baptism of the
                        Holy Ghost.

The earnest of our inheritance, until the redemption of the purchased possession, unto the praise of HIS glory.

THE HOLY SPIRIT OF PROMISE, IS THE HOLY GHOST,

1)   THAT AFTER YOU BELIEVED;

2)   YOU WERE SEALED WITH THAT <u>HOLY SPIRIT OF PROMISE</u>.
        IF you received the Baptism of the Holy Ghost

Lk 24:49   **And behold <u>I send the PROMISE of MY FATHER</u> *upon you*: but tarry ye in the city of Jerusalem, until ye be endued with power from on high.**

Speaking of THE HOLY GHOST that came down from heaven, on **THE DAY OF PENTECOST.**

As JESUS said: **"I AND THE FATHER ARE ONE."** HE also says:
"I SEND THE PROMISE OF MY FATHER UPON YOU."
(We cannot separate them.)

THE REASON TO STAY IN JERUSALEM, **"Until ye be endued with POWER FROM HEAVEN!"**

Acts 1:4   **"...*Wait* for the <u>PROMISE</u> of MY FATHER..."**

Acts 2:33   **"Therefore being by the right hand of GOD exalted, and having received of the FATHER, <u>PROMISE of the HOLY GHOST HE hath shed forth this, which ye NOW SEE and HEAR:</u>"**
                                (Other tongues which <u>IS</u> the evidence.)

Acts 2:38,39   **"Then Peter said unto them, Repent, and be baptized every one of you in the name of JESUS CHRIST for the remission of sins, and ye shall receive the gift of the HOLY GHOST.**

For the PROMISE is unto you, and to your
children, and to all that are afar off, *even* as
many as the LORD our GOD shall call."

Jn 12:48   "<u>He that rejecteth ME</u>, *(who is the HOLY
GHOST)* <u>and receiveth</u> NOT <u>MY WORDS, hath
one that judgeth him: the WORD that I have
spoken:</u> *THE SAME SHALL JUDGE him in
the LAST DAY.*" *(Jesus spake of the HOLY
GHOST to come.)*

He that REJECTS THE HOLY GHOST (who is JESUS) AND RECEIVES
NOT MY WORDS THAT I HAVE SPOKEN REGARDING THE BAPTISM
OF THE HOLY GHOST:
THE WORD WILL JUDGE HIM IN THE LAST DAY.

*Something for those that reject HIS WORD ON THE BAPTISM OF THE
HOLY GHOST, to give serious thought to!*

PAUL'S EXHORTATION TO THE CHURCH

THE PROMISE OF THE HOLY GHOST

Heb 4:1   "*Let us therefore FEAR, lest, a PROMISE* (of
the HOLY GHOST) **being left us of entering into
HIS REST, any of you should seem to come
short of it.**"

It is TIME TO FEAR THE LORD, lest the PROMISE OF THE HOLY GHOST
that was left us, we miss the opportunity by REJECTING THE HOLY GHOST
to ENTER GOD'S REST, which is the END OF OUR SALVATION!

LET US PAY SPECIAL ATTENTION TO THE GODHEAD

Again:
Col 2:8-9   "Beware lest any man spoil you through
philosophy and vain deceit, after the tradition
of men, after the rudiments of the world, and
not after Christ.

**FOR IN HIM DWELLETH ALL THE
FULLNESS OF THE GODHEAD BODILY."**

JESUS <u>IS</u> THE FATHER, THE SON AND THE HOLY GHOST. ALL THREE
MUST LIVE IN US THROUGH THE BAPTISM OF THE HOLY GHOST.
Christ in us our hope of Glory.

1 Jn 5:7   **"...And these <u>THREE ARE ONE</u>."**

For there are three that bear record in heaven, the **FATHER,** the **WORD**, and
the **HOLY GHOST:** <u>AND THESE THREE ARE ONE</u>.

Again:
 - THE FATHER - THE SON - THE HOLY GHOST "<u>ARE ONE</u>."

JESUS PREPARES THE DISCIPLES FOR HIS RETURN

Jn 14:28   **"Ye have heard how I said unto you, I go away,
                                and come again unto you. If ye loved ME, ye
                                would rejoice, because I said, I GO UNTO THE
                                FATHER: FOR MY FATHER IS GREATER
                                THAN I."**

JESUS returned as the HOLY GHOST on the DAY OF PENTECOST"
revealed in;

Jn 14:29   **"And NOW I have told you before *(THE DAY
                                OF PENTECOST)* it is COME TO PASS, THAT
                                WHEN IT IS COME TO PASS, ye
                                MIGHT BELIEVE."**

Jesus said, "I told you THE HOLY GHOST would come, that when it is come
to pass you might believe and TRUST IN ME." The Holy GHOST **HAS**
already come. And this is the message ministered unto us in the writing of
this book. Amen!!

JESUS IS THE COMFORTER - THE HOLY GHOST

Jn 14:18   "I will not leave you COMFORTLESS:
                         <u>I</u> WILL COME TO YOU."

JESUS IS THE COMFORTER and RETURNED on the DAY OF
PENTECOST.

Jn 16:7   "Nevertheless I tell you the truth; It is
                         expedient that I go away: for if I go not away,
                         THE COMFORTER will not come unto you;
                         But if I depart <u>I</u> WILL SEND HIM UNTO
                         YOU."

AS THE FATHER - THE SON - THE HOLY GHOST "ARE ONE" JESUS
returned as THE <u>PERSON</u> OF THE HOLY GHOST, THE COMFORTER.

Jn 16:16   "A little while, and ye shall not see ME: and
                         again, a little while, and ye shall see ME,
                         because I go to the FATHER."

Jn 14:20   "AT THAT DAY *(Day of Pentecost)* ye shall
                         know that,

                         1) I AM IN MY FATHER,
                         2) AND YE IN ME,
                         ("<u>THESE THREE ARE ONE</u>")
                         3) AND I IN YOU."

The above scripture reveals THE GODHEAD as it is this day to those that are
BAPTIZED IN THE HOLY GHOST.

FINALLY:

Matt 12:31,32 READ: WARNING - But whosoever speaks against
                         THE HOLY GHOST, it shall not be forgiven
                         him, in this world or the world to come! FOR
                         THESE THREE ARE ONE!

Wherefore I say unto you, All manner of sin and blasphemy shall be forgiven unto men: **but the blasphemy** *against* **the** *HOLY* **GHOST shall not be forgiven unto men.**

And whosoever speaketh a word against the Son of man, it shall be forgiven him: **BUT WHOSOEVER SPEAKETH AGAINST THE HOLY GHOST,**
it shall not be forgiven him, neither in this world, neither in the *world* **to come.**

ONE MIGHT ASK, "WHY IS THE HOLY GHOST SO IMPORTANT?"

BECAUSE THE HOLY GHOST IS THE GODHEAD, AND TO BLASPHEME THE GODHEAD, WE BLASPHEME NOT THE SON OF MAN, BUT THE SON OF GOD THAT DIED FOR OUR SINS ON CALVARY'S TREE!

How can we RESIST THE HOLY GHOST BAPTISM with such dire consequences.

UNDERSTAND, JESUS FINISHED THE WORK THE FATHER GAVE HIM TO DO.

NOW, WE ARE WORKERS TOGETHER WITH HIM, IF we don't RESIST THE POWER OF THE HOLY GHOST THAT WE MUST HAVE, TO FINISH THE WORK HE HAS GIVEN US TO DO. JESUS also said:

2 Corinth 6:16-18   **"And what agreement hath the temple of God with idols? For ye are the temple of the living God; as God hath said, I WILL DWELL IN THEM, AND WALK IN** *THEM***; AND I WILL BE THEIR GOD, AND THEY SHALL BE MY PEOPLE.**

Wherefore come out from among them, and be ye separate, saith the Lord, and touch not the unclean thing; and I will receive you,

And I will be a FATHER unto you, AND YE SHALL BE MY SONS AND DAUGHTERS, SAITH THE LORD ALMIGHTY."

Now we know THE TRUTH!

Chapter Nine

The Mystery Of Christ In Us

THE MYSTERY - HID FROM GENERATIONS

Gen 1:26   "...Let US make man in OUR image, after
                            OUR likeness:..."

Here we see the beginning of the great mystery plan of GOD, creating His
temple, or dwelling place that He would live in, during the latter days. Christ
in you, your hope of glory. (The RESURRECTION!)

Col 1:26-28 READ: "To whom GOD would make known what is the
                            riches of this MYSTERY among the Gentiles;
                            which is - CHRIST IN YOU, the hope of glory:"
                            (Eternal life)

THE MYSTERY KEPT SECRET SINCE THE WORLD BEGAN

Rom 16:25-26   "Now to <u>Him</u> that is of power to stablish you
                            according to MY GOSPEL, and the preaching
                            of Jesus Christ, according to the REVELATION
                            of the MYSTERY, which was kept secret since
                            the world began,

                            But now is made manifest, and by the
                            scriptures of the prophets, (Is 28:11 For with
                            stammering lips and another tongue will HE
                            speak unto this people) According to the
                            commandment of the everlasting GOD, made
                            known to All nations for the obedience of Faith:"

HOW CAN I BE A PARTAKER OF THIS MYSTERY?

Titus 3:5   "Not by WORKS of RIGHTEOUSNESS which
                            we have done, but according to HIS MERCY
                            He saved us, by the washing of regeneration and
                            renewing of the HOLY GHOST;"

WE BECOME HIS OFFSPRING

Acts 17:28   "For in Him we live, and move, and have our being; as certain also of your own poets have said, for we are also His offspring."

WE MUST EXAMINE OURSELVES

2 Corinth 13:5   "Examine yourselves, whether ye be in the faith; Prove your own selves. Know ye not your own selves, how that Jesus Christ is in you, except ye be reprobates?"

GOD'S TRUE DWELLING PLACE

Natural man has created and built beautiful buildings and called them "Churches" or "Houses of GOD," which are truly IDOLS of man!

MAN WANTS TO BUILD GOD A HOUSE

Acts 7:48   "Howbeit THE MOST HIGH dwelleth not in temples (Churches or buildings) **made with hands; as saith the Prophet,"** (Isaiah 66:2)

Acts 7:49   **HEAVEN IS MY THRONE, AND THE EARTH IS MY FOOTSTOOL:**

                         (1)   **What house will YE build ME? Saith the Lord:**

                         (2)   **What is the place of MY REST?"**

Acts 7:50   "Hath not MY HANDS made ALL these things?"

Acts 17:24   "God that made the World and ALL things therein, seeing that He is LORD of Heaven and Earth, **DWELLETH NOT IN TEMPLES MADE WITH HANDS;"**

WE ARE THE DWELLING PLACE OF THE LIVING GOD

2 Corinth 6:16 — "And what agreement has the temple of GOD (which we are) with IDOLS? For ye are the TEMPLE OF THE LIVING GOD; as GOD hath said, I WILL DWELL IN THEM, and WALK IN THEM; and I will be their GOD, and they shall be MY PEOPLE."

Heb 3:6 — "But Christ as a son over HIS OWN HOUSE; whose House are we, IF we hold fast the CONFIDENCE and the REJOICING of the HOPE firm unto THE END."

THE CONDITIONS FOR HIS INDWELLING PRESENCE

Jn 14:23 — "...If a man LOVE ME, he will keep MY WORDS: and MY FATHER will LOVE him, and WE will come unto him, AND MAKE OUR ABODE with him." This referring to the BAPTISM OF THE HOLY GHOST. THE FATHER AND SON who are THE HOLY GHOST, will come and make their ABODE with us.

1 Corinth 6:15 — "Know ye not that your bodies are the members of Christ?..."

1 Corinth 6:19 — "...Know ye not that your body is THE TEMPLE OF THE HOLY GHOST WHICH IS IN YOU, which ye have of GOD, and ye are not your own?"

1 Corinth 6:20 — "For ye are bought with a PRICE (on Calvary): therefore GLORIFY GOD in your body, and in your SPIRIT, which are GOD'S."

1 Corinth 3:16 — "Know ye not that ye are the TEMPLE OF GOD, and that the Spirit of GOD dwelleth in you?"

HIS POWER MUST WORK IN US
FOLLOWING THE BAPTISM OF THE HOLY GHOST!

1 Jn 2:27	"But the ANOINTING which ye have received of Him abideth IN you..." (this same ANOINTING teaches you all things.)
Eph 3:20	"Now unto him that is able to do exceedingly abundantly above ALL that we ask or think, <u>ACCORDING TO THE POWER THAT WORKETH IN US</u>," Through THE BAPTISM OF THE HOLY GHOST!
Philip 2:13	"For it is GOD which worketh in you both to WILL and TO DO of HIS GOOD PLEASURE."
1 Jn 4:4	"...Greater is HE that is in you, than he (Satan) that is in the world."
1 Corinth 4:20	"For the kingdom of GOD is NOT IN WORD, but in POWER."
1 Corinth 2:5	"That your FAITH should not stand in the wisdom of men, BUT IN THE POWER OF GOD."

EXHORTATION TO ENTER INTO THE POWER OF GOD

Philip 4:13	Paul said, "I can do <u>all things</u> through CHRIST (JESUS) which strengthens me."
Eph 3:16-21 READ:	"That He would grant you, according to the riches of His glory, to be strengthened with might by HIS SPIRIT IN THE INNER MAN;"

THE POWER HAS ALREADY BEEN DEMONSTRATED!

1 Corinth 4:19 READ: Paul said, **When I come, I will not know the words of them that are puffed up, but the POWER** (Which <u>IS</u> the Holy Ghost)!

1 Corinth 2:4   **"And my speech and my preaching, was NOT with enticing words of MAN'S WISDOM, but in DEMONSTRATION OF THE SPIRIT AND OF POWER."** (Of the Holy Ghost)

Acts 19:11-12   **"And GOD wrought special miracles by the hands of Paul: so that from his body were brought unto the sick handkerchiefs and aprons, and the diseases departed from them, and the evil spirits went out of them."**

Acts 5:3 READ: Ananias and Sapphira lie to the Holy Ghost dwelling in Peter and they died.

Acts 13:9-11 READ: Paul sets <u>his eyes</u> on Elymas the sorcerer and causes him to be blind, through THE POWER OF THE HOLY GHOST.

Acts 3:6 READ: Peter and John show the Lord's POWER, working in them: **"...Such as I have give I thee, in the NAME of JESUS CHRIST OF NAZARETH, RISE UP AND WALK!"**

BE MINDFUL ALWAYS THAT CHRIST IS IN YOU

1 Pet 4:11   **"If any man speak, let him speak as the oracles of GOD; if any man minister, let him do it as of the ability which GOD giveth:** (not the ability of natural man) **that GOD in ALL things may be glorified through Jesus Christ,..."**

2 Corinth 3:2-3   **"Ye are our epistle written in our hearts, known and read of all men: forasmuch as ye are**

manifestly declared to be the epistle of Christ ministered by us, written not with ink, but with the Spirit of the LIVING GOD; not in tables of stone, but in fleshly tables of THE HEART."

Philemon 6

"That the communication of thy faith may become effectual by the acknowledging of every good thing which is in you in Christ Jesus."

2 Corinth 5:19

"...God was IN Christ, reconciling the world unto Himself, NOT IMPUTING THEIR TRESPASSES UNTO THEM; and hath committed unto us the WORD of reconciliation." By our obedience to His Word, that we may be workers together as we commune with the Word day by day.

EXHORTATION TO LISTEN TO THE SPIRIT

Col 2:4

"And this I say, lest any man should beguile (or deceive) you with enticing words."

Col 2:6

"As ye have therefore received Christ Jesus the Lord, SO WALK YE IN HIM:" (And learn to listen to the Spirit for direction.)

UNDERSTANDING THE CHURCH - HIS DWELLING PLACE

Col 2:2

"That their HEARTS might be comforted, being knit together in LOVE, and unto all riches of the FULL ASSURANCE of UNDERSTANDING, to the acknowledgment of the MYSTERY OF GOD,..." (Which is Christ IN US our hope of glory) (or resurrection).

Eph 2:22

"In whom ye also (We) are builded together for an habitation of GOD through the Spirit."

Eph 1:23   "Which is HIS Body, the fullness of HIM that
                        filleth all IN ALL."

Eph 4:11-13 READ: "Till we all come in the unity of the faith, and
                        the knowledge of the Son of GOD, unto a
                        perfect man, unto the measure of the stature of
                        the FULLNESS of Christ:"

CONCLUSION OF THE MYSTERY

2 Corinth 5:10   "For we MUST all appear before the judgement
                        seat of Christ; that everyone may receive the
                        things done in HIS BODY, according to that he
                        hath done, whether it be good or bad."

REWARD OF THE FAITHFUL

Jn 15:7   Jesus said, "If ye abide in ME, and MY WORDS
                        abide in you, ye shall ask what ye will, and it
                        shall be done unto you."

Chapter Ten

Tongues The Language Of Angels

THROUGH OUR LACK OF SPIRITUAL UNDERSTANDING OF THE
SCRIPTURES, MANY IN THE BODY OF JESUS CHRIST ARE
RESISTING THE SPEAKING IN OTHER TONGUES WHICH <u>IS</u> THE
EVIDENCE WHEN A PERSON IS BAPTIZED IN THE HOLY GHOST.
**(Acts 2:4 And they were all filled with the Holy Ghost, and began to speak
with other tongues, as the Spirit gave them utterance.)**

REMEMBER: 1 Cor 2:14 "But the natural man receiveth NOT THE THINGS
OF THE SPIRIT OF GOD: for they are foolishness unto him: (neither can he
know them, because they are spiritually discerned)."

If you are one of those that cannot accept the SPEAKING OF OTHER
TONGUES, you are not alone, SATAN agrees with you!

In our "many experiences" through the years in the CASTING OUT OF
DEVILS, THE HOLY GHOST, SPAKE IN OTHER TONGUES and the
DEVILS became so upset that we had to hold the person down!

Did Satan understand what THE LORD was saying to him? Remember,
TONGUES ORIGINATED in heaven where Satan came from, and tongues
were sent down from HEAVEN on THE DAY OF PENTECOST through the
BAPTISM OF THE HOLY GHOST.

Before we continue to RESIST THE BAPTISM OF THE HOLY GHOST AND
SPEAKING IN OTHER TONGUES, please TAKE HEED to the <u>following
Scriptures,</u> lest we end up BLASPHEMING THE HOLY GHOST, which shall
not be forgiven in THIS WORLD, or THE WORLD TO COME!!
(Matthew 12:31)

Webster's Dictionary: **Tongues: Said to be possessed by Early
                                  Christians, (and was!)**

Question: **Are we different Christians than the
                                  Early Christians?**

LET US EXAMINE THE FOLLOWING SCRIPTURES BEFORE IT IS TOO LATE!

THE ANNOUNCEMENT BY THE PROPHETS THAT OTHER TONGUES WOULD COME.

Is 28:8-12 READ: **"Whom shall HE TEACH KNOWLEDGE? And whom shall HE make to UNDERSTAND DOCTRINE?**

Them that are weaned from THE MILK *(Spirit Birth)* **and DRAWN FROM THE BREASTS.** revealing that the Lord had more to say to us, beyond the Spirit Birth.

FOR WITH STAMMERING LIPS AND ANOTHER TONGUE WILL <u>HE</u> *(The LORD)* **SPEAK TO THIS PEOPLE."**

Will we still REJECT OTHER TONGUES, when it is THE LORD that is SPEAKING with STAMMERING LIPS and ANOTHER TONGUE through us today, HIS TEMPLE?!

PAUL THE APOSTLE SPEAKS THE SAME MESSAGE AS ISAIAH THE PROPHET

1 Corinth 14:20 **"Brethren, be NOT CHILDREN IN UNDERSTANDING: howbeit in malice be ye children, but in understanding be men."**

1 Corinth 14:21 **"IN THE LAW IT IS WRITTEN, WITH *MEN OF* OTHER TONGUES AND OTHER LIPS WILL <u>*I*</u> *SPEAK* UNTO THIS PEOPLE; AND YET FOR ALL THAT WILL THEY NOT HEAR ME, SAITH THE LORD."**

The above Scripture is a PROPHETIC WORD preached by PAUL THE APOSTLE to all those people that REJECT THE BAPTISM OF THE HOLY GHOST AND THE SPEAKING OF OTHER TONGUES, "will NOT HEAR ME" certainly applies to many local churches today!

My dear brother and sister IN THE FAITH, how can we LOVE THE LORD if we will NOT HEAR HIS VOICE, as HE SPEAKS IN OTHER TONGUES AND OTHER LIPS unto us today?

THE SPIRIT THAT IS GIVEN TO US, GAVE THE TONGUES AT PENTECOST

Acts 2:4
"AND THEY WERE ALL FILLED WITH THE HOLY GHOST, AND BEGAN TO SPEAK WITH OTHER TONGUES, AS THE <u>SPIRIT</u> GAVE THE UTTERANCE."

Remember, OUR BODIES ARE THE TEMPLE OF THE HOLY GHOST. When we are BAPTIZED IN THE HOLY GHOST the LORD SPEAKS in TONGUES out of HIS TEMPLE!

Will we still REJECT TONGUES, when it is our LORD THAT IS SPEAKING IN OTHER TONGUES?

ARE WE BLIND TO THE SPIRITUAL THINGS OF GOD, THAT THE SPIRIT THAT WE ARE BORN OF GAVE THE TONGUES?

I WOULD SAY, IF WE DON'T ACCEPT THE UTTERANCE OF THE SPIRIT THAT WE ARE BORN AGAIN OF, WE HAVE A SERIOUS PROBLEM!

1 Cor 2:14
"...NATURAL MAN RECEIVES NOT THE THINGS OF THE SPIRIT OF GOD:" (BECAUSE THEY ARE FOOLISHNESS UNTO HIM.)

JESUS IS THE ONE THAT BAPTIZES US WITH THE HOLY GHOST

Again:
Matt 3:11
"I indeed baptize you with water unto repentance: but <u>HE</u> that cometh after me is mightier than I, whose shoes I am not worthy to bear: HE SHALL BAPTIZE YOU WITH THE HOLY GHOST, AND *WITH* FIRE:"

QUESTION:	My dear brother and sister, HOW CAN WE REJECT THE BAPTISM OF THE HOLY GHOST AND THE SPEAKING IN OTHER TONGUES when JESUS OUR SAVIOR IS THE ONE THAT BAPTIZES US with THE HOLY GHOST AND THE SPEAKING IN "OTHER TONGUES"?

To all the pastors and TEACHERS OF THE WORD, are you BLIND also as the PHARISEES, when JESUS approached them with the MESSAGE OF SALVATION, they REJECTED HIM, and if they had had their way, we ALL would be in our sins without hope?

JESUS HAS NOW RETURNED AGAIN WITH THE MESSAGE OF THE BAPTISM OF THE HOLY GHOST AND SPEAKING IN OTHER TONGUES, AND MANY PASTORS AND TEACHERS ARE REJECTING HIM ONCE MORE!

MANY ARE TRUSTING IN THEIR CHURCH DENOMINATIONS, WHEN ALL OVER THE WORLD IN EVERY LANGUAGE, MEN AND WOMEN ARE BEING BAPTIZED IN THE HOLY GHOST BY OUR LORD JESUS.

DON'T YOU THINK IT IS TIME TO SEARCH THE WORD OF GOD FOR OURSELVES, AND STOP LISTENING TO MAN'S VOICE THAT CAN DECEIVE YOU, AND BEGIN TO LISTEN TO THE VOICE OF JESUS, WHO IS THE WORD?

REMEMBER:	*JESUS said:* **"YE SHALL RECEIVE POWER AFTER THAT THE HOLY GHOST IS COME UPON YOU."**
Acts 2:39	**"For the PROMISE is unto you, and to your children, and to all that are afar off, even as many as the LORD our GOD shall call."**

TODAY IF YOU WILL HEAR HIS VOICE: We cannot HEAR THE VOICE OF JESUS and then turn around and REJECT THE WORD, who IS JESUS OUR LORD!

1 Jn 5:7   **"FOR THERE ARE THREE** *(not two)* **THAT BEAR RECORD IN HEAVEN, THE FATHER, THE WORD,** *(OR SON)* **AND THE HOLY GHOST: <u>AND THESE THREE ARE ONE"</u>**

This Scripture reveals to us, that, if we REJECT THE HOLY GHOST AND THE SPEAKING IN OTHER TONGUES, WE REJECT THE FATHER, who LAID ALL THE FOUNDATIONS for us to build our faith on, we will also REJECT OUR LORD JESUS who died for our SINS and rose again from the DEAD to give us ETERNAL LIFE!

<u>BECAUSE THESE THREE ARE ONE</u>!!

There are many SCRIPTURES ON TONGUES I might give you at this time, but if we STILL DO NOT BELIEVE WHAT I HAVE ALREADY REVEALED, there is no purpose of continuing any further.

Many PASTORS and TEACHERS of the WORD OF GOD, are being challenged by THE WORD to LEAD THE CHILDREN of the LORD into THE TRUTH OF THE BAPTISM OF THE HOLY GHOST. Especially when they are searching THE SCRIPTURES for themselves and asking their PASTORS if the HOLY GHOST BAPTISM is for them today, or is it just for the thousands all over the world.

To ALL PASTORS I say, be careful with your answer! It is time my dear PASTORS that we begin to WAKE UP to the SPIRIT REVELATION of THE WORD and not man's OPINIONS and TRADITIONS of your local church.

We cannot receive JESUS OUR LORD as our SAVIOR and REJECT HIM as THE HOLY GHOST AND THE BAPTIZER WITH THE HOLY GHOST.

If we Pastors are not BAPTIZED IN THE HOLY GHOST and SPEAK IN OTHER TONGUES according to THE HOLY SCRIPTURES, how can we lead the children of GOD into THIS BEAUTIFUL EXPERIENCE? If we don't WAKE UP, we will find the sheep leading the shepherd!

THE LORD JESUS bless you mightily, as you search your hearts for THE TRUTH and HIS WILL FOR YOUR MINISTRY.

Chapter Eleven

The Spirit Birth Is A Separate Experience From The Baptism Of The Holy Ghost

THE BORN AGAIN EXPERIENCE

Jn 3:3-5   "Jesus answered and said unto him, Verily, verily, I say
                 unto thee, Except a man be born again he cannot see the
                 kingdom of God.
                 Nicodemus saith unto him, how can a man be born when
                 he is old? Can he enter the second time into his mother's
                 womb and be born?
                 Jesus answered, Verily, verily, I say unto thee, **EXCEPT
                 A MAN BE BORN OF WATER AND OF THE SPIRIT,
                 HE CANNOT ENTER INTO THE KINGDOM OF
                 GOD."** (THE SPIRIT BIRTH IS ONLY TO SEE AND
                 ENTER THE KINGDOM OF GOD. ONE MIGHT ASK,
                 "WHAT DO I DO NOW?!")

Rom 10:9   (The promise to all,) **"THAT IF THOU SHALT
                 CONFESS WITH THY MOUTH THE LORD JESUS,
                 AND SHALT BELIEVE IN THINE HEART THAT
                 GOD HAS RAISED HIM FROM THE DEAD,
                 THOU SHALT BE SAVED."**

THE BORN AGAIN EXPERIENCE INTO THE KINGDOM OF GOD, IS ONE OF THE MOST PRECIOUS MESSAGES IN THE HOLY SCRIPTURES, AND IS PREACHED BY THE TRUE CHURCH OF JESUS CHRIST ALL OVER THE WORLD!

BUT, MY DEAR BRETHREN, THE MESSAGE OF THE SPIRIT BIRTH into THE KINGDOM OF GOD is only THE BEGINNING of our JOURNEY unto the fullness of Christ in our SPIRITUAL WALK, as revealed in THE JOURNEY OF ISRAEL that is AN EXAMPLE for us to follow!

Jn 14:6   (Jesus revealed a Spiritual journey,)

"...I AM THE WAY, THE TRUTH, THE LIFE..."

The SPIRIT BIRTH IS THE WAY, THE TRUTH IS THE BAPTISM OF THE HOLY GHOST, (John 16:13 Howbeit when HE the Spirit of Truth is come, HE will guide you into all truth: for HE shall not speak of Himself; but whatsoever HE shall hear, that shall HE speak: and HE will shew you things to come.) and THE LIFE is the end and THE RESURRECTION.

We must _not_ bypass THE BAPTISM OF THE HOLY GHOST on our JOURNEY UNTO LIFE!

The purpose of this message is to reveal to us, BY THE WORD OF OUR LORD, THAT THE BAPTISM OF THE HOLY GHOST IS A SEPARATE EXPERIENCE FROM THE SPIRIT BIRTH.

REMEMBER, JESUS SAID, **"MY SHEEP HEAR MY VOICE, I KNOW THEM, THEY FOLLOW ME."**

I suggest from here forward THAT IF WE ARE HIS SHEEP, we should open our ears to what our Great Shepherd has to say, regarding THE BAPTISM OF THE HOLY GHOST.

We cannot deny HIS WORDS, IF WE ARE HIS SHEEP, and we should give serious concern to HIS WORD in the following scriptures.

THE MOST IMPORTANT MESSAGE TO THE BORN AGAIN CHURCH IN THIS HOUR!

This message by THE WORD OF GOD, is to CHALLENGE the RELIGIOUS ORDER and the TRADITIONS of those organizations that have resisted the BAPTISM OF THE HOLY GHOST as a separate experience from the BORN AGAIN experience.

Let the WORD OF GOD BE TRUE, and as we with open hearts receive this message on the BAPTISM OF THE HOLY GHOST we will find the preaching of the WORD is with POWER!
As Paul said, **"When I come, I will not know the preaching of them that are puffed up, BUT THE POWER."**

The LORD bless you as you open up your heart to the truth of the WORD OF GOD, as HIS COMING is very near!

This portion of the book is written to my dear pastors and brethren in THE FAITH, but especially to young men and women called of GOD into the MINISTRY of OUR LORD JESUS CHRIST.

ALSO, THAT YOU WILL SEARCH THE HOLY SCRIPTURES FOR YOUR SELVES, and let not your faith stand in the wisdom of man's preaching, but in THE DEMONSTRATION AND THE POWER OF HIS WORD, revealed in the following scriptures on THE BAPTISM OF THE HOLY GHOST! THE BAPTISM OF THE HOLY GHOST is indeed a **SEPARATE EXPERIENCE** beyond THE BORN AGAIN EXPERIENCE!

The Spirit Birth is only THE BEGINNING, to SEE and ENTER the KINGDOM OF GOD, accompanied by THE FRUITS OF THE SPIRIT and our LOVE FOR ONE ANOTHER.

This foundation must be established first, before THE BAPTISM OF THE HOLY GHOST can take effect in our lives!

This message of SALVATION IN CHRIST is preached in many parts of the world. At this time we are babes in CHRIST and MUST GROW UP with a VISION OF HIS PLAN AND PURPOSE FOR OUR CHRISTIAN LIVES, and that can only be accomplished through THE BAPTISM OF THE HOLY GHOST which is a SEPARATE EXPERIENCE from THE SPIRIT BIRTH which I shall reveal in this writing.

Even as I write, many evangelical churches are opening their eyes to THE TRUTH OF THE BAPTISM OF THE HOLY GHOST and SPEAKING IN OTHER TONGUES. Will we be left behind on THE JOURNEY OF TRUTH?

I know that many are resisting THE BAPTISM OF THE HOLY GHOST, because of their lack of SPIRITUAL UNDERSTANDING of the HOLY SCRIPTURES.

Prov 29:18   The scripture says, **"WHERE THERE IS NO VISION, THE PEOPLE PERISH:..."**

We are on a JOURNEY IN TRUTH, and where there is "NO VISION" there is BLINDNESS and many, many, refuse to go on this JOURNEY of TRUTH beyond the Spirit Birth, because in their BLINDNESS, they stumble at HIS HOLY WORD!

Though many local churches and denominations are resisting THE BAPTISM OF THE HOLY GHOST as a separate experience from THE SPIRIT BIRTH, I pray that they will reconsider and accept the following HOLY SCRIPTURES revealing the difference.

I thank the LORD for those pastors and teachers that believe, and teach the flock what THE WORD OF GOD says about THE BAPTISM OF THE HOLY GHOST!

MANY TODAY ARE STUMBLING AT THE WORD

1 Pet 2:7-8   **"Unto you therefore which believe HE is precious: but unto them which be disobedient, the stone which the builders disallowed, the same is made the head of the corner,**

And a stone of stumbling, and a rock of offence, even to them which stumble at the word, being disobedient: whereunto also they were appointed."

My dear brothers and sisters in Christ, DO NOT LET THIS HAPPEN TO YOU!

ARE WE GOING TO STUMBLE AT THE WORD? Will JESUS BE A ROCK OF OFFENCE who is also THE HOLY GHOST and the BAPTIZER with the HOLY GHOST?

Matt 3:11   **"I indeed baptize you with water unto repentance: but He that cometh after me is mightier than I, (whose shoes) I am not worthy to bear: He SHALL BAPTIZE YOU WITH THE HOLY GHOST and FIRE:"**

It is TIME my dear brethren in "THE FAITH" to seek SPIRITUAL UNDERSTANDING, and STOP being DISOBEDIENT TO THE WORD, WHO IS CHRIST OUR SAVIOUR, AND ALSO THE HOLY GHOST, that shall be revealed in this writing as we proceed.

WE ARE ON A JOURNEY UNTO LIFE ETERNAL

Prov 29:18   "WHERE THERE IS NO VISION, THE PEOPLE PERISH..."

PASTORS:

If we don't teach the people that there is more to our salvation than THE SPIRIT BIRTH, we have robbed them of THE VISION to take the JOURNEY IN TRUTH and the result is A SPIRITUALLY DEAD CHURCH!

ISRAEL'S JOURNEY TO THE PROMISED LAND TO ADMONISH US

1 Corinth 10:11-12   **"Now all these things happened unto them for ensamples: and they are written for our admonition, upon whom the ends of the world are come.**

                                 Wherefore let him that thinketh he standeth take heed lest he fall."

Note: This is a warning to those that THINK THEY ARE SAVED, when in TRUTH we are *being* SAVED, as we WALK on THE JOURNEY to our promised land in all TRUTH that is set before us, THROUGH THE BAPTISM OF THE HOLY GHOST!

PAUL SPEAKS OF ISRAEL'S JOURNEY

Heb 3:7-10   **"Wherefore as the Holy Ghost saith, To day if ye will hear his voice,** *(REGARDING THE BAPTISM OF THE HOLY GHOST!)*

                                   Harden not your hearts, as in the provocation, in the day of <u>temptation</u> in the wilderness:

                                   When your fathers tempted me, proved me, and saw my works forty years.

                                   Wherefore I was grieved with that generation, and said, <u>They do alway err in *their* heart; and they have not known my ways</u>."

JESUS SPEAKS OF A JOURNEY

Jn 14:6   **"...I AM THE WAY, THE TRUTH, THE LIFE..."**

Comment :   This is our JOURNEY in these last days.

1)   **THE WAY -** Our SPIRIT BIRTH into THE KINGDOM, now we must take the journey.

Many want to set up camp around THE BORN AGAIN EXPERIENCE and will resist THE WORD OF GOD, as Israel did and failed on their journey.

2)   **THE TRUTH (John 14:16-17)** THE SPIRIT OF TRUTH, THE HOLY GHOST. THAT WILL LEAD US INTO ALL TRUTH (not just a little truth).

Jn 14:16-17   **"And I will pray the Father, and he shall give you another Comforter, that he may abide with you for ever;**
Even the Spirit of truth; whom the world cannot receive, because it seeth him not, neither knoweth him: but ye know him; for he dwelleth with you, and shall be <u>in</u> you."

3)   **THE LIFE -** THE JOURNEY'S END as we begin in THE WAY (THE SPIRIT BIRTH) and as we take part and <u>receive</u> the SPIRIT OF TRUTH, AND <u>NOT RESIST</u> HIM, WHO IS THE HOLY GHOST, THAT WILL LEAD US ON OUR JOURNEY INTO LIFE ETERNAL.

I say this, UNTIL WE ARE BAPTIZED IN THE HOLY GHOST, we will have just an argument without a relationship with the Word, which <u>IS</u> Christ, until He comes.

If you still (I speak boldly) disagree with the HOLY SCRIPTURES that are written herein, you are listening to the WRONG VOICE!

Remember the PROPHET SAID: **Isaiah 8:20 "TO THE LAW AND TO THE TESTIMONY: IF THEY SPEAK NOT ACCORDING TO THIS WORD, IT IS BECAUSE THERE IS NO LIGHT IN THEM."**

THE PURPOSE OF THIS MESSAGE, IS TO REVEAL THE TRUTH ABOUT THE BAPTISM OF THE HOLY GHOST, <u>BY</u> THE WORD OF GOD, AND <u>NOT</u> MAN'S OPINIONS AND PHILOSOPHY.

TO REVEAL ALSO, HOW THE SO-CALLED "CHURCH LEADERS" WERE USED BY SATAN IN

<u>ACTS 19:2</u>: **"HE SAID UNTO THEM,** *HAVE YE RECEIVED* **THE <u>HOLY GHOST</u>** *SINCE* **YE BELIEVED? AND THEY SAID UNTO HIM, WE HAVE NOT SO MUCH AS HEARD WHETHER THERE BE ANY HOLY GHOST."**

AND BY SATAN'S SUBTLETY, *"CHANGED THE WORD" FROM "<u>SINCE</u>" TO "<u>WHEN</u>", TO DO AWAY WITH THE BAPTISM OF THE HOLY GHOST; THE THIRD PERSON OF THE GODHEAD!*

Reference: The New International Version of the Bible, Acts 19:2 Quote: and asked them, "Did you receive the Holy Spirit <u>when</u> you believed?"

Reference: The Living Bible, Acts 19:2 Quote: "Did you receive the Holy Spirit <u>when</u> you believed?" He asked them.

FOLLOWING THEIR UNGODLY ACT, NEW BIBLES WERE PUBLISHED TO DIMINISH THE POWER, AND CAUSE THE FAITH OF MANY TO FALTER.

REMEMBER, THE LORD SAID: *"I AM THE LORD AND I CHANGE NOT."* If we do not believe THE WORD OF GOD, that "THE SPIRIT BIRTH" <u>IS</u> a SEPARATE EXPERIENCE from THE HOLY GHOST BAPTISM, as revealed in the following scriptures, I can only say, *"EXAMINE YOURSELVES, WHETHER YE BE 'IN THE FAITH'!"*

I suggest that if you have one of these Bibles listed above, where the WORD OF GOD was changed, get rid of them, and acquire THE AUTHORIZED KING JAMES VERSION OF THE BIBLE, which has withstood it's critics for centuries.

For further UNDERSTANDING of the seriousness of the above, please turn to *"THE RESISTANCE TO THE BAPTISM OF THE HOLY GHOST"* that follows this writing.

PAUL'S WARNING

Col 2:8-10   **"Beware lest any man spoil you through Philosophy and VAIN DECEIT, After the TRADITIONS OF MEN, after the rudiments of the world and not after Christ."**

This MESSAGE is written to you young men and women that are not caught in THE TRADITIONS of the local church, BUT WILL SEARCH THE WORD OF GOD FOR YOURSELVES, and let not your faith stand in the WISDOM OF MAN'S PREACHING, but in the DEMONSTRATION AND POWER OF THE WORD, *THE BAPTISM OF THE HOLY GHOST!*

One might ask the question:
Why are there so many organized denominations resisting THE BAPTISM OF THE HOLY GHOST?

THE ANSWER:

BECAUSE OF THEIR lack of SPIRITUAL UNDERSTANDING OF THE GODHEAD,

1 Cor 2:14   **"But the natural man receiveth not the things of THE SPIRIT OF GOD: for they are foolishness unto him: neither can he know them, because they are SPIRITUALLY discerned."**

1 John 1:7 Says, **"BUT IF WE WALK IN THE LIGHT,** (the Word) **AS HE IS** (Jesus, the Word) **IN THE LIGHT, WE HAVE FELLOWSHIP ONE WITH ANOTHER, and the blood of Jesus Christ his Son cleanseth us from all sin."**

1 Jn 5:7   Again, **"FOR THERE ARE THREE THAT BEAR RECORD IN HEAVEN, THE FATHER, - THE WORD, AND - THE HOLY GHOST: AND THESE THREE ARE ONE."**

Revealing that if we reject <u>ANY</u> of the <u>THREE</u> we reject them ALL, BECAUSE **THESE THREE ARE ONE**!

SATAN'S PLAN IS TO DIVIDE THE CHURCH, OVER THE WORD OF GOD AND CONQUER as the deception is revealed today! The following scriptures will reveal that THE HOLY GHOST BAPTISM is SEPARATE from THE SPIRIT BIRTH, and if you still resist, you are resisting JESUS who <u>IS</u> THE HOLY GHOST, **"BECAUSE THESE THREE ARE ONE!"** And also that He <u>IS</u> the Baptizer with the Holy Ghost. Matthew 3:11 – John 1:33.

During my recent trip to INDIA, I was thrilled to see the Christians being BAPTIZED IN THE HOLY GHOST and SPEAKING IN OTHER TONGUES according to THE WORD OF GOD!

And not only in INDIA, but THOUSANDS upon THOUSANDS in every country I have visited are being BAPTIZED IN THE HOLY GHOST. Don't <u>you</u> want this GIFT FROM GOD? THAT <u>YOU</u> MAY have POWER IN YOUR MINISTRY and NOT JUST PREACH THE WORD ONLY?

Again I say, ONE WITH AN EXPERIENCE in the HOLY GHOST BAPTISM sent down from HEAVEN is worth more than TEN THOUSAND WITH AN ARGUMENT, because of their lack of Spiritual understanding of THE HOLY WORD OF GOD.

Heb 4:1   Paul said: **"LET US FEAR, lest a PROMISE BEING LEFT US** *(PROMISE OF THE HOLY GHOST)* **of entering into HIS REST, any of you should seem TO COME SHORT OF IT."**

After REVEALING THE TRUTH in the following SCRIPTURES, I do HOPE and PRAY that ALL THAT READ this WORD, will say:

*"**THUS SAITH THE LORD**" and not "**HATH GOD SAID?**" as Satan has been preaching!*

JESUS MAKES THE SEPARATION VERY CLEAR
JUST BEFORE THE HOLY GHOST WAS POURED OUT.

LET US NOW BEGIN TO REVEAL THE SEPARATION
BETWEEN THE SPIRIT BIRTH AND THE BAPTISM OF THE
HOLY GHOST

Jn 7:37-39		"In the LAST DAY, that GREAT DAY OF THE FEAST, (feast of the PASSOVER LAMB) **JESUS STOOD UP AND CRIED, saying, If any man thirst let him come unto ME, and drink.**"
		"He that BELIEVETH on ME, as the scripture has said, OUT of his belly shall flow RIVERS OF LIVING WATER."
Jn 7:39	(1)	"BUT THIS SPAKE HE OF THE SPIRIT, WHICH THEY THAT BELIEVE ON HIM SHOULD RECEIVE: *(THE SPIRIT BIRTH)*
	(2)	<u>FOR THE HOLY GHOST WAS NOT YET GIVEN;</u> Because that JESUS was not yet glorified."

Quite a challenge my dear brethren, if you reject HIS WORDS above. May I ask who's sheep are you? How much clearer could our dear LORD make the difference between THE HOLY SPIRIT and the HOLY GHOST BAPTISM?

Lk 6:46-49 READ:	JESUS SAID, **"AND WHY CALL YE ME, LORD, LORD AND DO NOT THE THINGS WHICH I SAY?"**
Jn 10:27	JESUS SAID FURTHER, **"MY SHEEP HEAR MY VOICE, I KNOW THEM, THEY FOLLOW ME:"**
QUESTION:	ARE WE HEARING HIS VOICE?

An honest question: "How can we follow HIM if we reject THE BAPTISM OF THE HOLY GHOST that HE said would come, to lead us into ALL TRUTH?"

Jn 14:26   **"But the Comforter, *which is* the Holy Ghost, whom the Father will send in my name, he shall teach you All things, and bring All things to your remembrance, whatsoever I have said unto you."**

PETER'S MESSAGE EXPLAINING THE HOLY GHOST FOLLOWING THE DAY OF PENTECOST

Acts 2:37   **"Now when they heard this, they were PRICKED IN THEIR HEARTS,** *(same as today)* **And said unto Peter and the rest of the APOSTLES, MEN AND BRETHREN,**

- "WHAT SHALL WE DO?"

PETER GIVES THE ANSWER TO ALL CHRISTIANS:

Acts 2:38   **"Then Peter said unto them,**
          (1)   **REPENT, AND BE BAPTIZED EVERY ONE OF YOU IN THE NAME OF (THE LORD) JESUS CHRIST, for the REMISSION OF SINS,**

          (2)   **AND YE SHALL RECEIVE THE GIFT OF THE HOLY GHOST."**

Acts 2:39   **"FOR THE PROMISE IS UNTO YOU, AND TO YOUR CHILDREN, and to all that are AFAR OFF, even as many as THE LORD OUR GOD SHALL CALL."**

Comment: Here we see again 1) THE SPIRIT BIRTH and 2) the BAPTISM OF THE HOLY GHOST! Will we not obey what PETER said and stop RESISTING the BAPTISM OF THE HOLY GHOST?!

SIMON THE SORCERER IS BAPTIZED
AND DESIRES TO PURCHASE THE HOLY GHOST

Acts 8:9-13

"But there was a certain man, called Simon, which beforetime in the same city used sorcery, and bewitched the people of Samaria, giving out that himself was some great one:

To whom they all gave heed, from the least to the greatest, saying, This man is the great power of God.

And to him they had regard, because that of long time he had bewitched them with sorceries."

THE SPIRIT BIRTH

Acts 8:12   (1)

"But when they believed Philip, preaching the things concerning to the KINGDOM of GOD and THE NAME OF JESUS CHRIST, THEY WERE BAPTIZED, both men and women." *(Water baptism and Spirit birth)*

Acts 8:13

"Then SIMON himself believed also, AND WHEN HE WAS WATER BAPTIZED, he continued with Philip, AND WONDERED, beholding the MIRACLES and SIGNS, which were done." *(POWER OF THE HOLY GHOST.)*

THE BAPTISM OF THE HOLY GHOST

Acts 8:18   (2)

"When SIMON SAW THAT THROUGH THE LAYING ON OF THE APOSTLES HANDS, THE HOLY GHOST WAS GIVEN, HE (SIMON) OFFERED THEM MONEY," (to purchase it)

Note: Simon was Born of the Spirit, BAPTIZED IN WATER and heard them speak in OTHER TONGUES revealing the BAPTISM of the HOLY GHOST.

SIMON as a SORCERER thought he could make money by laying hands on people to hear them SPEAK IN other TONGUES and miracles and signs would follow!

**THE APOSTLES HEAR THAT
SAMARIA HAD RECEIVED THE WORD OF GOD**

BORN OF THE SPIRIT

Again:

Acts 8:14-17   "Now when the Apostles, which were at JERUSALEM, heard that SAMARIA HAD RECEIVED THE WORD OF GOD, they sent unto them Peter and John:"

Note: The people of Samaria were Born of the Spirit.

HOLY GHOST

Acts 8:15   "Who, when they were come DOWN, prayed for them, that they might receive THE HOLY GHOST:"

BAPTIZED IN WATER

Acts 8:16   "(For as yet HE was fallen upon none of them:
         (1)   Only they were BAPTIZED IN THE NAME OF THE LORD JESUS.)" (Water)

FOLLOWING WATER BAPTISM THE HOLY GHOST WAS GIVEN

Acts 8:17   (2)   "Then laid they their hands on them, AND THEY RECEIVED THE HOLY GHOST."

Again it is revealed, THE SPIRIT BIRTH IS SEPARATE FROM THE BAPTISM OF THE HOLY GHOST!

PETER PREACHES THE GOSPEL TO CORNELIUS A GENTILE

Acts 10:1-48 READ: Peter is sent by GOD TO PREACH THE GOSPEL to Cornelius.

Note: Peter was called to preach the GOSPEL ONLY TO THE JEWS.

THE HOLY GHOST FELL ON THEM

Acts 10:44 "While Peter yet SPAKE THESE WORDS, THE HOLY GHOST FELL ON THEM, which <u>HEARD</u> THE WORD."

THE GIFT OF THE HOLY GHOST

Acts 10:45 (1) "And they of the circumcision *(JEWS)* which BELIEVED WERE ASTONISHED, as many as came with Peter, BECAUSE that on the GENTILES also WAS POURED OUT THE GIFT OF THE HOLY GHOST."

THE EVIDENCE - SPEAKING IN OTHER TONGUES

Acts 10:46 "FOR THEY <u>HEARD</u> THEM SPEAK WITH TONGUES, and MAGNIFY GOD..."

Revealing that TONGUES <u>IS</u> THE FIRST EVIDENCE that we are BAPTIZED in the HOLY GHOST.

WATER BAPTISM

Acts 10:47 (2) "CAN ANY MAN FORBID WATER, THAT THESE SHOULD NOT BE BAPTIZED? WHICH HAVE RECEIVED THE HOLY GHOST AS WELL AS WE?"

Many times people have been BAPTIZED IN THE HOLY GHOST and spake with other tongues before they were Baptized in water, or at the same time they were being Baptized in water.

Acts 10:48	**"And he commanded them to be BAPTIZED IN THE NAME OF THE LORD..."**
Note:	Again it is REVEALED, THE HOLY GHOST BAPTISM IS SEPARATE FROM WATER BAPTISM and THE SPIRIT BIRTH.

PETER'S DEFENSE TO THE JEWS
FOR MINISTERING TO CORNELIUS (A GENTILE)

Acts 11:1-13 READ:	*THE JEWS challenge Peter for ministering to CORNELIUS, A GENTILE.*

PETER'S ANSWER TO THE JEWS

An ANGEL instructs Cornelius to send men to Joppa for Peter - Direction came from Heaven!

Acts 11:14	**(1)**	**"Who shall tell thee (CORNELIUS) WORDS, whereby thou and all thy house (SHALL BE *(future)* SAVED."** *This message was given by Peter.*
Acts 11:15	**(2)**	**"And as I began to SPEAK, THE HOLY GHOST FELL ON THEM, AS ON US AT THE BEGINNING"** (The day of Pentecost)

(And is <u>still</u> taking place today in many churches that do not resist THE HOLY GHOST BAPTISM!)

Acts 11:16	**"Then remembered I the WORD OF THE LORD, how that HE SAID: John indeed BAPTIZED WITH WATER, BUT YE SHALL BE BAPTIZED WITH THE HOLY GHOST."**

Acts 11:17	**(1)**	**"For as much then, as GOD GAVE THEM THE LIKE <u>GIFT</u>, AS HE DID UNTO US,** *(THE GIFT OF THE BAPTISM OF THE HOLY GHOST.)*
	(2)	**"WHO BELIEVED ON THE LORD JESUS CHRIST;** *(SPIRIT BIRTH)* <u>**WHAT WAS I THAT I COULD WITHSTAND GOD?"**</u>

As Paul said, I think we should examine ourselves, whether we be in "THE FAITH" because many local churches in the land today who preach the SPIRIT BIRTH in their churches, <u>WITHSTAND GOD</u> over THE GIFT OF THE HOLY GHOST BAPTISM and THE EVIDENCE OF SPEAKING IN OTHER TONGUES!

Question	Peter an apostle WOULD NOT WITHSTAND GOD, how then can we take the opposite stand to Peter, and withstand GOD on THE BAPTISM OF THE HOLY GHOST?

THE EARLY CHURCH OUR EXAMPLE
(AUTHORIZED KING JAMES BIBLE REVEALS THE TRUTH)

Acts 19:1	**"And it came to pass, that, while Appolos was at Corinth, and Paul having passed through the upper coasts, came to Ephesus: AND FINDING CERTAIN DISCIPLES,"** *(a group of believers)*
Acts 19:2	Paul said unto these BELIEVERS, **"HAVE YE RECEIVED THE HOLY GHOST <u>SINCE YE BELIEVED</u>?"** **And they said unto him, "We have not so much as heard, whether there be any HOLY GHOST."**
Comment:	To those who preach that "HOLY GHOST" means "HOLY SPIRIT" (which is true) in this case, is confusion, for they were DISCIPLES of Jesus, Born of HIS SPIRIT. They were truthfully

answering Paul, "We have not so much as heard
whether there be any HOLY GHOST." (Not Holy
Spirit) Paul did **NOT say**, "Did ye receive THE
HOLYSPIRIT, **WHEN** YE BELIEVED!"

Reference: The New International Version of the Bible, Acts 19:2 Quote: and
asked them, "Did you receive the Holy Spirit when you believed?"

Reference: The Living Bible, Acts 19:2 Quote: "Did you receive the Holy
Spirit when you believed?" He asked them.

Regarding the N.I.V. and the Living Bible quoted above: In their desire to
eliminate the Holy Ghost, they got into confusion in asking this question.
"Did you receive the Holy Spirit when you believed?" Our truthful answer to
all Christians would be "YES! I DID RECEIVE THE HOLY SPIRIT WHEN
I BELIEVED." "HOWEVER, REGARDING THE BAPTISM OF THE HOLY
GHOST, I DID **NOT** RECEIVE THE HOLY GHOST WHEN I BELIEVED,
BUT **AFTER** I BELIEVED! According to the Holy Scriptures."

Acts 19:3   **Paul said unto them, "...unto what then were ye
                            BAPTIZED?
                            And they said, unto John's Baptism."**

Acts 19:4   **"Then said Paul, "John verily BAPTIZED with
                            the BAPTISM OF REPENTANCE, saying unto
                            the people, that they should believe on HIM
                            which should come after him that is on
                            CHRIST JESUS."**

WATER BAPTISM

Acts 19:5   1)   **"When they heard this, THEY WERE
                            BAPTIZED IN THE NAME OF THE LORD
                            JESUS."** *(Revealing WATER BAPTISM and the
                            Spirit Birth.)*

HOLY GHOST BAPTISM

Acts 19:6	2)	**"And when Paul laid his hands on them, THE HOLY GHOST CAME ON THEM, AND THEY SPAKE WITH TONGUES AND PROPHESIED."**

Comment:	These two verses alone, in the N.I.V. and the Living Bible expose the lies and subtlety of Satan in "THEIR VERSION" of **Acts 19:2**, when they changed THE WORD to read: **"DID YOU RECEIVE THE HOLY SPIRIT 'WHEN' YE BELIEVED,"** when the scriptures reveal the opposite!

Acts 19:5 READ:	Comment: THEY WERE BAPTIZED IN WATER **'WHEN'** THEY BELIEVED. (NOT THE HOLY GHOST BAPTISM.)

Acts 19:6 READ:	Comment: THEY WERE BAPTIZED IN THE HOLY GHOST, **AFTER** THEY BELIEVED.

With the above scriptures revealing THE TRUTH of THE BAPTISM OF THE HOLY GHOST, will we still reject JESUS who IS THE HOLY GHOST? AND IN Matthew 3:11 it is revealed that JESUS IS THE ONE THAT BAPTIZES WITH THE HOLY GHOST?!

We MUST LEAVE THE PRINCIPLES OF THE DOCTRINE OF CHRIST - (SPIRIT BIRTH) and GO ON. We are on a Spiritual Journey. If we don't keep walking from - 1) SPIRIT BIRTH 2) WATER BAPTISM 3) HOLY GHOST BAPTISM (Doctrine of BAPTISMS) we will GO BACKWARDS, as ISRAEL DID ON THEIR JOURNEY TO THE PROMISED LAND.

PAUL'S EXHORTATION ALSO TO GO BEYOND THE BORN AGAIN EXPERIENCE

Heb 5:11-14	**"Of whom we have many things to say, and hard to be uttered, SEEING YE ARE DULL OF HEARING. 1 Corinthians 14:21 "...and yet for all that, will they not hear me, saith the Lord."**

For when for the time ye ought to be teachers, ye have need that one teach you again which *be* the first principles of the oracles of GOD; and are become such as have need of milk, and not of strong meat."

"For every one that useth milk *is* unskilful in the word of righteousness: FOR HE IS A BABE.

But strong meat belongeth to them that are of full age, *even* those who by reason of use have their senses exercised to discern both good and evil."

THE PROPHETS SPEAK OF THE HOLY GHOST TO COME

Again:
Is 28:11   "For with stammering lips and another tongue will <u>HE</u> speak to this people."

Revealing that it is THE LORD that speaks in tongues out of HIS TEMPLE, a human body that HE made in the beginning for this purpose. Genesis 1:26 "And GOD said, Let us make man in our image, after our likeness:"

PAUL REVEALS THE RESISTANCE TO THE HOLY GHOST

1 Corinth 14:21   "In the law it is written, With *men of* other tongues and other lips will <u>I</u> speak unto this people; and yet for all that will they not hear me, saith the LORD." - Paul quotes Isaiah 28:11 above.

JESUS <u>IS</u> THE BAPTIZER WITH THE HOLY GHOST

Jn 1:33   "And I knew him not: but he that sent me to baptize with water, the same said unto me, Upon

whom thou shalt see
(1) the Spirit descending, and remaining on him,
(2) **THE SAME IS HE WHICH BAPTIZETH WITH THE HOLY GHOST."**

Matt 3:11   **"I indeed baptize you with water unto repentance: but He that cometh after me is mightier than I, whose shoes I am not worthy to bear: He SHALL BAPTIZE YOU WITH THE HOLY GHOST and FIRE:"**

QUESTION: AS JESUS IS THE ONE THAT BAPTIZES WITH THE HOLY GHOST, HOW CAN WE RESIST THE BAPTISM OF THE HOLY GHOST?!!

REMEMBER,   If we are HIS SHEEP we will HEAR HIS VOICE. Again, don't you think we should examine ourselves?

CHALLENGING WORD FOR ALL OF US REGARDING OUR FAITH

Mk 16:15-18 READ: **"THESE SIGNS SHALL FOLLOW THEM THAT BELIEVE;**

1)   **IN MY NAME SHALL THEY CAST OUT DEVILS;** (By the power of the HOLY GHOST)
2)   **THEY SHALL SPEAK WITH NEW TONGUES;"** (Only if baptized in the HOLY GHOST)
3)   **"...THEY SHALL LAY HANDS ON THE SICK, AND THEY SHALL RECOVER"** (By the power of the HOLY GHOST)

Question: Ask yourself do I have these signs as a believer without the Baptism of the HOLY GHOST or am I deceived?

Comment: The SPIRIT BIRTH ALONE, CANNOT ACCOMPLISH the Scripture ABOVE!

WE MUST GO ON, for ONLY IN THE POWER OF THE HOLY GHOST, AND IN THE NAME OF JESUS WILL THESE THINGS BE ACCOMPLISHED.

Acts 1:8 **"But ye shall RECEIVE POWER, after that the HOLY GHOST is come upon you:"**

JESUS has a plan for your ministry my dear brother and sister in CHRIST, **"Know ye not YOUR BODY IS THE TEMPLE OF THE HOLY GHOST?"**

Chapter Twelve

Resistance To The Baptism Of The Holy Ghost

First, it is strange that there are at least twenty-four published bibles today that have deleted or added to the HOLY WORD OF GOD by man's opinions and have attacked THE KING JAMES BIBLE that holds ALL THE TRUTH for the child of GOD, and this truth has endured SATAN'S ATTACK on THE WORD which is OUR LORD JESUS CHRIST for hundreds of years!

In this writing, I WILL CHALLENGE THE SUBTLETY OF SATAN **BY THE HOLY WORD OF GOD**, as certain men, deceived by Satan, crept in unawares to CHANGE THE WORD OF GOD through the BLINDNESS OF THEIR HEART, the most important message from THE LORD in this hour, THE BAPTISM OF THE HOLY GHOST!

THE FOLLOWING SCRIPTURES REVEAL THE SUBTLETY OF SATAN AND THE REASON FOR THIS WRITING, TO WAKE UP THE CHURCH! FOUND IN THE AUTHORIZED KING JAMES BIBLE.

Acts 19:1 **"And it came to pass, that while Apollos was at Corinth, Paul having passed through the upper coasts, came to Ephesus: and FINDING CERTAIN DISCIPLES,"** (who were Christian believers).

Acts 19:2 *And Paul said, unto these Christian believers,* **"...HAVE YE RECEIVED THE HOLY GHOST SINCE YE BELIEVED?..."** Paul was speaking to his disciples that were BORN OF THE SPIRIT.

Comment:
The above scriptures reveal that THE HOLY GHOST BAPTISM IS A SEPARATE EXPERIENCE that **follows** the "BORN AGAIN" experience.

THE HOLY WORD OF GOD WAS CHANGED TO READ in The New International Version of the Bible, and I quote Acts 19:2, "DID YOU RECEIVE THE HOLY SPIRIT, **WHEN** YOU BELIEVED." Also The Living Bible, and I quote Acts 19:2, "Did you receive the Holy Spirit when you believed? He asked them."

These individuals crept in unawares who through the BLINDNESS of their HEARTS, resisted THE HOLY WORD OF GOD regarding THE BAPTISM OF THE HOLY GHOST, when CHRIST **IS** THE HOLY GHOST, **AS THE FATHER** - **THE SON** and **THE HOLY GHOST** are **ONE**. ALSO, JESUS **IS** THE ONE THAT BAPTIZES WITH THE HOLY GHOST.

Matt 3:11	**"I indeed baptize you with water unto repentance: but He that cometh after me is mightier than I, whose shoes I am not worthy to bear: He shall baptize you with the HOLY GHOST AND WITH FIRE!"**

I say "WAKE UP CHURCH" to the TRUTH OF GOD'S WORD and not man's traditions and opinions that are attempting to divide and destroy THE CHURCH, when JESUS prayed that we may BE ONE!

OUR LORD JESUS WARNS US OF THE DAYS WE LIVE

Matt 24:4	*JESUS said these WORDS,* **"...TAKE HEED THAT NO MAN DECEIVE YOU."**
Matt 24:5	**"FOR MANY SHALL COME IN MY NAME, SAYING, I AM CHRIST; AND SHALL DECEIVE MANY."**

These two verses of scripture are being fulfilled in this hour!

Comment:	There is no greater way to DECEIVE the CHRISTIAN CHURCH in this hour, but to **CHANGE THE HOLY WORD OF GOD in whom we trust,** in an attempt to do away with THE BAPTISM OF THE HOLY GHOST!! AND, ALSO PRINT NEW BIBLES TO SUBSTANTIATE THEIR UNGODLY ACT.
QUESTION:	**Where are THE FATHERS and PILLARS of THE CHURCH?**, that they have not cried out against "THE CHANGING OF THE WORD?" Are they DECEIVED BY SATAN as well? Are they in darkness, that they cannot see where they are leading THE CHURCH OF JESUS CHRIST?

Is 8:20	THE PROPHET SAID, "To the law and to the testimony: if they speak not according to THIS WORD, IT IS BECAUSE THERE IS NO LIGHT IN THEM."

CHALLENGING SCRIPTURES REGARDING CHANGING OF THE WORD

Gen 2:7 READ:	Comment: Shall THE SOUL that was CREATED BY THE WORD, now CHANGE THE WORD that created him?
Comment:	One might ask, "WHAT PORTION OF THE HOLY WORD OF GOD WILL THESE MEN ATTEMPT TO CHANGE NEXT?"
Malachi 3:6	*When THE LORD SAID;* "FOR I AM THE LORD, (THE WORD) I CHANGE NOT;..."

TO CHANGE THE WORD IS TO CHANGE JESUS WHO IS THE WORD!

WARNING TO US REGARDING THOSE THAT CHANGE THE WORD

Prov 24:21	"...MEDDLE NOT WITH THEM THAT ARE GIVEN TO CHANGE:"

FEARFUL WARNINGS TO THEM THAT WOULD CHANGE "THE WORD" OR ADD TO IT
(As Satan deceived Eve in the garden when he omitted and added to the Word.)

THE BEGINNING OF THE BIBLE

Duet 4:1-4	"Now therefore hearken, O Israel, unto the statutes and unto the judgments, which I teach you, for to do them, that ye may live, and go in and possess the land which the Lord God of your fathers giveth you.

The reason:

YE SHALL NOT <u>ADD</u> UNTO THE WORD WHICH I COMMAND YOU NEITHER SHALL YE <u>DIMINISH</u> OUGHT FROM IT, THAT   YE   MAY   KEEP   THE <u>COMMANDMENTS OF THE LORD</u>...”

Your eyes have seen what the Lord did because of Baal-peor: for all the men that followed Baal-peor, the Lord thy God hath destroyed them from among you.
But ye that did cleave unto the Lord your God are alive every one of you this day.”

HOW SHALL WE KEEP THE COMMANDMENTS OF THE LORD IF THE WORD IS BEING CHANGED?!

“Thus saith <u>THE LORD</u>” and **“IT IS WRITTEN”** is what we put our hope in.
AND NOT THUS SAITH <u>MAN</u>, AS HE ATTEMPTS TO CHANGE THE WORD TO AGREE WITH <u>HIS</u> NATURAL, SINFUL MIND, AND ALSO PRINT NEW BIBLES TO SUBSTANTIATE HIS UNGODLY WAYS!

Rev 22:18

“...IF ANY MAN SHALL <u>ADD</u> UNTO THESE THINGS, GOD SHALL <u>ADD</u> UNTO HIM THE PLAGUES THAT ARE WRITTEN IN THIS BOOK:”

Rev 22:19

**“AND IF ANY MAN SHALL <u>TAKE AWAY</u> FROM THE WORDS OF THE BOOK OF THIS PROPHECY,
GOD SHALL <u>TAKE AWAY</u> HIS PART OUT OF THE BOOK OF LIFE...”**

Comment:

Don't you think we should examine ourselves, and **<u>CHANGE OURSELVES</u>** to be obedient to THE WORD OF GOD and NOT **<u>CHANGE THE WORD</u>** OF GOD to be obedient to us and our sinful ways!

Remember, Is 8:20	"To the law and to the testimony: if they speak not according to THIS WORD, IT IS BECAUSE THERE IS NO LIGHT IN THEM."

PAUL REVEALS THE FOOLISHNESS OF THE CHANGE IN ACTS 19:2

Eph 1:13	Paul reveals THE TRUTH, "In whom ye also trusted, <u>after</u> that ye heard the word of truth, the gospel of your salvation."

      1)   IN WHOM ALSO, **AFTER** THAT YE BELIEVED (NOT **WHEN**),

      2)   YE WERE SEALED WITH THAT HOLY <u>SPIRIT</u> OF <u>PROMISE</u>,
(THE BAPTISM OF THE HOLY GHOST) revealed in the following scriptures.

Acts 1:4	He commanded them NOT to depart from Jerusalem, but WAIT for **THE PROMISE OF THE FATHER.** - (THE HOLY GHOST)

Lk 24:49	**And behold, I send THE PROMISE OF MY FATHER upon you:**
(THE HOLY GHOST)

Acts 2:33	Having received of the FATHER, <u>THE PROMISE OF THE HOLY GHOST</u>. He hath shed forth this, which ye now **SEE** and **HEAR**. - (THE HOLY GHOST BAPTISM)

IT IS TIME TO ASK OURSELVES SOME QUESTIONS:

1)   Who are these people, who CHANGED THE WORD OF GOD in **Acts 19:2** and published NEW BIBLES to support their UNGODLY DECEPTION?

2)   Did the LORD CHANGE HIS MIND? When the LORD SAID, **"I AM THE LORD AND I CHANGE NOT!"**

I strongly suggest we get rid of THE NEW VERSIONS and obtain **THE AUTHORIZED KING JAMES BIBLE**, that has endured its critics for centuries.

NOTE: If your pastor continues to preach that you received the Holy Ghost <u>when</u> you believed, I suggest you not only get rid of the NEW VERSION BIBLE, but think seriously of changing your pastor, before it's too late, for the coming of the Lord is very near, signs are everywhere!

WE BEGIN WITH THE WORD OF EXHORTATION FROM PAUL JESUS IS SPEAKING TO US TODAY

Heb 1:1-2   **"GOD, who at sundry times and in diverse manners, spake in TIMES PAST unto THE FATHERS by THE PROPHETS,"**

Heb 1:2   **"HATH IN THESE LAST DAYS SPOKEN UNTO US BY HIS SON,** (who is the Holy Ghost) **whom HE hath APPOINTED HEIR of ALL THINGS BY WHOM also HE made the worlds;"**

Comment: JESUS our LORD spake more than all regarding the coming OF THE HOLY GHOST to give POWER to HIS CHURCH to finish the WORK HE has called us to do.

FURTHER EXHORTATION FROM PAUL

Heb 2:1-4   **"THEREFORE, WE OUGHT TO GIVE THE MORE EARNEST HEED TO THE THINGS WHICH WE HAVE HEARD, LEST AT ANY TIME WE SHOULD LET THEM SLIP.** (And that includes THE BAPTISM OF THE HOLY GHOST!)

> For if THE WORD SPOKEN by the ANGELS was STEADFAST, and EVERY TRANSGRESSION and DISOBEDIENCE received a JUST RECOMPENSE OF REWARD;
>
> HOW SHALL WE ESCAPE, if we NEGLECT SO <u>GREAT SALVATION</u>; which at the FIRST began to be spoken by THE LORD, and was confirmed to us by them that HEARD HIM;"

Our **"GREAT SALVATION"** includes THE BAPTISM OF THE GHOST and NOT JUST "THE SPIRIT BIRTH," which is only the beginning!

> GOD also bearing them witness, both with SIGNS and WONDERS, and with DIVERSE MIRACLES, and <u>GIFTS OF THE HOLY GHOST</u>..."

Comment: Again the scripture reveals, that the SPIRIT BIRTH is only the beginning of OUR SALVATION, and as we GO ON TO PERFECTION, THE HOLY GHOST will be presented to us as PART OF OUR SALVATION. Now we MUST MAKE A DECISION TO ACCEPT or REJECT THE POWER FROM HEAVEN FOR OUR MINISTRY.

TODAY, *PLEASE* HEAR HIS VOICE

Heb 3:7   **"WHEREFORE AS THE HOLY GHOST SAITH,**
                                 <u>**TODAY IF YE WILL HEAR HIS VOICE**</u>,"

THE JOURNEY OF ISRAEL GIVEN AS AN EXAMPLE (Which is a shadow of the Church)

Heb 3:8   **"Harden <u>NOT YOUR HEARTS</u>, as in the PROVOCATION, in the DAY OF TEMPTATION in the WILDERNESS:"**

Heb 3:9	"When your fathers TEMPTED ME, proved ME, and saw MY WORKS for forty years."
Heb 3:10	**"<u>WHEREFORE, I WAS GRIEVED WITH THAT GENERATION</u>, and said, THEY DO ALWAY ERR IN THEIR HEART; AND THEY HAVE NOT KNOWN MY WAYS."**
Comment:	Many have resisted THE HOLY GHOST BAPTISM because they have no vision of GOD'S plan for their lives. It appears that our generation is the one JESUS is speaking to:

1) SPOKEN UNTO US BY HIS SON;

2) We need to give MORE EARNEST HEED to the <u>WORD</u>;

3) HOW shall we ESCAPE IF WE NEGLECT SO GREAT SALVATION.

(THE WORD ABOVE SPEAKS FOR ITSELF!)

AARON'S ROD THAT BUDDED

THE WORD WAS CHALLENGED BY OTHER MINISTRIES IN THE PAST, WHO HAD NO POWER

Num 17:2-10	**"Speak unto the children of Israel, and take of every one of them a rod according to the house of *their* fathers, of all their princes according to the house of their fathers twelve rods: write thou every man's name upon his rod.**
	And thou shalt write Aaron's name upon the rod of Levi: for one rod *shall be* for the head of the house of their fathers.

And thou shalt lay them up in the tabernacle of the congregation before the testimony, where I will meet with you.

And it shall come to pass, *that* the man's rod, whom I shall choose, shall blossom: and I will make to cease from me the murmurings of the children of Israel, whereby they murmur against you.

And Moses spake unto the children of Israel, and every one of their princes gave him a rod apiece, for each prince one, according to their fathers' houses, *even* twelve rods: and the rod of Aaron *was* among their rods.

And Moses laid up the rods before the LORD in the tabernacle of witness.

And it came to pass, that on the morrow Moses went into the tabernacle of witness; and, behold, the rod of Aaron for the house of Levi was budded, and brought forth buds, and bloomed blossoms, and yielded almonds.

And Moses brought out all the rods from before the LORD unto all the children of Israel: and they looked, and took every man his rod.

And the LORD said unto Moses, Bring Aaron's rod again before the testimony, to be kept for a token against the rebels; and thou shalt quite take away their murmurings from me, that they die not."

- Israel challenged the ROD and the LORD intervened.
- Jesus was challenged when HE came unto HIS OWN.

- Many challenge or resist the Holy Ghost Power today.
- Many still want to remove Aaron's Rod from THE ARK of the Covenant - where we find the revelation of the GODHEAD -

  1) Tables of Stone,
  2) Golden Pot of Manna,
  3) Aaron's Rod that Budded - revealing the POWER you could have in your ministry by the BAPTISM OF THE HOLY GHOST.

I know there are a few LANGUAGES in the world that interpret HOLY SPIRIT for HOLY GHOST which is true, but their motive is hidden, which is to remove the BAPTISM OF THE HOLY GHOST, and even publish NEW BIBLES, to subvert the CHRISTIAN CHURCH regarding THE HOLY GHOST BAPTISM and CHANGE THE WORD to ACCOMPLISH THIS!

AN HONEST QUESTION - "DO YOU THINK, THE LORD should CHANGE HIS HOLY WORD in these last days, to AGREE with your problem regarding THE HOLY GHOST, OR SHOULD YOU CHANGE YOUR INTERPRETATION OF THE HOLY GHOST TO AGREE WITH THE HOLY WORD OF GOD?!"

Many are so caught up in the RESISTANCE to the HOLY GHOST BAPTISM, that their EARS ARE CLOSED to what the PROPHET and our LORD JESUS is saying today, about THE HOLY GHOST!

One might say, "MY MIND IS MADE UP through the TRADITIONS and TEACHING of our local church. DON'T CONFUSE ME WITH THE WORD, which is CHRIST!"

Don't let this happen to you. Search THE WORD to see what the LORD has said, and not man's opinions and traditions.

1 Jn 5:7   *READS:*   *"THERE ARE THREE (persons) THAT BEAR RECORD IN HEAVEN,*
1) THE FATHER,
2) THE WORD, (JESUS); AND
3) THE HOLY GHOST: <u>AND THESE THREE ARE ONE</u>."

REVEALING:

- There are THREE PERSONS IN THE GODHEAD (NOT TWO)
- **"<u>AND THESE THREE ARE ONE</u>."**

Comment: If you believe in THE FATHER and THE SON, you <u>MUST</u> BELIEVE in the HOLY GHOST also, BECAUSE "<u>THESE THREE ARE ONE</u>!"

EXAMPLE:

We have THREE beautiful gothic windows in our Church building:

-   *They are <u>ALL</u> WINDOWS and <u>ALL</u> have the same purpose (The same as the Father, Son and Holy Ghost).*

-   *They represent the <u>GODHEAD</u>, - <u>THREE PERSONS</u>, - FATHER - SON - HOLY GHOST.*

-   *If we say FATHER - SON - and Holy Spirit, we are saying FATHER - SON - and window, for they are <u>ALL</u> WINDOWS and we do away with the meaning of the THIRD WINDOW, which represents the HOLY GHOST.*

If we take away the THIRD PERSON OF THE GODHEAD, we have destroyed THE GODHEAD.

BECAUSE - <u>"THESE THREE ARE ONE!"</u>

SATAN THE DECEIVER

I will REVEAL in the WORD OF GOD, as I proceed, that **IF** we RESIST or REJECT the BAPTISM OF THE HOLY GHOST, WE RESIST or REJECT OUR LORD JESUS, who **IS** THE HOLY GHOST - "FOR THE FATHER, THE SON AND THE HOLY GHOST ARE ONE!" AND ALSO, THAT JESUS IS THE BAPTIZER WITH THE HOLY GHOST

Matt 3:11
> "I indeed baptize you with water unto repentance: but He that cometh after me is mightier than I, whose shoes I am not worthy to bear: He shall baptize you with the Holy Ghost, and *with* fire:"

LET US GO BACK TO THE BEGINNING, WHERE RESISTANCE BEGAN

Gen 3:1
> "NOW, THE SERPENT was more SUBTLE than any beast of the FIELD, which the LORD GOD had made..."

> And Satan said unto THE WOMAN, "YEA HATH GOD SAID?"

Comment:
"YEA, HATH GOD SAID?" Is what we shall focus on at this time. The SUBTLETY OF SATAN in questioning THE WORD OF GOD, IS REPEATING itself in the CHURCH in this hour! WAKE UP CHURCH! It is not a time to SLEEP. JESUS said, **"THE HOUSE DIVIDED AGAINST ITSELF, SHALL COME TO DESOLATION."** SATAN is attempting in THESE LAST DAYS to diminish the POWER OF THE WORD in the CHURCH, (through men and women that resist THE BAPTISM OF THE HOLY GHOST) that brings the POWER to cast out DEVILS!

REMEMBER, there is ONLY ONE CHURCH - THE BODY OF CHRIST!

SATAN'S plan is to divide and conquer! For he knows THE CHURCH divided against itself will come to desolation. It is DIVIDED today over THE WORD that the HOLY GHOST is for all today.

JESUS SAID DIVISION WOULD COME BECAUSE OF HIS WORDS

Lk 12:51-53   **"SUPPOSE YE THAT I HAVE COME TO GIVE PEACE ON THE EARTH? I TELL YOU, NAY; BUT RATHER A DIVISION:"**

Did HE not also say, "Your enemies shall be they of your own household." (or CHURCH of JESUS CHRIST). Which we are finding out who these enemies are through their rejection of the HOLY GHOST BAPTISM, AND CHANGING THE WORD OF GOD AND ADDING TO IT!

These are surprising words from our LORD, and that DIVISION is caused by the rejection of THE BAPTISM OF THE HOLY GHOST when JESUS **IS** THE HOLY GHOST **AND THE** BAPTIZER WITH THE HOLY GHOST.

LET US EXAMINE OURSELVES IF WE BE IN THE FAITH

"HATH GOD SAID" - Because in your language, HOLY GHOST means HOLY SPIRIT, does NOT mean you can REJECT THE BAPTISM OF THE HOLY GHOST!

"HATH GOD SAID" - You can CHANGE THE WORD in **Acts 19:2** to READ: *"Did you receive the HOLY SPIRIT <u>WHEN</u> ye believed,"* and write NEW BIBLES to promote it?

"HATH GOD SAID" You could WITHSTAND GOD, regarding THE HOLY GHOST baptism?

PETER WOULD NOT WITHSTAND GOD
WHEN PREACHING THE GOSPEL TO CORNELIEUS

Acts 11:14-17

"Who shall tell thee words, whereby thou and all thy house shall be saved.

And as I began to speak, the Holy Ghost fell on them, as on us at the beginning.

Then remembered I the word of the Lord, how that he said, John indeed baptized with water; but ye shall be baptized with the Holy Ghost."

WHEN PETER SAID: (When Cornelius and his household were being baptized in the HOLY GHOST) "**For as much then as GOD GAVE THEM THE LIKE GIFT,** (The Baptism of the Holy Ghost) **AS HE DID UNTO US,** (Who were Born Again of the Spirit) **WHO BELIEVED ON THE LORD JESUS CHRIST: WHAT WAS I, THAT I COULD WITHSTAND GOD!?**

QUESTION:

How can we RESIST THE BAPTISM OF THE HOLY GHOST, when PETER, an APOSTLE **would not** WITHSTAND GOD?

Comment:

If you do not AGREE WITH GOD'S WORD as revealed above,
YOU ARE LISTENING TO THE WRONG VOICE and reading the WRONG BIBLE!!

HISTORY IS REPEATING ITSELF

When JESUS, our PRECIOUS LORD, presented HIMSELF to the Religious Leaders of that day, HE took them completely by surprise, although the HOLY PROPHETS gave sufficient warning HE WAS COMING, as did THE HOLY PROPHETS REGARDING THE HOLY GHOST! (Isaiah 28:11, Matthew 3:11, John 1:33)

Is 28:11-12	"FOR WITH STAMMERING LIPS AND ANOTHER TONGUE WILL HE SPEAK TO THIS PEOPLE.
	TO WHOM HE SAID, THIS *IS* THE REST *WHEREWITH* YE MAY CAUSE THE WEARY TO REST; AND THIS *IS* THE REFRESHING: YET THEY WOULD NOT HEAR."
Matt 3:11	"I INDEED BAPTIZE YOU WITH WATER UNTO REPENTANCE: BUT HE THAT COMETH AFTER ME IS MIGHTIER THAN I, WHOSE SHOES I AM NOT WORTHY TO BEAR: HE SHALL BAPTIZE YOU WITH THE HOLY GHOST, AND *WITH* FIRE:"
Jn 1:33	"AND I KNEW HIM NOT: BUT HE THAT SENT ME TO BAPTIZE WITH WATER, THE SAME SAID UNTO ME, UPON WHOM THOU SHALT SEE THE SPIRIT DESCENDING, AND REMAINING ON HIM, THE SAME IS HE WHICH BAPTIZETH WITH THE HOLY GHOST."

Revealing that THE SPIRIT BIRTH and THE HOLY GHOST are separate.

The established Religious Leaders REJECTED HIM, calling HIM, Beelzebub (devil), False Prophet, and many other names, BECAUSE HIS MESSAGE UPSET THEIR TRADITIONS AND RELIGIOUS ORDER, AS THE MESSAGE OF THE BAPTISM OF THE HOLY GHOST IS UPSETTING THESE SAME (so called) RELIGIONS IN OUR DAY!

Comment:	If the Leaders of that day, when JESUS came THE FIRST TIME, had had their way, we would still be in our SINS without hope of the RESURRECTION of LIFE!
	If the (so called) leaders of today, that have REJECTED THE BAPTISM OF THE HOLY GHOST had their way (AND THEY HAVE NOT) we would be still preaching THE GOSPEL without Power until JESUS comes!

PETER GIVES US WARNING

2 Pet 2:1-12

"But there were **FALSE PROPHETS** also among the people, even as there shall be **FALSE TEACHERS** among you, who privily shall bring in **DAMNABLE HERESIES**, even denying the **LORD** that bought them, (Do away with the virgin birth, rejecting THE HOLY GHOST who is JESUS), **and bring upon themselves swift DESTRUCTION.**

AND MANY SHALL FOLLOW THEIR PERNICIOUS WAYS; by reason of whom <u>THE WAY OF TRUTH</u> (THE HOLY GHOST) **SHALL BE EVIL SPOKEN OF.** (AS IS TAKING PLACE TODAY!)

And through covetousness shall they with feigned words make merchandise of you: whose judgment now of a long time lingereth not, and their damnation slumbereth not.

For if God spared not the angels that sinned, but cast *them* **down to hell, and delivered** *them* **into chains of darkness, to be reserved unto judgment;**

And spared not the old world, but saved Noah the eighth *person*, **a preacher of righteousness, bringing in the flood upon the world of the ungodly;**

And turning the cities of Sodom and Gomorrha into ashes condemned *them* **with an overthrow, making** *them* **an ensample unto those that after should live ungodly;**

And delivered just Lot, vexed with the filthy conversation of the wicked:

(For that righteous man dwelling among them, in seeing and hearing, vexed *his* righteous soul from day to day with *their* unlawful deeds;)

The Lord knoweth how to deliver the godly out of temptations, and to reserve the unjust unto the day of judgment to be punished:

But chiefly them that walk after the flesh in the lust of uncleanness, and despise government. Presumptuous *are they*, selfwilled, they are not afraid to speak evil of dignities.

Whereas angels, which are greater in power and might, bring not railing accusation against them before the Lord.

But these, as natural brute beasts, made to be taken and destroyed, speak evil of the things that THEY UNDERSTAND NOT; and shall utterly perish in their own corruption;"

THE TRADITIONS OF MAN CHALLENGED ONCE AGAIN

Jn 14:20, 23, 28 READ: JESUS came the FIRST TIME as the SON OF GOD, to SAVE US FROM OUR SINS, and was rejected by many.

JESUS came the SECOND TIME as THE HOLY GHOST, to take possession of HIS TEMPLE (our bodies) that we would have POWER to finish HIS WORK on the earth, and is rejected by many today.

Brothers and sisters in CHRIST, wake up to the call of GOD for your ministry, and let not the traditions of man's church hinder you! For we shall all stand before the JUDGMENT SEAT OF CHRIST, to give an account of what we have done in our ministries!

ALTHOUGH, THE PROPHETS SPAKE OF THE HOLY GHOST
TO COME

Is 28:11-12   "FOR WITH STAMMERING LIPS and
                      another TONGUE,
                      will _HE_ speak to this people.
                      (THE LORD Speaking)
                      To whom he said, This *is* the rest *wherewith* ye
                      may cause the weary to rest; and this *is* the
                      refreshing: YET THEY WOULD NOT HEAR."

PAUL AGREES WITH IS 28:11

1 Corinth 14:21   Paul said, "In the law it is written, With men of
                      other   tongues   and   other   lips   will
                      _I_ speak unto this people; and yet for all that
                      will they NOT HEAR ME, saith THE LORD."
                      (This scripture is being fulfilled by those who
                      reject the Baptism of the Holy Ghost today.)

Joel 2:28   "And it shall come to pass afterward, that _I_
                      will pour out OF MY SPIRIT upon ALL
                      FLESH; and your sons and your daughters
                      SHALL PROPHESY, your old men shall dream
                      dreams, your young men shall see visions:"
                      (Only by THE HOLY GHOST)

LAST OF THE PROPHETS
REVEALING - JESUS IS THE ONE THAT BAPTIZES WITH THE
HOLY GHOST

Matt 3:11   He that cometh after me, "...SHALL BAPTIZE
                      YOU WITH THE HOLY GHOST and FIRE."

IF WE DO NOT BELIEVE THE PROPHETS, then what do we believe? For
THE PROPHETS are the foundations of our faith!

OUR FOUNDATIONS

Eph 2:20	**"AND (WE) ARE BUILT UPON THE FOUNDATION OF THE APOSTLES AND PROPHETS, JESUS CHRIST HIMSELF BEING THE CHIEF CORNER STONE."** (And the Baptizer with the Holy Ghost.)
Comment:	The above scripture reveals THE CORNER STONE of a BUILDING which is JESUS CHRIST OUR LORD, and HIS NAME IS WRITTEN IN THE CORNER STONE! If we leave out of our BUILDING, THE APOSTLES and PROPHETS, who reveal the BAPTISM OF THE HOLY GHOST, we are building on a very shaky foundation and there is NO PLACE FOR THE CORNER STONE.

THESE ARE HIS FINAL WORDS BEFORE HIS BETRAYAL

Jn 10:27	**"My sheep hear my voice, and I know them, and they follow me:"**

JESUS SPAKE OF THE HOLY GHOST TO COME AS A PERSON

Jn 14:12-31	**"Verily, verily, I say unto you, He that believeth on me, the works that I do shall he do also; and greater *works* than these shall he do; because I go unto my Father.** (And send down the HOLY GHOST.) **And whatsoever ye shall ask in my name, that will I do, that the Father may be glorified in the Son.** **If ye shall ask any thing in my name, I will do *it*. If ye love me, keep my commandments.** (And his commandments are to receive the Holy Ghost on the day of Pentecost).

And I will pray the Father, and He shall give you another <u>COMFORTER,</u> (which <u>IS</u> the Holy Ghost) **that He may abide with you for ever;**

Even **the Spirit of Truth;** (which <u>IS</u> the Holy Ghost) **whom the world cannot receive, because it seeth <u>HIM</u> not, neither knoweth <u>HIM</u>: but ye know <u>HIM</u>; for <u>HE</u> dwelleth with you, and shall be <u>IN</u> you.''** Special mention here, "The Spirit of Truth" which is the Holy Ghost. Since when do we call the Spirit a person "HIM" or "HE", if not referring to the person of the Holy Ghost? (Which IS the Father and the Son)

"I will not leave you comfortless: I will come to you." (Jesus <u>IS</u> THE HOLY GHOST that would come down on the day of Pentecost.)

"Yet a little while, and the world seeth me no more; but ye see me: because I live, ye shall live also".

"At that day ye shall know that I *am* in my Father, and ye in me, and I in you."
The GODHEAD then has taken up residence, through THE BAPTISM OF THE HOLY GHOST. AS THE GODHEAD, FATHER, SON AND HOLY GHOST, were in the beginning, so the Father, Son and Holy Ghost WILL now live in us at the end, through THE BAPTISM OF THE HOLY GHOST which IS the GODHEAD.

"He that hath my commandments, and keepeth them, he it is that loveth me: and he that loveth me shall be loved of my Father, and I will love him, and will manifest myself to him." (Luke 6:46 "And why call ye me, Lord, Lord, and do not the things which I say?)"

THESE ARE HIS FINAL WORDS BEFORE HIS BETRAYAL

JESUS SPAKE OF THE HOLY GHOST TO COME AS A PERSON (cont.)

Judas saith unto him, not Iscariot, Lord, how is it that thou wilt manifest thyself unto us, and not unto the world?

Jesus answered and said unto him, If a man love me, he will keep my words: and my Father will love him, and <u>WE</u> will come unto him, and make our abode with him." (Revealing that the Father and the Son <u>ARE</u> the Holy Ghost, and will come and make their abode with us, THROUGH THE BAPTISM OF THE HOLY GHOST.)

He that loveth me not keepeth not my sayings: and the word which ye hear is not mine, but the Father's which sent me.

These things have I spoken unto you, being *yet* **present with you."**

But the <u>COMFORTER</u>, *which <u>IS</u>* **the <u>Holy Ghost</u>, whom the Father will send in my name, <u>HE</u> shall teach you all things, and bring all things to your remembrance, whatsoever I have said unto you."** (Jesus reveals that the Comforter <u>IS</u> the Holy Ghost and HE is a person, and that person IS THE FATHER AND THE SON.)

Peace I leave with you, my peace I give unto you: not as the world giveth, give I unto you. Let not your heart be troubled, neither let it be afraid.

Ye have heard how I said unto you, <u>I go away, and come</u> *again* **<u>unto you</u>. If ye loved me, ye would rejoice, because I said, I go unto the Father: for my Father is greater than I.** (AND RETURN ON THE DAY OF PENTECOST, as the HOLY GHOST.)

And now I have told you before it come to pass, that, when it is come to pass, ye might believe. (IT HAS NOW COME TO PASS. **DO YOU NOW BELIEVE?**)

Hereafter I will not talk much with you: for the prince of this world cometh, and hath nothing in me." (As he has come today to try to destroy the Baptism of the Holy Ghost.)

"But that the world may know that I love the Father; and as the Father gave me commandment, even so I do. Arise, let us go hence."

Jn 16:7-16

"Nevertheless I tell you the truth; It is expedient for you that I go away: for if I go not away, the Comforter (which is the Holy Ghost) **will not come unto you; but if I depart, I will send <u>HIM</u> unto you.**

And when <u>*HE*</u> is come, <u>*HE*</u> will reprove the world of sin, and of righteousness, and of judgment: (Again, since when do we call the Spirit a **He instead of the Holy Ghost**?)

MINISTRY OF THE HOLY GHOST:

Of sin, BECAUSE THEY BELIEVE NOT ON ME;

Of righteousness, because I go to my Father, and ye see me no more; (in the flesh) But return on the DAY OF PENTECOST in THE PERSON OF THE HOLY GHOST.

Of judgment, because the prince of this world is judged.

I have yet many things to say unto you, but ye cannot bear them now.

Howbeit when _HE_, the Spirit of Truth, (the Holy Ghost) is come, _HE_ will guide you into all truth: for _HE_ shall not speak of <u>HIMSELF</u>; but whatsoever _HE_ shall hear, *that* shall _HE_ speak: and _HE_ will shew you things to come. Again, notice HE as JESUS refers to THE HOLY GHOST, which is HIMSELF.

_HE_ shall glorify me: for _HE_ shall receive of mine, and shall shew *it* unto you.

All things that the Father hath are mine: therefore said I, that _HE_ shall take of mine, and shall shew *it* unto you.

A little while, and ye shall not see me: and again, a little while, and ye shall see me, because I go to the Father," (and return as THE HOLY GHOST).

JESUS' FINAL WORDS REGARDING THE BAPTISM OF THE HOLY GHOST

Acts 1:8   "But ye shall receive <u>POWER,</u> after that the <u>HOLY GHOST</u> is come upon you:..." Remember, Jesus said, "MY SHEEP HEAR MY VOICE, I KNOW THEM, THEY FOLLOW ME."

THE HOLY GHOST CAME ON THE DAY OF PENTECOST

Acts 2:4   "And they were ALL FILLED WITH THE HOLY GHOST, AND BEGAN TO SPEAK WITH OTHER TONGUES AS THE SPIRIT gave them utterance."

REMEMBER, <u>JESUS RETURNED</u>, FOR HE <u>IS</u> THE BAPTIZER WITH THE HOLY GHOST

QUESTION:　　　　　How could they be BAPTIZED IN THE HOLY GHOST IF JESUS HAD NOT RETURNED, FOR JESUS IS THE BAPTIZER WITH THE HOLY GHOST.

Matt 3:11 Confirms:　**"I INDEED BAPTIZE YOU WITH WATER UNTO REPENTANCE: BUT HE THAT COMETH AFTER ME IS MIGHTIER THAN I, WHOSE SHOES I AM NOT WORTHY TO BEAR: HE SHALL BAPTIZE YOU <u>WITH THE HOLY GHOST, AND *WITH* FIRE</u>:"**

Comment:　After the PROPHETS, and OUR LORD JESUS announce the coming of THE HOLY GHOST, and after that <u>HE</u> CAME ON THE DAY OF PENTECOST, many of our leaders still REJECT THE HOLY GHOST because HE UPSET THEIR NATURAL PHILOSOPHY and TRADITION as they did on HIS FIRST COMING, when HE was presented to the leaders of that day.

JESUS THE STUMBLING STONE APPEARS AS THE HOLY GHOST

1 Pet 2:7-8　**"Unto you therefore WHICH BELIEVE, HE IS PRECIOUS: BUT UNTO THEM WHICH BE DISOBEDIENT,** *(TO THE WORD).* **THE STONE WHICH THE BUILDERS DISALLOWED, THE SAME** *(PRAISE GOD)* **IS MADE THE HEAD OF THE CORNER,**

　And A STONE OF STUMBLING and a ROCK OF OFFENSE, even to <u>THEM THAT STUMBLE AT THE WORD</u>, (revealing the BAPTISM OF THE HOLY GHOST) **being <u>DISOBEDIENT</u>: whereunto also they were APPOINTED."**

JESUS THE STUMBLING STONE APPEARS AS THE HOLY GHOST (cont.)

Is 8:14	THE PROPHET SPAKE, **"And he shall be for a STONE OF STUMBLING and for a ROCK OF OFFENSE..."** (To them that STUMBLE at THE WORD.)
Comment:	The above scriptures are being fulfilled before our very eyes today, as those who stumble at the Word which IS Christ who IS the Baptizer with The Holy Ghost.
Rom 9:33	Paul quotes THE PROPHETS, **"As it is written, BEHOLD, I lay in Zion, a STUMBLING STONE AND A ROCK OF OFFENSE:..."** (Confirming there are those who stumble at the Word which IS Christ.)
Ps 118:22	**"THE STONE WHICH THE BUILDERS REFUSED** *(THE HOLY GHOST)* **IS BECOME THE HEADSTONE OF THE CORNER."**
Comment:	When we are BAPTIZED IN THE HOLY GHOST my dear brethren in THE FAITH, we will not reject our LORD JESUS who IS THE HOLY GHOST, any more, and HE WILL NOT BE YOUR STUMBLING STONE.

JESUS, THE HOLY GHOST STUMBLING STONE

Though,   1) REVEALED IN THE PROPHETS,
                 2) PROMISED BY OUR LORD JESUS,
                 3) CONFIRMED ON THE DAY OF PENTECOST,
many have totally REJECTED THE BAPTISM OF THE HOLY GHOST, and IT HAS BECOME THEIR STUMBLING STONE.

THIS IS SOMETHING FOR US PASTORS AND TEACHERS, TO GIVE
SERIOUS CONSIDERATION. FOR WHAT ANSWER WILL WE GIVE
THE LORD IN "THAT DAY", WHEN WE HAVE MISLED HIS PEOPLE,
BY NOT MINISTERING THE BAPTISM OF THE HOLY GHOST, THAT
THEY MAY HAVE A FULL AND COMPLETE CHRISTIAN LIFE, AND
HAVE <u>POWER</u> OVER ALL THE WORKS OF SATAN.

I know many pastors, young and old are now confronted with "THEIR
STUMBLING STONE", which is our LORD JESUS, concerning THE
BAPTISM OF THE HOLY GHOST. You know it is "THE TRUTH" and also
know that you could loose your ORDINATION and your living if you
minister THE BAPTISM OF THE HOLY GHOST in your local church, mainly
because it will upset THEIR TRADITIONS. JESUS help you to make the
right DECISION, so that HE will not be your STUMBLING STONE!

A CHALLENGING SCRIPTURE FOR THOSE WHO
WITHSTAND GOD

Acts 11:15-17   Again, (Peter's defense of Acts 10:34-48) **"And**
                            as I began to speak the HOLY GHOST fell on
                            them, as on us at the BEGINNING. <u>**Then**</u>
                            <u>**remembered I, THE WORD OF THE LORD,**</u>
                            how that HE said, John indeed BAPTIZED with
                            WATER, (Revealing the separation of the baptism
                            in water and The Baptism of the Holy Ghost)
                            but ye shall be BAPTIZED with the
                            HOLY GHOST."

                            "For as much then, as GOD GAVE THEM THE
                            LIKE GIFT, (The Baptism of the Holy Ghost) **as**
                            HE did unto us, who BELIEVED ON THE
                            LORD JESUS CHRIST. <u>**WHO WAS I, THAT**</u>
                            <u>**I COULD WITHSTAND GOD?"**</u>

QUESTIONS:

1)   Are we more spiritual and greater than Peter that we should
       WITHSTAND GOD and HIS HOLY WORD?
2)   My dear Pastor, if Peter would not WITHSTAND GOD on the
       BAPTISM OF THE HOLY GHOST, how can we today?

THE CHALLENGE TO EVERY PASTOR IN THIS HOUR

QUESTION:

THE BAPTISM OF THE HOLY GHOST and **SPEAKING IN OTHER TONGUES** that came down from **HEAVEN** on the DAY OF PENTECOST, **is this of man**, **the devil**, or is it from GOD? Is the speaking in other tongues through the BAPTISM of the HOLY GHOST written in HIS HOLY WORD, false doctrine?

These questions we Pastors must answer one day or else turn to THE LORD now and RECEIVE THE BAPTISM OF THE HOLY GHOST **THAT IS WRITTEN IN HIS HOLY WORD**, THE AUTHORIZED KING JAMES BIBLE IN ACTS 19:2.

THE WARNING OF RESISTING THE HOLY GHOST AS REVEALED IN THE WORD OF GOD

RESISTANCE TO THE BAPTISM OF THE HOLY GHOST A DANGEROUS ROAD TO FOLLOW!

CERTAIN PASTORS AND TEACHERS, BLIND TO THE HOLY GHOST BAPTISM, even though THOUSANDS upon THOUSANDS all over the WORLD are being BAPTIZED in the HOLY GHOST and SPEAK IN OTHER TONGUES according to the HOLY SCRIPTURES, are still STUMBLING AT THE WORD, and CHANGED and ADDED TO THE WORD OF GOD, (as Satan did in Genesis 3:1) to CONFORM to their DOCTRINE and TRADITIONS, AND ATTEMPT BY DECEIT to do away with THE HOLY GHOST, the **THIRD PERSON OF THE GODHEAD, AND JESUS OUR LORD, WHO IS THE HOLY GHOST!**

AGAIN REMEMBER: **"1 John 5:7 FOR THERE ARE THREE that bear record in heaven, THE FATHER, THE WORD, AND THE HOLY GHOST: AND THESE THREE ARE ONE."**
Therefore; JESUS IS THE HOLY GHOST! Are we still going to reject HIM, KNOWING HE IS THE HOLY GHOST?

I REPEAT THE WARNING FROM THE LORD FOR CHANGING HIS WORD AND ADDING TO HIS WORD IN ACTS 19:2

Rev 22:14-21

"Blessed are they THAT DO HIS COMMANDMENTS (How can the children of the Lord hear and obey the commandments, when man has changed the Word?) **that they may have RIGHT TO THE TREE OF LIFE, and may enter in through THE GATES OF THE CITY.**"

Rev 22:18

"FOR I TESTIFY unto EVERY MAN, that HEARETH THE WORDS of the prophecy of this BOOK, *IF ANY MAN SHALL ADD UNTO THESE THINGS,* GOD SHALL ADD UNTO HIM THE PLAGUES, that are written in this BOOK:"

Rev 22:19

"AND IF ANY MAN SHALL TAKE AWAY FROM THE WORDS of the BOOK of this PROPHECY, GOD shall take away his part out of THE BOOK OF LIFE,..."

Deut 4:1-4

(THE FATHER SPEAKS,) "Now therefore hearken, O Israel, unto the statutes and unto the judgments, which I teach you, for to do *them*, that ye may live, and go in and possess the land which the LORD God of your fathers giveth you."

Ye shall not ADD unto the word which I command you, neither shall ye DIMINISH *ought* from it, that ye may keep the commandments of the LORD your God which I command you.

Your eyes have seen what the LORD did because of Baalpeor: for all the men that followed Baalpeor, the LORD thy God hath destroyed them from among you.

But ye that did cleave unto the LORD your God *are* alive every one of you this day."

TO THOSE THAT RESIST THE HOLY GHOST

"STEPHEN'S LAST WORDS TO US, BEFORE HE DIED REGARDING THE BAPTISM OF THE HOLY GHOST.

Acts 7:51-55   YE STIFF NECKED and uncircumcised in HEART and EARS, ye do always RESIST THE <u>HOLY GHOST</u>: as your fathers *did, so do ye.*"

Which of the prophets have not your fathers persecuted? And they have slain them which shewed before of the coming of the Just One; of whom ye have been now the betrayers and murderers:

Who have received the law by the disposition of angels, and have not kept *it*.

When they heard these things, they were cut to the heart, and they gnashed on him with *their* teeth.

But he, being full of the <u>HOLY GHOST</u>, looked up steadfastly into heaven, and saw the glory of GOD, and JESUS standing on the right hand of GOD,"

Comment:	STIFF-NECKED the meaning - WILL NOT CHANGE - MIND is made up, DON'T CONFUSE ME WITH THE WORD OF TRUTH! UNCIRCUMCISED IN HEART AND EARS - THE BLOOD of JESUS and CALVARY has not had effect on our HEART, and our EARS are <u>not</u> open to HIS VOICE! BLIND TO THE SPIRIT VISION, and without a VISION THE PEOPLE PERISH (Proverbs 29:18).

EXHORTATION TO THE BODY OF CHRIST TODAY

Please do not set up a RESISTANCE in your heart, against the BAPTISM OF THE HOLY GHOST, through TEACHINGS and TRADITIONS of your local church. Prove those TEACHINGS, by STUDYING THE WORD OF GOD for your own selves! You will be challenged, by THE WORD OF GOD written in this BOOK to make a DECISION, a <u>VERY IMPORTANT DECISION</u>, that THE WORD OF GOD <u>IS</u> TRUE, and THE BAPTISM OF THE HOLY GHOST <u>IS</u> for <u>ALL</u> CHRISTIANS following the SPIRIT BIRTH John 3:3.

You will at that time HAVE AN <u>EXPERIENCE</u>, instead of an <u>ARGUMENT</u>! THOUSANDS of CHRISTIANS all over the world, <u>ARE</u> being BAPTIZED IN THE HOLY GHOST and SPEAK IN OTHER TONGUES, according to the WORD OF GOD!

QUESTION:	Will you RESIST or REJECT THE WORD OF GOD? It is <u>your</u> DECISION!

CHALLENGE TO THOSE THAT THINK THEY BELIEVE

Mk 16:15-18 READ:	"And these SIGNS SHALL FOLLOW THEM THAT BELIEVE;..."
1)	"...They shall LAY HANDS ON THE SICK, and they <u>shall</u> recover." *(By the POWER of the HOLY GHOST which <u>IS</u> the Father and the Son.)*

2)   **They shall SPEAK WITH NEW TONGUES.**
        (Sent down from heaven) - *(THE BAPTISM OF THE HOLY GHOST)*

3)   **"...In MY NAME, THEY SHALL CAST OUT DEVILS;..."** (The only thing the devil is afraid of is a Christian with the anointing and power of the Holy Ghost)

Comment: You may not accomplish these things now my dear brethren, but THE BAPTISM OF THE HOLY GHOST will give you the POWER, as you study HIS WORD that is written in this book and <u>DO IT</u>. What a wonderful experience is waiting for you! For none of the above can take place in your ministry, but only through the power of the Holy Ghost Baptism.

FINAL EXHORTATION TO THE CHILDREN OF GOD:

First, the experience MUST begin with your Pastor, and if he refuses THE WORD OF GOD on the BAPTISM of the HOLY GHOST, there is a good possibility you are in the WRONG LOCAL CHURCH, and taking your instruction from the wrong Bible, that has been changed by natural man who receives **NOT THE THINGS OF THE SPIRIT OF GOD, for they are foolishness unto him** as we see today.

TO ALL MY *DEAR BROTHERS* THAT ARE PASTORS

Seek THE TRUTH of the HOLY GHOST BAPTISM revealed in the WORD OF GOD, with a TRUE HEART and through your FAITH, it <u>WILL</u> happen in your church as it did in the Early Church. You THEN WILL HAVE A REVIVAL with LOVE on your hands and won't be attempting to explain away the TRUTH of the BAPTISM OF THE HOLY GHOST any more!

Exhortation:

Dear Pastor, if you were to build a CHURCH according to THE WORD OF GOD, why not look to THE EARLY CHURCH and THE WORDS OF JESUS.

A VISION OF THE THREE BROTHERS
BUILDING A HOUSE FOR OTHERS

The Vision the Lord revealed to me, regarding the CHURCH and THE BAPTISM OF THE HOLY GHOST.

- I saw in a VISION, THREE BROTHERS, who reveal the FATHER, SON, and HOLY GHOST.

- These THREE BROTHERS, FATHER, SON, and HOLY GHOST, AGREED AS ONE to BUILD A BEAUTIFUL HOUSE for us to dwell in.

- This is a SHADOW and VISION of the THREE PERSONS OF THE GODHEAD for all to UNDERSTAND, THEIR purpose: to BUILD THE TRUE HOUSE OF GOD, THE CHURCH.

- Many souls accept THE FATHER, and THE SON, but REJECT THE HOLY GHOST who IS THE FATHER and THE SON, "BECAUSE **THESE THREE ARE ONE**."

- I repeat, THE HOUSE IS NOT COMPLETE WITHOUT THE BAPTISM OF THE HOLY GHOST!

- THE THREE BROTHERS mentioned above are ALL BUILDERS, revealed as THE GODHEAD, and **WE MUST HAVE ALL THREE to complete the HOUSE!**

- THE FATHER LAID THE FOUNDATIONS, JESUS IS THE CHIEF CORNER STONE, what purpose has THE BUILDING if it has NO POWER IN it, THE BAPTISM OF THE HOLY GHOST.

THE VISION

John, a carpenter, (as THE FATHER,) who LAID THE FOUNDATIONS to BUILD THE HOUSE ON.

Joseph, a plumber, (as THE WORD) to bring WATER (SPIRIT) into THE HOUSE, example: Washing of WATER by THE WORD - Rivers of Living Water (**John 7:38-39**).

David, an electrician, (as THE HOLY GHOST,) to wire and PREPARE the HOUSE for the POWER and LIGHT to SEE THE BEAUTY OF THE HOUSE, "THE CHURCH"

THE STUDY OF THE PLANS

When the PLANS WERE REVIEWED, and the FINAL PREPARATIONS WERE MADE, the TIME HAD COME to BEGIN BUILDING THE HOUSE.

The strangest thing happened! The people that the HOUSE WAS BEING BUILT FOR, <u>DIDN'T UNDERSTAND THE PLANS</u>. GREAT CONFUSION and DISAGREEMENT was the result over DAVID, the electrician, (THE HOLY GHOST,) who was to install <u>POWER</u> IN THE HOUSE!

CHANGE OF THE PLANS

The people that the HOUSE was to be built for HAD NO VISION for the completed plan, so began to change THE PLAN, as in <u>Acts 19:2</u>, to suit themselves. (King James Bible.)

- They agreed with JOHN, (as THE FATHER,) THAT LAID THE FOUNDATIONS.

- They agreed with JOSEPH, (as THE WORD,) that brought WATER (THE SPIRIT) into THE HOUSE.

- They DISAGREED with DAVID (THE HOLY GHOST) the electrician, and for no reason whatsoever REJECTED Him who was to install **THE POWER IN THE HOUSE!**

AS THE THREE BROTHER'S agreed in THE BEGINNING to BUILD THE HOUSE TOGETHER, they could not BUILD THE HOUSE without DAVID, (THE HOLY GHOST) <u>no matter what changes were made</u> to THE PLANS, as it is this day in the rejection of the **POWER**, we receive through the power of the Holy Ghost.

- A HOUSE BUILT WITHOUT THE POWER installed is not much of a house, it **ONLY LOOKS LIKE ONE!**

2 Tim 3:5   **"HAVING A FORM OF GODLINESS, BUT
                            DENYING THE POWER THEREOF:..."**
                            (Which is the Holy Ghost).

THE FINAL RESULT

THEREFORE, THE THREE BROTHER'S, (FATHER, SON, and HOLY
GHOST) went out to SEEK OTHERS who would ACCEPT THE PLANS
and not reject DAVID, the ELECTRICIAN (HOLY GHOST) that would
install **POWER** IN THE HOUSE!
THE ABOVE REVEALS THE PERFECT PLAN OF THE FATHER, THE
SON and the HOLY GHOST, and THEIR PLANS **CAN NOT BE CHANGED**
as was attempted in ("The Living Bible **Acts 19:2**, and I quote, "Did you
receive the Holy Spirit when you believed?"). As we can see in our day, many
want to change GOD'S PLANS for BUILDING THE CHURCH, and do away
with THE **POWER** of **HOLY GHOST**. DO NOT let the Lord pass you by,
for HE IS SEEKING OTHERS THAT WILL ACCEPT HIS PLANS AND
BUILD ACCORDING TO HIS WORD AND NOT MAN'S OPINIONS!

Chapter Thirteen

Before The Day Of Pentecost

JESUS IS THE HOLY GHOST

Col 2:9

"FOR IN HIM DWELLETH ALL THE FULLNESS OF THE GODHEAD BODILY." (THE FATHER, THE SON AND THE HOLY GHOST.)

1 Jn 5:7

"FOR THERE ARE THREE THAT BEAR RECORD IN HEAVEN, THE FATHER, THE WORD, AND THE HOLY GHOST: AND THESE THREE ARE ONE." (JESUS IS ALSO THE HOLY GHOST.)

Jn 14:26

"But the COMFORTER, which IS the HOLY GHOST, whom the FATHER will send in MY NAME, HE shall TEACH YOU ALL THINGS, and bring all things to your REMEMBRANCE, whatsoever I have said unto you."

Jn 14:28

"...I GO AWAY AND COME AGAIN UNTO YOU. ..." (On the day of PENECOST JESUS reveals that HE IS the Holy Ghost.)

Jn 14:29

"And NOW, I have told you before *(THE DAY OF PENTECOST)* it COME TO PASS, THAT, WHEN IT IS COME TO PASS, ye MIGHT BELIEVE."

Acts 2:4

"And they were all filled with the Holy Ghost, and began to speak with other tongues, as the Spirit gave them utterance." How can we not believe when it has come to pass?

Jn 14:18

"I will not leave you COMFORTLESS: *I* WILL COME TO YOU." (Jesus reveals that HE is the HOLY GHOST, and will come on THE DAY OF PENTECOST.)

Jn 16:7	**"...It is expedient for you that I** (in HIS human body) **go away: for if I go not away, THE COMFORTER will not come unto you; But if I depart, I WILL SEND HIM UNTO YOU."** (Jesus returns as the Comforter which <u>is</u> the Holy Ghost.)
Jn 16:16	**"A little while, and ye shall not see ME: and again, a little while, and ye shall se ME,..."** (Because Jesus will return as the Holy Ghost which is the Father and the Son.)
Jn 14:20	**"AT THAT DAY** *(Day of Pentecost)* **ye shall know that** **1) I AM IN MY FATHER,** **2) AND YE IN ME,** **3) AND I IN YOU."** (This is the completeness of his plan and purpose through the Baptism of the Holy Ghost to make us one.)
Comment:	The above scripture reveals THE GODHEAD as it is this day to those that are BAPTIZED IN THE HOLY GHOST.

THE GODHEAD began their work in the HEAVENS – 1 John 5:7.
THE GODHEAD ends their work on THE EARTH, taking up residence in THEIR TEMPLE that THE FATHER and SON made in THEIR IMAGE and LIKENESS. – Revealed in Genesis 1:26.

OUR LORD'S FINAL WORDS BEFORE LEAVING THIS WORLD

Jn 10:27	**"My sheep hear my voice, and I know them, and they follow me:"**
Heb 3:7	**"Wherefore as THE HOLY GHOST SAITH, TODAY IF YE WILL HEAR HIS VOICE,"**
Acts 1:4-5	**"And, being assembled together with them, commanded them that they should not depart from Jerusalem, but WAIT FOR THE PROMISE OF THE FATHER, which, saith he, ye have heard of me."**

"For John truly baptized with water; but YE SHALL BE BAPTIZED WITH THE HOLY GHOST, not many days hence." (A direct command for the future on the Baptism of the Holy Ghost that was coming, <u>FOR THE SPIRIT BIRTH IS NOT A COMMAND</u> BUT "<u>WHOSOEVER WILL MAY COME</u>"!) Revealing again that the Spirit Birth is Separate from the Holy Ghost Baptism.

Acts 1:8,9   "<u>BUT YE SHALL RECEIVE POWER</u>, AFTER THAT THE HOLY GHOST IS COME UPON YOU: AND YE SHALL BE WITNESSES UNTO ME BOTH IN JERUSALEM, AND IN ALL JUDAEA, AND IN SAMARIA, AND UNTO THE UTTERMOST PART OF THE EARTH." (For none yet have received power through the Spirit Birth, for it is only your entrance into the Kingdom of God.) "And when He had spoken these things, while they beheld, he was taken up; and a cloud received Him out of their sight."

Acts 5:32   "And we are his witnesses of these things; and *so is* also the Holy Ghost, whom God hath given to them that obey him." (Peter speaking of the fact that the disciples were actually His witnesses when Jesus walked on the earth.)

Now that He is gone to heaven, WE then become His witnesses by the Baptism of the Holy Ghost, who follow after. Revealing also that He was <u>not</u> speaking of the Spirit Birth, (that we must be obeying Him before we can have salvation), but rather they must obey His commandments to receive the Baptism of the Holy Ghost.

Chapter Fourteen

The Day
Of
Pentecost

WHAT REALLY WAS ACCOMPLISHED ON THE DAY OF PENTECOST?

1.   HIS MYSTERY PLAN FULFILLED!

Gen 1:26   **"...LET US** *(THE GODHEAD)* **make man in OUR IMAGE, after OUR LIKENESS:..."** (Showing the persons of the Godhead the Father and the Son.)

Comment: On the DAY OF PENTECOST, THE GODHEAD that was in the BEGINNING, came down from heaven to take up RESIDENCE in our bodies (which are his temples) through THE BAPTISM OF THE HOLY GHOST to FULFILL ALL THINGS written by THE HOLY PROPHETS since the world began.

2.   THE HOLY GHOST WAS TO COME ON THE DAY OF PENTECOST

ISAIAH - FULFILLED:

Is 28:9   **"Whom shall HE TEACH KNOWLEDGE? And whom shall HE make to UNDERSTAND DOCTRINE?..."**

ANSWER: **THEM THAT ARE WEANED** *(left the area of the SPIRIT BIRTH)* **FROM THE MILK AND DRAWN FROM THE BREASTS** *(babes in CHRIST).*

Comment: The Prophet reveals that THE LORD wants to teach us KNOWLEDGE and UNDERSTAND HIS DOCTRINE (established TRUTH) and HE is not able to, until we have left the area of THE SPIRIT BIRTH, for in that state, we are BABES IN CHRIST, and will reject the STRONG MEAT; **"THE BAPTISM OF THE HOLY GHOST,** as they do in many local churches today.

THE HOLY GHOST WAS TO COME ON THE DAY OF PENTECOST (cont.)

Is 28:11 - Fulfilled:	**"FOR WITH STAMMERING LIPS AND ANOTHER TONGUE WILL <u>HE</u> speak to this people."**
Note:	**"<u>HE</u>"** is <u>THE LORD</u> who speaks out of His temples which we are.
Acts 2:4	**"And they were ALL FILLED with THE HOLY GHOST, and began to speak with other tongues, as the <u>SPIRIT</u> gave them UTTERANCE."**
Note:	It is <u>THE SPIRIT</u> that <u>gave them</u> the utterance of other tongues, to confirm the evidence that we are BAPTIZED IN THE HOLY GHOST!

THE APOSTLE PAUL REFERS TO Isaiah 28:11

1 Cor 14:20	**"Brethren, BE NOT CHILDREN IN UNDER STANDING:...** **BUT IN UNDERSTANDING BE MEN."** (NOT babes as the "Spirit Birth".)
1 Cor 14:21	**"In the law IT IS WRITTEN, WITH MEN OF OTHER TONGUES AND OTHER LIPS WILL <u>I</u> SPEAK UNTO THIS PEOPLE;** **AND YET FOR ALL THAT, WILL THEY NOT HEAR ME, SAITH THE LORD."** We should ask ourselves, "Are we hearing the Lord or are we hearing man's opinions of the flesh?"

PLEASE ASK YOURSELF THIS QUESTION:
AM I one of those that WILL NOT HEAR?!

THE HOLY GHOST WAS TO COME ON THE DAY OF
PENTECOST (cont.)

THE PROPHET JOEL - FULFILLED:

Joel 2:28-32   "And it shall come to pass afterward, THAT I
                          WILL POUR <u>OUT MY</u> SPIRIT UPON ALL
                          FLESH; (The Baptism of the Holy Ghost.)
RESULT: And your SONS AND DAUGHTERS SHALL
                          PROPHECY, YOUR OLD MEN SHALL
                          DREAM DREAMS, YOUR YOUNG MEN
                          SHALL SEE VISIONS:"

NOTE: We will never fulfill this scripture written by the PROPHET
                 Joel, without THE BAPTISM OF THE HOLY GHOST.

**THE APOSTLE PETER SPEAKS OF THE OUT-POURING OF THE
HOLY GHOST**

PETER QUOTES THE PROPHET JOEL:

Acts 2:16   "But this *(the outpouring of the HOLY GHOST)*
                          is that which was spoken by the prophet Joel;
                          "...I will POUR OUT OF MY SPIRIT upon ALL
                          FLESH: and your SONS and DAUGHTERS
                          shall prophecy,..."

                          JOHN THE BAPTIST THE LAST OF
                          THE OLD TESTAMENT PROPHETS
                          -FULFILLED:

Matt 3:11   "I indeed baptize you with WATER unto
                          REPENTANCE: But HE that cometh after me
                          is MIGHTIER than I, whose shoes I am not
                          worthy to bear: <u>HE</u> SHALL BAPTIZE YOU
                          WITH THE HOLY GHOST, AND
                          WITH FIRE:"

THE HOLY GHOST WAS TO COME ON THE DAY OF PENTECOST (cont.)

FULFILLED

Acts 2:4   **"And they were ALL FILLED with THE HOLY GHOST, and began to speak with other tongues, as the <u>SPIRIT</u> gave them UTTERANCE."**

Comment: We can see in THE OUTPOURING OF THE HOLY GHOST that the above PROPHECY was fulfilled, as CLOVEN TONGUES as of FIRE sat upon each of them, and they were BAPTIZED IN THE HOLY GHOST and spake in other tongues.

JOHN THE BAPTIST
"HE SHALL BAPTIZE YOU WITH THE HOLY GHOST AND FIRE."
Many are baptized with THE HOLY GHOST but lack THE FIRE!

One might ask, "WHY THE FIRE?"

Answer: THE FIRE is likened to a FOREST FIRE, not very pleasant at the time, as we watch the FIRE DESTROY everything in its path, to make a way for our NEW LIFE to take place through THE BAPTISM OF THE HOLY GHOST.

With GREAT EFFORT we try to put THE FIRE OUT, in our lives, because we don't want to change from our old ways, and many die in the process!   But not UNDERSTANDING, that all the UNDER GROWTH (traditions of man) and OLD LOGS that are dead lying around on the GROUND, preventing NEW LIFE from springing up are burned up by THE FIRE!

When the FIRE is finished, NEW LIFE APPEARS! NOW THE HOLY GHOST will begin to be revealed with POWER in our lives.

THE HOLY GHOST WAS TO COME ON THE DAY OF PENTECOST (cont.)

So with us, THE FIRE OF THE HOLY GHOST will BURN UP all the dead things in our lives, that the NEW LIFE IN CHRIST may appear!

There is a good example in the pine forests in Northern California. A few years ago, a forest fire swept through the land destroying everything in its path.
But the pine tree has an acorn that sustains life inside (as with us) and as the forest fire passes through the acorns open up and the seed is released to the forest floor.

The acorn must have 140 degrees of heat to open up and deposit the new seed, creating a new forest because of the fire!

Inside we have THE SPIRIT OF GOD'S SON in our hearts, and we need THE HOLY GHOST AND FIRE, to cause us to open up our hearts to THE HOLY GHOST to allow new life in THE CHURCH to appear!

WITHOUT THE FIRE OF THE HOLY GHOST, WE WILL NOT CHANGE OUR OLD WAYS AND THE UNDER GROWTH, (and we know these things in our lives) WILL PREVENT US FROM ALLOWING OUR NEW LIFE TO SPRING FORTH!

THE LAST WORDS OF OUR LORD JESUS - FULFILLED

Acts 1:4   **"...WAIT FOR THE PROMISE OF THE FATHER,..."**

Acts 1:5   **"...YE SHALL BE BAPTIZED IN THE HOLY GHOST NOT MANY DAYS HENCE."**

Acts 1:8	**"BUT YE SHALL RECEIVE POWER, <u>AFTER</u> THAT THE HOLY GHOST IS COME UPON YOU: AND YE SHALL BE WITNESSES UNTO ME..."**
Jn 14:16	**"And I will pray THE FATHER, and <u>HE</u> shall give you another COMFORTER,..."** (Which IS the Holy Ghost.) in the person of the Father and Son.
Jn 14:18	**"<u>I</u> will not LEAVE YOU COMFORTLESS: <u>I</u> WILL COME TO YOU."** (Revealing again that Jesus IS the Holy Ghost, revealing also the Father and the Son <u>are</u> the Holy Ghost.)
Jn 14:26	**"BUT THE <u>COMFORTER, WHICH IS THE HOLY GHOST,</u> <u>WHOM</u> THE FATHER WILL SEND IN MY NAME, <u>HE</u> SHALL TEACH YOU ALL THINGS, AND BRING ALL THINGS TO YOUR REMEMBRANCE, whatsoever I have SAID UNTO YOU."**
Jn 14:28	**"...I GO AWAY, and COME AGAIN unto you."** (Revealing that Jesus <u>IS</u> the Holy Ghost and returned again on the day of Pentecost.)
Jn 14:29	**"And NOW I HAVE TOLD YOU, BEFORE IT COME TO PASS, that, when it is COME TO PASS, YE MIGHT BELIEVE."** *(The outpouring of the HOLY GHOST.)*

Do you still not believe the words of our Lord and Saviour, Jesus Christ?

THE HOLY GHOST WAS TO COME ON THE DAY OF PENTECOST
(cont.)

THE LAST WORDS OF OUR LORD JESUS - FULFILLED

Jn 16:7   **"Nevertheless I tell you THE TRUTH; It is
                                EXPEDIENT for you that I go away: For if I
                                go NOT AWAY, THE COMFORTER will not
                                come unto you; BUT IF I DEPART, I WILL
                                SEND <u>HIM</u> UNTO YOU."**

Jn 16:16   **"A little while, and ye shall not see ME: And
                                again, a little while, and ye shall SEE ME,
                                because I go to THE FATHER."** *(And RETURN
                                IN THE PERSON OF THE HOLY GHOST.)*

1 Jn 5:7 (Again,)   **"FOR THERE ARE THREE THAT BEAR
                                RECORD IN HEAVEN, THE FATHER, THE
                                WORD, and HOLY GHOST: <u>AND THESE
                                THREE ARE ONE</u>."**

Comment: In the beginning, THE GODHEAD (**Genesis 1:26**) made
                 man in THEIR OWN IMAGE, which was to be THEIR
                 TEMPLE to live in during THEIR FINAL BATTLE WITH
                 SATAN. NOW, on the DAY OF PENTECOST, THE
                 FATHER, SON and HOLY GHOST came down to LIVE
                 IN THAT TEMPLE, TO BEGIN THAT WARFARE!

JESUS <u>IS</u> THE FATHER, SON AND HOLY GHOST

Col 2:8   **"BEWARE LEST ANY MAN SPOIL YOU
                                THROUGH PHILOSOPHY AND VAIN
                                DECEIT, AFTER THE TRADITIONS OF
                                MEN, AFTER THE RUDIMENTS OF THE
                                WORLD, AND NOT AFTER CHRIST."**
                                Paul warns us of those that would change the Word
                                through their fleshly desires, for these desires are
                                not our Lord.

Col 2:9	**"FOR IN HIM DWELLETH ALL THE FULLNESS OF THE GODHEAD BODILY."** *(or in HIS BODY).*
Comment:	The VAIN DECEIT and TRADITIONS of man, can BLIND US FROM ONE OF THE GREATEST TRUTHS IN THE BIBLE. "FOR IN HIM DWELLETH ALL THE FULLNESS OF THE GODHEAD" (In HIS BODY, as with us). For if we do away with the Godhead, we do away with Christ, because <u>THESE THREE ARE ONE</u>!

JESUS AND THE FATHER ARE ONE IN THE PERSON OF THE HOLY GHOST

Jn 14:9	**"...HE THAT HAS SEEN ME, HAS SEEN THE FATHER;..."**
Jn 10:30	**"I AND MY FATHER ARE ONE."**
Jn 14:23	**"Jesus answered and said unto him, If a man love me, he will keep my words: and my Father will love him, and WE WILL COME UNTO HIM, AND MAKE OUR ABODE WITH HIM."**
Acts 2:1	**"And when the DAY OF PENTECOST was fully come, they were ALL WITH <u>ONE ACCORD</u> in <u>ONE PLACE</u>."**

What an exciting time to live! It was announced by the FATHER through the PROPHETS the coming of the HOLY GHOST, and confirmed by OUR LORD JESUS, THE DAY of the outpouring of THE HOLY GHOST, sent down from heaven had arrived!

Acts 2:2	**"And suddenly there came a SOUND FROM HEAVEN as of a RUSHING MIGHTY WIND, and it filled all the house where they were sitting."** When the Lord breathed the first

time man became a living soul and now God breathed again on the day of Pentecost and man became a quickening Spirit.

Acts 2:3   **"And there appeared unto them CLOVEN TONGUES like as of FIRE,..."** *(Matthew 3:11 fulfilled)*

Matt 3:11   **"...He shall baptize you with the Holy Ghost, and *with* fire:"**

Acts 2:4   1)   **"AND THEY WERE ALL FILLED WITH THE HOLY GHOST,**

AND BEGAN TO SPEAK WITH OTHER TONGUES,

2)   **AS THE <u>SPIRIT</u> GAVE THEM UTTERANCE."**

Chapter Fifteen

After The Day Of Pentecost

THE PEOPLE REACT TO THE OUTPOURING OF THE HOLY GHOST

Acts 2:12   "And they were ALL AMAZED,
                     And WERE IN DOUBT,
                     Saying one to another, WHAT MEANETH
                     THIS?"

Comment: My dear brethren, the situation has not changed today.
                     1) Fulfilling the WORD of the PROPHETS!
                     2) Fulfilling the WORDS OF OUR LORD JESUS!
                     Now you know **"WHAT MEANETH THIS."**

Acts 2:13   "Others MOCKING said, These men are full
                     of new wine."

Comment: To certain Pastors, who have RESISTED THE HOLY
                     GHOST BAPTISM, I found it was time to challenge three
                     pastors that I know on this issue, and I said, "IS THE HOLY
                     GHOST BAPTISM, OF GOD? - IS IT FROM THE
                     DEVIL?" SILENCE FOLLOWED, as I reminded them of
                     blaspheming the Holy Ghost. They walked away, having
                     nothing to say!

Matt 12:31-32   "Wherefore I say unto you, All manner of SIN
                     and BLASPHEMY shall be forgiven unto men:
                     BUT THE BLASPHEMY *AGAINST* THE
                     HOLY GHOST (The Father and the Son) SHALL
                     NOT BE FORGIVEN UNTO MEN."

                     "And whosoever speaketh a word against the
                     Son of man, it shall be forgiven him: but
                     whosoever speaketh against the HOLY GHOST,
                     it shall not be forgiven him, neither in this world,
                     neither in the *world* to come."

BECAUSE THE FATHER, THE SON, THE HOLY GHOST ARE ONE. IF
WE SPEAK AGAINST THE HOLY GHOST, WE HAVE SPOKEN AGAINST
THE FATHER AND THE SON, ALSO.

Comment: This is something for us ALL to think about, FOR ONE DAY WE WILL ALL HAVE TO GIVE AN ANSWER to our LORD JESUS, and then TIME for man will have RUN OUT!

PETER'S FIRST SERMON AFTER THE HOLY GHOST WAS POURED OUT

NOTE: Many (including Pastors) know about THE HOLY GHOST BAPTISM and that it IS for us today. If they do not respond TO THE WORD OF GOD regarding THE HOLY GHOST, THEY HAVE RESISTED THE HOLY GHOST as others have done in the PAST!

Acts 2:14-18   "But Peter, standing up with the eleven, lifted up his voice, and said unto them, Ye men of Judea, and all *ye* that dwell at Jerusalem, be this known unto you, and hearken to my words:

For these are not drunken, as ye suppose, seeing it is *but* the third hour of the day.

BUT THIS IS THAT WHICH WAS SPOKEN BY THE PROPHET JOEL;

AND IT SHALL COME TO PASS IN THE LAST DAYS, SAITH GOD, I WILL POUR OUT OF MY SPIRIT UPON ALL FLESH: AND YOUR SONS AND YOUR DAUGHTERS SHALL PROPHESY, AND YOUR YOUNG MEN SHALL SEE VISIONS, AND YOUR OLD MEN SHALL DREAM DREAMS:

AND ON MY SERVANTS AND ON MY HANDMAIDENS I WILL POUR OUT IN THOSE DAYS OF MY SPIRIT; AND THEY SHALL PROPHESY:"

PETER'S FIRST SERMON AFTER THE HOLY GHOST WAS POURED OUT (cont.)

Acts 2:33
"**Therefore being by the right hand of GOD exalted, and having received of the FATHER the promise of the HOLY GHOST, HE hath shed forth this, which ye now <u>SEE</u> and <u>HEAR</u>.**" (They were speaking in other tongues.)

THE REACTION TO PETER'S FIRST SERMON

Acts 2:37
"**Now when they heard this,** *(Peter's sermon)* **they were pricked in their heart, and said unto PETER and to the rest of the APOSTLES, <u>MEN AND BRETHREN, WHAT SHALL WE DO?</u>**"

I pray to God that the Church would respond with a true heart to Peter's message and ask the same question, "What shall we do?"

PETER GIVES THE ANSWER!

Acts 2:38-40   1)
"**...REPENT, and be BAPTIZED** *(water baptism)* **every one of you IN THE NAME OF JESUS CHRIST FOR THE REMISSION OF SINS,**

                2)
AND YE SHALL RECEIVE THE GIFT OF THE HOLY GHOST."

The above scripture reveals: (1) Water Baptism and Spirit Birth; (2) That the Holy Ghost Baptism follows the Spirit Birth according to the scriptures.

Acts 2:39
"**For THE PROMISE** *(THE HOLY GHOST)* **is unto you, and TO YOUR CHILDREN, and to ALL that are afar off, even as many as the LORD our GOD shall call.**"

PETER'S FIRST SERMON AFTER THE HOLY GHOST WAS POURED OUT (cont.)

Acts 2:40   **"And with many other WORDS did he testify and exhort, saying, SAVE YOURSELVES FROM THIS UNTOWARD GENERATION."**

This is the reason for this writing on the Baptism of the Holy Ghost, for it will give you a victorious life in the power of Jesus' name and save you from this untoward God generation, that have changed the Holy Word of God to agree with the blindness of their heart and their fleshly minds and <u>NOT</u> after Christ!

THE BEGINNING OF THE HOLY GHOST CHURCH

Acts 2:41-47 READ: **"Then they that gladly received his word were baptized: and the same day there were added *unto them* about three thousand souls. And they continued steadfastly in the <u>apostles' doctrine</u>** (Baptism of the Holy Ghost) **and fellowship, and in breaking of bread, and in prayers.**
And <u>FEAR</u> came upon every soul: and many wonders and signs were done by the apostles."

THIS IS A PATTERN FOR THE CHURCH TO FOLLOW TODAY.

For we are not a different church, but the same church continuing on in the Truth of the Baptism of the Holy Ghost.

POWER OF THE HOLY GHOST REVEALED IN HEALING

Acts 3:1-11 READ: (Peter and John HEAL THE LAME MAN.)
                                   "And Peter, fastening his eyes upon him with John, said, Look on us."

"And he gave heed unto them, expecting to receive something of them.

Then Peter said, Silver and gold have I none; but such as I have give I thee: (The Power of the anointing by the Holy Ghost.) **In the name of JESUS CHRIST OF NAZARETH RISE UP AND WALK.**

And he took him by the right hand, and lifted *him* up: and **IMMEDIATELY** his feet and ankle bones received strength.

And he leaping up stood, and walked, and entered with them into the temple, **WALKING, AND LEAPING, AND PRAISING GOD.**"

PETER PREACHES THE FULFILLING OF THE PROPHETS AND THE RESURRECTION

Acts 3:18-26

"But those things, which God before had shewed by the mouth of all his prophets, that Christ should suffer, he hath so fulfilled.

Repent ye therefore, and be converted, that your sins may be blotted out, when the times of refreshing shall come from the presence of the Lord;

And he shall send Jesus Christ, which before was preached unto you:

Whom the heaven must receive until the times of restitution of all things, which God hath spoken by the mouth of all his holy prophets since the world began.

For Moses truly said unto the fathers, A prophet shall the Lord your God raise up unto you of your brethren, like unto me; him shall ye hear in all things whatsoever he shall say unto you."

"And it shall come to pass, *that* every soul, which will not hear that prophet, shall be destroyed from among the people.

Yea, and all the prophets from Samuel and those that follow after, as many as have spoken, have likewise foretold of these days.

Ye are the children of the prophets, and of the covenant which God made with our fathers, saying unto Abraham, And in thy seed shall all the kindreds of the earth be blessed.

Unto you first God, having raised up his Son Jesus, sent him to bless you, in turning away every one of you from his iniquities."

THE RESISTANCE TO THE POWER OF THE GOSPEL BEGINS

PETER AND JOHN PUT IN PRISON

Acts 4:1-3

"And as they spake unto the people, the priests, and the captain of the temple, and the Sadducees, came upon them,

Being grieved that they taught the people, and preached through JESUS THE RESURRECTION FROM THE DEAD.

And they laid hands on them, and put *them* in hold unto the next day: for it was now eventide."

Note:

In the midst of the persecution, while the Sadducees, were not aware, five thousand souls came to the Lord!

FIVE THOUSAND SOULS BELIEVED

Acts 4:4   "Howbeit many of them which heard the word believed; and the number of the men was about five thousand."

THEY ARE THREATENED:
SPEAK NO MORE TO ANY MAN IN THE NAME OF JESUS

Acts 4:17   "But that it spread no further among the people, let us straitly threaten them, that they speak henceforth to no man in this name."

THEY PRAY FOR BOLDNESS AND ALL FILLED WITH THE HOLY GHOST
AND SPAKE THE WORD OF GOD WITH BOLDNESS

Acts 4:28-32   "For to do whatsoever thy hand and thy counsel determined before to be done.

And now, Lord, behold their threatenings: and grant unto thy servants, that with all boldness they may speak thy word,

By stretching forth thine hand to heal; and that signs and wonders may be done by the name of thy holy child Jesus.

And when they had prayed, the place was shaken where they were assembled together; and they were all filled with the Holy Ghost, and they spake the word of God with boldness.

And the multitude of them that believed were of one heart and of one soul: neither said any *of them* that ought of the things which he possessed was his own; but they had all things common."

**ANANIAS AND SAPPHIRA DIE AFTER LYING TO THE HOLY
GHOST**

Acts 5:1-11   *"READ:* Deception and lying will not be tolerated
                                   when dealing with the HOLY GHOST!"

**WHEN FEAR COMES ON ALL THE CHURCH
SIGNS AND WONDERS WILL HAPPEN**

Acts 5:11-16   **"AND GREAT <u>FEAR</u> CAME UPON <u>ALL THE</u>
                                   <u>CHURCH,</u> AND UPON AS MANY AS HEARD
                                   THESE THINGS.**

                                   **And by the hands of the apostles were many
                                   signs and wonders wrought among the people;
                                   (and they were all with one accord in
                                   Solomon's porch.**

                                   **And of the rest durst no man join himself to
                                   them: but the people magnified them.**

                                   **And believers were the more added to the Lord,
                                   multitudes both of men and women.)**

                                   **Insomuch that they brought forth the sick into
                                   the streets, and laid *them* on beds and couches,
                                   that at the least the shadow of Peter passing by
                                   might overshadow some of them.**

                                   **There came also a multitude *out* of the cities
                                   round about unto Jerusalem, bringing sick
                                   folks, and them which were vexed with unclean
                                   spirits: and they were healed <u>every one</u>."**

WITHOUT THE FEAR OF GOD (HIS WORD) WHICH IS THE
BEGINNING OF WISDOM, THE SIGNS AND WONDERS WILL
<u>NEVER</u> TAKE PLACE.

APOSTLES AGAIN PUT IN PRISON BY THE HIGH PRIEST

Acts 5:17-18   "Then the high priest rose up, and all they that were with him, (which is the sect of the Sadducees,) and were filled with indignation,

And laid their hands on the apostles, and put them in the common prison."

ANGEL OF THE LORD SETS THE APOSTLES FREE

Acts 5-19-28   "But the angel of the Lord by night opened the prison doors, and brought them forth, and said,

Go, stand and speak in the temple to the people all the words of this life.

And when they heard *that*, they entered into the temple early in the morning, and taught. But the high priest came, and they that were with him, and called the council together, and all the senate of the children of Israel, and sent to the prison to have them brought.

But when the officers came, and found them not in the prison, they returned, and told,

Saying, The prison truly found we shut with all safety, and the keepers standing without before the doors: but when we had opened, we found no man within.

Now when the high priest and the captain of the temple and the chief priests heard these things, they doubted of them whereunto this would grow.

Then came one and told them, saying, Behold, the men whom ye put in prison are standing in the temple, and teaching the people."

"Then went the captain with the officers, and brought them without violence: for they feared the people, lest they should have been stoned.

And when they had brought them, they set *them* before the council: and the high priest asked them,

Saying, Did not we straitly command you that ye should not teach in this name? And, behold, ye have filled Jerusalem with your doctrine, and intend to bring this man's blood upon us."

THE DAILY ADMINISTRATION OF THE CHURCH

Acts 6:1-6

"And in those days, when the number of the disciples was multiplied, there arose a murmuring of the Grecians against the Hebrews, because their widows were neglected in the daily ministration.

Then the twelve called the <u>multitude of the disciples</u> *unto them*, and said, It is not reason that we should leave the word of God, and serve tables.

Wherefore, brethren, look ye out among you seven men of honest report, full of the <u>Holy Ghost and wisdom</u>, whom we may appoint over this business.

But we will give ourselves continually to prayer, and to the ministry of the word.

And the saying pleased the whole multitude: and they chose Stephen, a man full of faith and of <u>the Holy Ghost</u>, and Philip, and Prochorus, and Nicanor, and Timon, and Parmenas, and Nicolas a proselyte of Antioch:"

"Whom they set before the apostles: and when they had prayed, they laid *their* hands on them."
(Through the power of the Holy Ghost.)

SEVEN BRETHREN CHOSEN OF HONEST REPORT
FULL OF THE HOLY GHOST

Acts 6:3   "Wherefore, brethren, look ye out among you SEVEN MEN OF HONEST REPORT, FULL OF THE HOLY GHOST AND WISDOM, WHOM WE MAY APPOINT OVER THIS BUSINESS."

Comment: As these SEVEN MEN were all "BORN AGAIN" of the SPIRIT, the scripture reveals that once more the HOLY GHOST BAPTISM IS SEPARATE from the SPIRIT BIRTH!

STEPHEN FULL OF THE HOLY GHOST
IS STONED TO DEATH FOR PREACHING THE TRUTH

Acts 7:51   (And Stephen said,) "YE STIFFNECKED AND UNCIRCUMCISED IN HEART AND EARS, YE DO ALWAYS RESIST THE HOLY GHOST: AS YOUR FATHERS *DID*, SO *DO* YE."

Acts 7:54-55   "WHEN THEY HEARD THESE THINGS, THEY WERE CUT TO THE HEART, AND THEY GNASHED ON HIM WITH *THEIR* TEETH.

BUT HE, BEING FULL OF THE HOLY GHOST, LOOKED UP STEDFASTLY INTO HEAVEN, AND SAW THE GLORY OF GOD, AND <u>JESUS STANDING</u> ON THE RIGHT HAND OF GOD,"

PHILIP'S REVIVAL IN SAMARIA

Acts 8:12

"But when THEY BELIEVED PHILIP preaching the things concerning the KINGDOM OF GOD, AND THE NAME OF JESUS CHRIST, THEY WERE BAPTIZED, *(in water)* both MEN and WOMEN."

Acts 8:14-17

"Now when the apostles which were at Jerusalem heard that Samaria had received the word of God, they sent unto them Peter and John:
WHO, WHEN THEY WERE COME DOWN, PRAYED FOR THEM, THAT THEY MIGHT RECEIVE THE HOLY GHOST:"

SPIRIT BIRTH

"(For as yet <u>HE</u> was fallen upon none of them: only they were baptized in the name of the LORD JESUS.)"

HOLY GHOST BAPTISM

"THEN LAID THEY *THEIR* HANDS ON THEM, AND THEY RECEIVED THE HOLY GHOST."

Positively revealing that they were 1) Born Again and Baptized in water, 2) <u>And then</u> they were Baptized in the Holy Ghost.

SIMON THE SORCERER BELIEVES AND IS BAPTIZED

Acts 8:9-13 READ:

"But there was a certain man, called Simon, which beforetime in the same city used sorcery, and bewitched the people of Samaria, giving out that himself was some great one:"

"And to him they had regard, because that of long time he had bewitched them with sorceries. <u>But</u> when they believed Philip preaching... they were baptized, both men and

women. "(They were Born Again and Baptized in water.)

"Then Simon himself believed also: and when he was baptized, he continued with Philip, and wondered, beholding the miracles and signs which were done."

(By the Holy Ghost and speaking in tongues. Simon also was Born Again and Baptized in water.)

SIMON OFFERS MONEY FOR THE GIFT OF THE HOLY GHOST

Acts 8:18-24

"And when Simon saw that through LAYING ON OF THE APOSTLES' HANDS THE HOLY GHOST WAS GIVEN, he offered them money,

Saying, Give me also this POWER, that on whomsoever I lay hands, he may receive the HOLY GHOST. (And speak in other tongues.)

But Peter said unto him, Thy money perish with thee, because thou hast thought that THE GIFT OF GOD (which is the Holy Ghost) **may be purchased with money.**

Thou hast neither part nor lot in this matter: for thy HEART IS NOT RIGHT IN THE SIGHT OF GOD.

Repent therefore of this thy wickedness, and pray GOD, if perhaps the thought of thine heart may be forgiven thee.

For I perceive that thou art in the gall of bitterness, and *in* the bond of iniquity.

Then answered Simon, and said, Pray ye to the LORD FOR ME, that none of these things which ye have spoken come upon me."

Comment: Simon **HEARD** the people SPEAK IN TONGUES.

THE MIRACLES CONTINUE

Acts 8:26-35 READ: "Philip preaches THE GOSPEL unto the EUNICH."

PHILIP BAPTIZES THE EUNICH IN WATER - (FULL SUBMERSION)

Acts 8:36-39 READ: "And they WENT DOWN both into the water, ...and HE BAPTIZED HIM."

PAUL IS CONVERTED TO CHRISTIANITY

Acts 9:1-31   "Then had the CHURCHES REST throughout all Judea and Galilee and Samaria,..."

                               PETER HEALS A MAN SICK WITH THE PALSY - ALL TURNED TO THE LORD"

Acts 9:32-35   "And it came to pass, as Peter passed throughout all *quarters*, he came down also TO THE SAINTS WHICH DWELT AT LYDDA.

                               And there he found a certain man named Aeneas, which had kept his bed eight years, and was SICK OF THE PALSY.

                               And Peter said unto him, AENEAS, JESUS CHRIST MAKETH THEE WHOLE: ARISE, AND MAKE THY BED. AND HE AROSE IMMEDIATELY.

                               And all that dwelt at Lydda and Saron SAW HIM, *(be healed)* AND TURNED TO THE LORD."

                               "Oh Lord, we need your power working in us to fulfill the deliverances mentioned above!"

THE MIRACLES CONTINUE

PETER RAISES TABITHA
FROM THE DEAD AND MANY BELIEVED IN THE LORD

Acts 9:36-42 READ: "Now there was at Joppa a CERTAIN
                          DISCIPLE named Tabitha, which by
                          interpretation is called Dorcas: this woman was
                          full of good works and almsdeeds which she did.

                          And it came to pass in those days, that she was
                          sick, and died: whom when they had washed,
                          they laid *her* in an upper chamber.

                          And the disciples had heard that Peter was there,
                          they sent unto him two men, desiring *him* that
                          he would not delay to come to them.

                          Then Peter arose and went with them. When
                          he was come, they brought him into the upper
                          chamber: and all the widows stood by him
                          weeping, and shewing the coats and garments
                          which Dorcas made, while she was with them.

                          BUT PETER PUT THEM ALL FORTH, AND
                          KNEELED DOWN, AND PRAYED; AND
                          TURNING *HIM* TO THE BODY SAID,
                          TABITHA, ARISE. AND SHE OPENED HER
                          EYES: AND WHEN SHE SAW PETER, SHE
                          SAT UP.

                          And he gave her *his* hand, and lifted her up, and
                          when he had called the saints and widows,
                          PRESENTED HER ALIVE.
                          And it was known throughout all Joppa; AND
                          MANY BELIEVED IN THE LORD."

CORNELIUS THE GENTILE CALLS FOR PETER, WHOSE
MINISTRY WAS TO THE JEWS
THE ACCOUNT:

Acts 10-1-33 READ:	Peter is sent by GOD TO PREACH THE GOSPEL to Cornelius.
Note:	Peter was called to preach the GOSPEL ONLY TO THE JEWS.
Comment:	**Cornelius, of the Italian *band*, *A* devout *man*, feared God with all his house, gave much alms to the people, and prayed to God always. He saw in a vision an angel of God coming in to him, and saying unto him, Cornelius. And he was afraid, and said, What is it, Lord? And he said unto him, THY PRAYERS AND THINE ALMS ARE COME UP FOR A MEMORIAL BEFORE GOD.**

"And now send men to Joppa, and call for *one* Simon, whose surname is Peter:... HE SHALL TELL THEE WHAT THOU OUGHTEST TO DO.

***(Simon sent men and*, as they drew nigh unto the city,) "Peter went up upon the housetop TO PRAY about the sixth hour: And he became very hungry, and would have eaten: but while they made ready, he <u>FELL INTO A TRANCE</u>,**

And saw heaven opened, and a certain vessel descending unto him, as it had been a great sheet knit at the four corners, and let down to the earth: Wherein were all manner of fourfooted beasts of the earth, and wild beasts, and creeping things, and fowls of the air. And there came a voice to him, Rise, Peter; kill, and eat. But Peter said, NOT SO, LORD; FOR I HAVE NEVER EATEN ANY THING THAT IS COMMON OR UNCLEAN.

CORNELIUS THE GENTILE CALLS FOR
PETER, WHOSE MINISTRY WAS TO THE JEWS (cont.)

And the voice spake unto him again the second
time, WHAT GOD HATH CLEANSED, THAT
CALL NOT THOU COMMON.

Now while Peter doubted in himself what this
vision which he had seen should mean, behold,
the men which were sent from Cornelius
had made enquiry for Simon's house, and stood
before the gate, and called, and asked whether
Simon, which was surnamed Peter, were lodged
there.

While Peter thought on the vision, the Spirit said
unto him, BEHOLD, THREE MEN SEEK
THEE. ARISE THEREFORE, AND GET
THEE DOWN, AND GO WITH THEM,
DOUBTING NOTHING: FOR I HAVE
SENT THEM."

"Then Peter went down...and said, Behold, I am
he whom ye seek: what is the cause wherefore
ye are come?

And they said, Cornelius the centurion,... was
WARNED FROM GOD by an HOLY ANGEL
to send for thee into his house, and to HEAR
WORDS OF THEE.

Then called he them in, and lodged them. And
on the morrow Peter went away with them, and
certain brethren from Joppa accompanied him.
...And Cornelius waited for them, and had called
together his kinsmen and near friends."

"And he said unto them, YE KNOW HOW
THAT IT IS AN UNLAWFUL THING FOR A

MAN THAT IS A JEW TO KEEP COMPANY,
OR COME UNTO ONE OF ANOTHER
NATION; BUT GOD HATH SHEWED ME
THAT I SHOULD NOT CALL ANY MAN
COMMON OR UNCLEAN.

Therefore came I *unto you* without gainsaying,
as soon as I was sent for: I ask therefore for
what intent ye have sent for me?"

(Cornelius repeats the vision.")

PETER MINISTERS SALVATION UNTO
THE HOUSE OF CORNELIUS - A GENTILE

Acts 10:34-43

"Then Peter OPENED *HIS* MOUTH, AND
SAID, OF A TRUTH I PERCEIVE THAT GOD
IS NO RESPECTER OF PERSONS:

BUT IN EVERY NATION HE THAT
FEARETH HIM, AND WORKETH
RIGHTEOUSNESS, IS ACCEPTED
WITH HIM.

THE WORD WHICH *GOD* SENT UNTO THE
CHILDREN OF ISRAEL, PREACHING
PEACE BY JESUS CHRIST: (HE IS LORD
OF ALL:)

THAT WORD, *I SAY*, YE KNOW, WHICH
WAS PUBLISHED THROUGHOUT ALL
JUDAEA, AND BEGAN FROM GALILEE,
AFTER THE BAPTISM WHICH JOHN
PREACHED;
HOW GOD ANOINTED JESUS OF
NAZARETH WITH THE HOLY GHOST AND
WITH POWER: WHO WENT ABOUT
DOING GOOD, AND HEALING ALL THAT
WERE OPPRESSED OF THE DEVIL; FOR
GOD WAS WITH HIM.

PETER MINISTERS SALVATION UNTO
THE HOUSE OF CORNELIUS - A GENTILE (cont.)

AND WE ARE WITNESSES OF ALL THINGS
WHICH HE DID BOTH IN THE LAND OF
THE JEWS, AND IN JERUSALEM; WHOM
THEY SLEW AND HANGED ON A TREE:

HIM GOD RAISED UP THE THIRD DAY,
AND SHEWED HIM OPENLY;

NOT TO ALL THE PEOPLE, BUT UNTO
WITNESSES CHOSEN BEFORE OF GOD,
EVEN TO US, WHO DID EAT AND DRINK
WITH HIM AFTER HE ROSE FROM
THE DEAD.

AND HE COMMANDED US TO PREACH
UNTO THE PEOPLE, AND TO TESTIFY
THAT IT IS HE WHICH WAS ORDAINED
OF GOD *TO BE* THE JUDGE OF QUICK
AND DEAD.

TO HIM GIVE ALL THE PROPHETS
WITNESS, THAT THROUGH HIS NAME
WHOSOEVER BELIEVETH IN HIM SHALL
RECEIVE REMISSION OF SINS."

Acts 10:44-48   "While Peter YET SPAKE THESE WORDS,
THE HOLY GHOST FELL ON ALL THEM
WHICH HEARD THE WORD.
And they of the circumcision which believed
were astonished, as many as came with Peter,
because THAT ON THE GENTILES ALSO
WAS POURED OUT THE GIFT OF THE
HOLY GHOST."

"For they HEARD THEM SPEAK WITH
TONGUES, and magnify GOD. Then answered

Peter, Can ANY MAN FORBID water, that these should not be baptized, which have RECEIVED THE HOLY GHOST as well as we? And he COMMANDED THEM TO BE BAPTIZED IN THE NAME OF THE LORD. Then prayed they him to tarry certain days."

Revealing again that the Spirit Birth through water Baptism is a separate experience from the Baptism of the Holy Ghost.

PETER REHEARSES HIS DEFENSE TO THE APOSTLES AT JERUSALEM FOR PREACHING TO CORNELIUS - A GENTILE

Acts 11:15-18	"And as I began to speak, THE HOLY GHOST FELL ON THEM, AS ON US AT THE BEGINNING. Then <u>REMEMBERED I THE WORD OF THE LORD</u>, how that he said, John indeed baptized with water; BUT YE SHALL BE BAPTIZED WITH THE HOLY GHOST."
Matt 3:11	..."He shall baptize you with the Holy Ghost, and *with* fire:"
Acts 11:17-18	"Forasmuch then as GOD GAVE THEM THE LIKE GIFT AS *HE DID* UNTO US, WHO BELIEVED ON THE LORD JESUS CHRIST; WHAT WAS I, THAT I COULD WITHSTAND GOD? When they heard these things, they held their peace, and glorified GOD, saying, <u>Then hath God also to the Gentiles granted repentance unto life</u>."

Acts 12:1-25 READ.

JAMES IS KILLED WITH A SWORD AND PETER IS PUT IN PRISON BUT THE ANGEL OF GOD FREES HIM

THE HOLY GHOST DIRECTS PAUL AND BARNABAS TO PREACH TO THE GENTILES

Acts 13:1-52 READ: "As they ministered to the Lord, and fasted, the Holy Ghost said, Separate me Barnabas and Saul for the work whereunto I have called them.

And when they had fasted and prayed, and <u>laid</u> <u>*their* hands</u> on them, they sent *them* away."

THE SPIRIT BIRTH - WATER BAPTISM HOLY GHOST BAPTISM REVEALED AS SEPARATE

Acts 19:1-5   **SPIRIT BIRTH**

"And it came to pass, that, while Apollos was at Corinth, Paul having passed through the upper coasts came to Ephesus:
AND FINDING CERTAIN DISCIPLES, *(believers),*

He said unto them, HAVE YE RECEIVED THE HOLY GHOST <u>SINCE</u> YE BELIEVED?

And they said unto him, we have not so much as heard whether there be any HOLY GHOST."

(Paul said unto them,) "...unto what then were ye BAPTIZED?
And they said, unto, John's Baptism.
Then said Paul, John verily BAPTIZED with the BAPTISM OF REPENTANCE, saying unto the people, that they should believe on HIM which should come after him, that is, on CHRIST JESUS.

When they heard this, **THEY WERE BAPTIZED IN THE NAME OF THE LORD JESUS."**

HOLY GHOST BAPTISM

Acts 19:6 **"And when Paul had laid his hands upon them, THE HOLY GHOST CAME ON THEM; and they SPAKE WITH TONGUES, AND PROPHESIED."**

Revealing: THE SPIRIT BIRTH - HOLY GHOST BAPTISM

Chapter Sixteen

The Doctrine Of The Laying On Of Hands

INTRODUCTION:

Heb 6:2 READ: (And of the **DOCTRINE OF THE LAYING ON OF HANDS.**)

Many are confused and do not understand "THE LAYING ON OF HANDS" and well they should be confused, if THEY HAVE REJECTED THE BAPTISM OF THE HOLY GHOST that puts the POWER in your hands to deliver! For JESUS is now living in HIS TEMPLE by THE BAPTISM OF THE HOLY GHOST and our HANDS become HIS HANDS, to HEAL, BLESS and to impart THE SPIRITUAL GIFTS.

QUESTION: What purpose is there in THE LAYING ON OF HANDS if there is NO POWER in them? FOR THIS POWER ONLY COMES BY THE BAPTISM OF THE HOLY GHOST!

CHALLENGING SCRIPTURES TO ALL CHRISTIANS

Mk 16:17   **"And THESE SIGNS SHALL FOLLOW THEM THAT BELIEVE; IN MY NAME shall they cast out DEVILS; They shall SPEAK WITH NEW TONGUES;"**

Mk 16:18   **"...THEY SHALL LAY HANDS ON THE SICK, AND THEY SHALL RECOVER."**

These scriptures reveal, dear children of the Lord, that we have not developed our faith beyond the BORN AGAIN EXPERIENCE, for babes have NO POWER!

Acts 1:8   **"BUT YOU SHALL RECEIVE POWER, AFTER THAT THE HOLY GHOST is come upon you:"**

QUESTION: Will you still RESIST THE BAPTISM OF THE HOLY GHOST that will give you this POWER, and fulfill the above scripture in your Spiritual life?

NOTE: In the following pages, you will find the UNDERSTANDING of the LAYING ON OF HANDS to help you on your way.

SPIRITUAL HANDS TODAY

Heb 6:2 **"Of the doctrine of baptisms, and of LAYING ON OF HANDS, and of resurrection of the dead, and of eternal judgment."**

Every Christian who is **BAPTIZED in the HOLY GHOST** knows and experiences that the Lord *has taken over their body as HIS HOUSE OR TEMPLE.* Now Jesus can *express HIMSELF* through human flesh, to bring about the END of ALL THINGS through the *LAYING ON OF HIS HANDS* <u>*with POWER!*</u>

NOTE: As was evident in the early church, He has called <u>MATURE</u> individuals out of His body of believers and given them a DEFINITE MINISTRY by the LEADING of the HOLY GHOST. This PROPHETIC MINISTRY in some areas is being operated today by the LAYING ON OF HANDS! Through the PROPHETIC WORD, the Lord wants to impart to us HIS GIFTS and DIRECTION for our lives to finish HIS WORK here on Earth.

FOUR OPERATIONS FOR THE LAYING ON OF HANDS

(1) **HEALING**

Mk 16:18 **"...They shall LAY HANDS on the sick and they shall recover."**

(2) **BAPTISM OF THE HOLY GHOST**

Acts 19:6 **"And when Paul had laid HIS HANDS upon them, the HOLY GHOST came on them;"**

SPIRITUAL HANDS TODAY (cont.)

(3)   GIFTS OF THE SPIRIT

1 Tim 4:14   "Neglect not the gift that is in thee, which was given thee by prophecy, with the laying on of the hands of the presbytery."

(4)   SEPARATE UNTO CALLING OF GOD

Acts 13:2-3   "...And FASTED, THE HOLY GHOST said, Separate Barnabas and Saul for the work where unto I have called them. And when they had FASTED and PRAYED, and LAID their hands on them, they sent them away."

(1)   HEALING BY LAYING ON OF HANDS

Lk 4:40-41   "Now when the sun was setting, all they that had any sick with divers diseases brought them unto HIM; and he LAID HIS HANDS ON EVERY ONE OF THEM, AND HEALED THEM."

Lk 13:11-13 READ: Woman with Spirit of Infirmity of 18 years JESUS LAID HIS HANDS on her: and IMMEDIATELY she was made straight, & glorified GOD.

Lk 5:12-13   "And he put forth HIS HAND and touched him, saying, I WILL: BE THOU CLEAN. And IMMEDIATELY the leprosy departed from him."

Mk 16:15-20   "And these signs shall follow them that BELIEVE; ...THEY SHALL LAY HANDS ON THE SICK, and they shall recover."

NOTE: *It is for us today if we really **BELIEVE**!*

(2)   **BAPTISM OF THE HOLY GHOST**

Acts 8:9-19 READ: (Philip's revival in Samaria. **Then Peter and John LAID HANDS ON THEM and they received the HOLY GHOST.**)

Acts 9:10-18 READ: (Paul receives his sight and is BAPTIZED in the HOLY GHOST when Ananias LAYS HANDS on him.)

Acts 19:1-6 READ: **(When Paul LAID HIS HANDS on them, the HOLY GHOST came on them; and they spake with TONGUES, AND PROPHESIED.)**

(3)   **NINE GIFTS OF THE HOLY GHOST**

Heb 2:4   **"God also bearing them witness, both with SIGNS AND WONDERS, and with divers miracles, and gifts of the HOLY GHOST,..."**

1 Cor 12:1-12 READ: **"Now concerning SPIRITUAL GIFTS, brethren, I would not have you ignorant."**

This chapter cannot be understood unless you <u>are</u> *BAPTIZED in the HOLY GHOST!* These gifts are **given** *by the* **HOLY GHOST**, *by the* **LAYING ON OF HANDS** of the presbytery or mature vessels called to this ministry.

REVEALED METHOD:
FASTING - LAYING ON OF HANDS - PROPHECY

EXAMPLES:

Rom 1:11   (Paul to church at Rome,) **"For I long to see you, that I may impart unto you some SPIRITUAL GIFT, to the end that ye may be established;"**

1 Tim 1:18   **"This CHARGE I commit unto thee, son Timothy, according to the prophecies that went**

before on thee, that THOU, BY THEM, MIGHTEST WAR A GOOD WARFARE;"

1 Tim 4:14   "Neglect not the GIFT that is in thee, which was given thee BY PROPHECY, with the LAYING ON OF THE HANDS of the PRESBYTERY."

2 Tim 1:6   "Wherefore I put thee in REMEMBRANCE, that thou STIR UP THE GIFT OF GOD, which is in THEE by the laying on of my hands."

1 Tim 4:15   "MEDITATE UPON THESE THINGS; give thyself wholly to them; that thy profiting may appear to all."

1 Tim 5:22   _(WARNING:)_ "LAY HANDS SUDDENLY on no man, (and prophecy) neither be partaker of other men's sins: keep thyself pure."

Comment: Let every man prove himself, if we lay hands and prophecy over them and they are in sin, we become part of their sins.

(4) SEPARATED TO GOD'S CALLING BY THE LAYING ON OF HANDS

Acts 6:1-6 READ: _Daily administration_ - "seven men chosen of honest report and full of the HOLY GHOST, whom they set before the Apostles: and when they had prayed, they LAID THEIR HANDS ON THEM."

Acts 13:1-4 READ: Comment: Paul and Barnabas were _SEPARATED_ to preach to the Gentiles and when the APOSTLES HAD FASTED AND PRAYED, they laid their hands on them and sent them away.

Chapter Seventeen

Gifts
Of The
Spirit

This portion of the book is written to those that are BAPTIZED IN THE HOLY GHOST AND SPEAK IN OTHER TONGUES.

THE GIFTS OF THE SPIRIT ARE GIFTS OF THE HOLY GHOST, and we will not understand THE GIFTS, neither will we have them, until we are BAPTIZED IN THE HOLY GHOST.

For example, how can we have the GIFT OF TONGUES AND THE INTERPRETATION if we are not BAPTIZED IN THE HOLY GHOST AND SPEAK IN TONGUES?

1 Corinthians 12:1   **"Now concerning SPIRITUAL *GIFTS*, brethren, I would not have you ignorant."**

This epistle is written to those that are BAPTIZED IN THE HOLY GHOST, and to give understanding that the Holy Ghost is the giver of the GIFTS OF THE SPIRIT.

For many stumble at THE GIFTS, and have not received them, because they have rejected THE HOLY GHOST that gave them!

THE NINE GIFTS ARE LISTED

1 Corinth 12:7-10   **"But the manifestation of the Spirit is given to every man to profit withal.**

For to one is given by the Spirit the word of wisdom; to another the word of knowledge by the same Spirit;

To another faith by the same Spirit; to another the gifts of healing by the same Spirit;

To another the working of miracles; to another prophecy; to another discerning of spirits; to another *divers* kinds of tongues; to another the interpretation of tongues:"

THE STRUCTURE OF THE CHURCH IN MINISTRY

1 Corinth 12:27-28   "Now ye are the body of Christ, and members
                        in particular.

                        And God hath set some in the church, first
                        apostles, secondarily prophets, thirdly teachers,
                        after that miracles, then gifts of healings, helps,
                        governments, diversities of tongues."

COVET EARNESTLY THE BEST GIFTS

1 Corinth 12:30-31   "Have all the gifts of healing? Do all speak with
                        tongues? Do all interpret?

                        But covet earnestly the best gifts: and yet shew
                        I unto you A MORE EXCELLENT WAY."

Many love "THE MORE EXCELLENT WAY", that they may excuse
themselves from THE GIFTS OF THE SPIRIT, because they know they don't
have them, neither have they "THE MORE EXCELLENT WAY" because
"THE LOVE OF GOD IS SHED ABROAD IN OUR HEARTS BY THE
HOLY GHOST."

THE LOVE CHAPTER

1 Corinth 13:1-13 READ: (1) "Though I speak with the tongues of
                              men and of angels, and have not
                              charity, I am become *as*
                              sounding brass, or a tinkling cymbal."

These verses are speaking to ALL Christians, especially those that are
BAPTIZED IN THE HOLY GHOST! Revealing that ALL GIFTS, no matter
how wonderful they are in operation, ARE NOTHING WITHOUT
CHARITY! Many that resist THE BAPTISM OF THE HOLY GHOST also
resist THE GIFTS and are in complete confusion over THE GIFTS
because Paul said, "THAT CHARITY WAS A MORE EXCELLENT WAY."

1 Corinth 14:1	When Paul also said, **"FOLLOW AFTER CHARITY, AND DESIRE SPIRITUAL** *GIFTS,..."*

HOW TO OPERATE THE GIFTS OF THE SPIRIT

1 Corinth 14:1	Again, **"FOLLOW AFTER CHARITY, AND DESIRE SPIRITUAL *GIFTS*, but rather that ye may PROPHESY."**

Let us understand in the beginning, THAT PROPHESY IS NOT PREACHING as many without THE BAPTISM OF THE HOLY GHOST are saying today! Jesus is living in our human bodies, HIS TEMPLE, and will speak from time to time through Spiritual PROPHECY unto the people.

Rev 19:10	(John said,) "And I fell at his feet to worship him. And he said unto me, See *thou do it* not: I am thy fellowservant, and of thy brethren that have the TESTIMONY OF JESUS: WORSHIP GOD: **"FOR THE TESTIMONY OF JESUS IS THE SPIRIT OF PROPHECY."**

THE UNKNOWN TONGUE AND PROPHECY

1 Corinth 14:2	**"For he that speaketh in an *unknown* tongue speaketh not unto men, but unto God:** (Tongues are a heavenly, Spiritual language that ONLY GOD can understand) **for no man understandeth *him*; HOWBEIT IN THE SPIRIT HE SPEAKETH MYSTERIES."**

To hear from heaven through THE BAPTISM OF THE HOLY GHOST AND SPEAKING IN OTHER TONGUES is one of the greatest experiences we will have on this earth, as many Christians pray in tongues to the Father daily, to gain strength and comfort themselves.

Jude 20	"BUT YE, BELOVED, BUILDING UP YOURSELVES ON YOUR MOST HOLY FAITH, **PRAYING IN THE HOLY GHOST,"** (Speaking in tongues.)

HOW TO OPERATE THE GIFTS OF THE SPIRIT (cont.)

PROPHECY

1 Corinth 14:3   **"But he that prophesieth speaketh unto men** *to* **EDIFICATION, and EXHORTATION, and COMFORT."**

This is the Testimony of Jesus coming from HIS TEMPLE, THE SPIRIT OF PROPHECY to meet a need in the common language of that country and not speaking in other tongues that they cannot understand.

1 Corinth 14:4   **"He that speaketh in an** *unknown* **tongue edifieth himself; but he that prophesieth (by THE SPIRIT of prophecy) edifieth the CHURCH."**

1 Corinth 14:5   **"I would that ye all spake with tongues, but rather that ye prophesied: for greater** *is* **he that prophesieth than he that speaketh with tongues, <u>EXCEPT HE INTERPRET</u>, that the CHURCH may receive edifying."**

Many times a brother or sister may give A MESSAGE in tongues and after give the interpretation. If they do not have the interpretation, the message only edifies themselves.

1 Corinth 14:9   **"So likewise ye, except ye utter by the tongue words easy to be understood, how shall it be known what is spoken? For ye shall speak into the air."**

1 Corinth 14:12-15   **"Even so ye, forasmuch as ye are zealous of spiritual** *gifts*, **seek that ye may excel to THE EDIFYING OF THE CHURCH."**

                           "WHEREFORE LET HIM THAT SPEAKETH IN AN *UNKNOWN* **TONGUE PRAY THAT HE MAY INTERPRET."**

HOW TO OPERATE THE GIFTS OF THE SPIRIT (cont.)

"For if I pray in an *unknown* tongue, MY SPIRIT PRAYETH, but my understanding is unfruitful.

WHAT IS IT THEN? I WILL PRAY WITH THE SPIRIT, (Tongues) AND I WILL PRAY WITH THE UNDERSTANDING <u>ALSO</u>: I WILL SING WITH THE SPIRIT, (Tongues) AND I WILL SING WITH THE UNDERSTANDING ALSO."

Many times, brothers and sisters sang in unknown tongues, and afterwards sang beautifully with the UNDERSTANDING.

1 Corinth 14:18   "I THANK MY GOD, I SPEAK WITH TONGUES MORE THAN YE ALL:"

I believe Paul was a good example for all of us!

1 Corinth 14:19-22   "Yet in THE CHURCH I had rather speak five words with my understanding, that *by my voice* I might teach others also, than ten thousand words in an *unknown* tongue."

1 Corinth 14:20   "Brethren, be NOT CHILDREN IN UNDERSTANDING: howbeit in malice be ye CHILDREN, (extreme ill will) but in UNDERSTANDING BE MEN."

1 Corinth 14:21   "In the law IT IS WRITTEN, WITH *MEN OF* OTHER TONGUES AND OTHER LIPS <u>WILL I SPEAK UNTO THIS PEOPLE</u>; AND YET FOR ALL THAT WILL THEY NOT HEAR ME, SAITH THE LORD"

1 Corinth 14:22   "Wherefore TONGUES ARE FOR A SIGN, not to them that believe, BUT TO THEM THAT BELIEVE NOT:..."

1 Corinth 14:23-25   "If therefore the whole church be come together into one place, and all speak with tongues, and here come in *those that are* unlearned, or unbelievers, will they not say that ye are mad?

But if all prophesy, and there come in one that believeth not, or *one* unlearned, he is convinced of all, he is judged of all:

And thus are the secrets of his heart made manifest; and so falling down on *his* face he will worship God, and report that GOD IS IN YOU OF A TRUTH."

FUNCTION OF THE HOLY GHOST FILLED CHURCH

1 Corinth 14:26   "How is it then, brethren? When ye come together, every one of you hath A PSALM, hath a DOCTRINE, hath a TONGUE, hath a REVELATION, hath an interpretation. LET ALL THINGS BE DONE UNTO EDIFYING."

1 Corinth 14:27-33   "If any man speak in an *UNKNOWN* TONGUE, *let it be* by TWO, or at the most *by* THREE, and *that* by course; and let one interpret. (THIS IS THE GIFT OF TONGUES AND INTERPRETATION OF THE TONGUES)

But if there be no interpreter, let him keep silence in THE CHURCH; and let him speak to himself, and to GOD.

Let the prophets speak two or three, and let the other judge.

If *any thing* be revealed to another that sitteth by, let the first hold his peace. (Honour preferring one another)

"For ye may all **PROPHESY one by one,** (Not preaching) **that ALL MAY LEARN, and all may be comforted.**

And the SPIRITS of the PROPHETS are subject to THE PROPHETS.

For GOD is not *the AUTHOR* **OF CONFUSION, but of peace, as in ALL CHURCHES of the saints."**

1 Corinth 14:39-40   "Wherefore,   brethren,   COVET   TO **PROPHESY,** <u>AND FORBID NOT TO SPEAK WITH TONGUES</u>.

LET ALL THINGS BE DONE decently and in order."

THE GIFTS OF OUR HEAVENLY FATHER TO THE CHURCH

(1)   LORD JESUS
(2)   THE HOLY GHOST

THE GIFTS OF THE HOLY GHOST TO THE CHURCH NINE GIFTS OF THE SPIRIT

1 Cor 12:8-10   (Again:) "For to one is given by the SPIRIT the **WORD OF WISDOM**; to another **THE WORD OF KNOWLEDGE** by the same SPIRIT; to another **FAITH** by the same SPIRIT; to another the gifts of **HEALING** by the same SPIRIT; to another the **WORKING OF MIRACLES**; to another **PROPHECY**; to another **DISCERNING OF SPIRITS**; to another **DIVERS KINDS OF TONGUES**; to another the **INTERPRETATION OF TONGUES**."

THE GIFTS OF JESUS TO THE CHURCH
FIVE MINISTRIES

Eph 4:11-13	"And HE gave some, **APOSTLES**; and some, **PROPHETS**; and some, **EVANGELISTS**; and some, **PASTORS**, and **TEACHERS**; for the *perfecting of the saints*, for the work of the ministry, *for the EDIFYING of the BODY OF CHRIST:*"
NOTE:	*These five ministries should be operating in the church.*
1 Cor 2:12-14	**"Now we have received, not the spirit of the world, but the spirit which is of God; that we might <u>know the things that are freely given to us of God.</u>**
	Which things also we speak, not in the words which man's wisdom teacheth, but which the Holy Ghost teacheth; comparing spiritual things with spiritual.
	But the natural man <u>receiveth not the things of the Spirit of God</u>: for they are <u>foolishness unto him</u>: neither can he know *them*, <u>because they are spiritually discerned</u>."

SPIRITUAL GIFTS

READ: **1 Corinth 12:1-31**	<u>**"Now concerning SPIRITUAL GIFTS, brethren, I would not have you to be ignorant."**</u>
Comment:	<u>NATURAL WEDDING</u> IN BOTH WEDDINGS, GIFTS WILL BE OFFERED <u>SPIRITUAL WEDDING</u>

SPIRITUAL GIFTS (cont.)

Where there is a **TRUE** love affair, GIFTS WILL BE GIVEN - *(no love affair, NO GIFTS!)*
Where there is a Bride preparing for the MARRIAGE SUPPER of the LAMB, GIFTS WILL BE GIVEN.

QUESTION: *Do I have some of the GIFTS OF THE SPIRIT?*

ANSWER: *Do you love the brethren, to which the GIFTS are given for?*

THE GREATEST SPIRITUAL SANDWICH

1 Corinth 12:1-31   **"Now concerning SPIRITUAL GIFTS, brethren, I WOULD NOT HAVE YOU IGNORANT."**

1 Corinth 13:1-13   **(Without LOVE or CHARITY there is NO PURPOSE for the SANDWICH!)**

1 Corinth 14:1-40   **"FOLLOW AFTER CHARITY, and DESIRE SPIRITUAL GIFTS,..."**

Comment: LOVE IS THE MEAT IN THE SANDWICH - NO MEAT, NO SANDWICH!

**THE NINE GIFTS OF THE SPIRIT
WHICH OPERATE BY THE HOLY GHOST**

1 Corinth 12:7-10   **"But the manifestation of THE SPIRIT is given to every man to profit withal."**

THE NINE GIFTS

1 Corinth 12:8 READ:

    1) THE WORD OF WISDOM
    2) THE WORD OF KNOWLEDGE

SPIRITUAL GIFTS (cont.)

1 Corinth 12:9 READ:
> 3) THE GIFT OF FAITH
> 4) THE GIFT OF HEALING

1 Corinth 12:10 READ:
> 5) THE GIFT OF THE WORKING OF MIRACLES
> 6) THE GIFT OF PROPHECY
> 7) THE GIFT OF DISCERNING OF SPIRITS
> 8) THE GIFT OF DIVERS KINDS OF TONGUES
> 9) THE GIFT OF INTERPRETATION OF TONGUES

Note: These GIFTS OF THE SPIRIT <u>cannot</u> be operated without the BAPTISM OF THE HOLY GHOST <u>AND</u> SPEAKING IN TONGUES.

GIFTS FROM GOD OUR HEAVENLY FATHER

Romans 6:23   **(<u>SALVATION</u>) "For the wages of sin is death; but the GIFT OF GOD is Eternal Life through Jesus Christ our Lord."**

Eph 2:8-9   **(<u>GRACE</u>) "For by Grace are ye saved through faith; and that not of yourselves: it is the gift of God: not of works, lest any man should boast."**

2 Corinth 9:15   **(<u>JESUS</u>) "Thanks be unto GOD for HIS UNSPEAKABLE GIFT."**

Heb 6:4   **(<u>JESUS</u>) "...And have tasted of THE HEAVENLY GIFT,"**

Acts 2:38   **(<u>HOLY GHOST</u>) "...Repent, and be Baptized every one of you in the NAME of JESUS CHRIST for the Remission of sins, and ye shall receive the GIFT OF THE HOLY GHOST."**

Acts 10:44-48 READ: **(<u>HOLY GHOST</u>) (GIFT of GOD poured out on Cornelius—heard them speak in TONGUES.)**

Acts 8:18-20 READ: (<u>HOLY GHOST</u>) (Simon tries to purchase THE
                            GIFT OF THE HOLY GHOST with money.)
                            (Heard them speak in tongues.)

ADDITIONAL SCRIPTURES ON THE GIFTS

Heb 2:4 READ: "...Bearing them witness,... with divers miracles
                            and GIFTS OF THE HOLY GHOST,..."

Rom 1:11 READ: "...That I may impart unto you some
                            SPIRITUAL GIFT."

1 Tim 4:14 READ: (Neglect not THE GIFT given thee, by the
                            laying on of my hands.)

2 Tim 1:6 READ: (Stir up the GIFT that was given thee by the
                            laying on of my hands.)

Chapter Eighteen

Ye Are My Witnesses And So Is The Holy Ghost

INTRODUCTION

To be a Witness for JESUS and lead SOULS BACK TO THE FATHER IS ONE OF THE **MOST IMPORTANT TRUTHS IN THE BIBLE!**

This **TRUTH** is the reason the BIBLE was written, it contains the message of salvation to the world! **(BE FRUITFUL AND MULTIPLY)**

It is the **reason** our HEAVENLY FATHER gave the SUPREME SACRIFICE, His only begotten SON on Calvary's Cross. **"YE ARE MY WITNESSES!"**

THE BEGINNING OF OUR CHRISTIAN LIFE

Jn 3:3   (Jesus said,) **"Verily, verily, I say unto thee, Except a man be BORN AGAIN,** (of the SPIRIT), **he cannot *SEE* the Kingdom of God."**

Jn 3:5   **"...Verily, verily, I say unto thee, Except a man be BORN OF WATER and of the SPIRIT, he cannot *ENTER* INTO THE KINGDOM OF GOD."**

Comment: At this stage in our Christian lives, it is only the beginning. "We are babes."

COMPARE THE NATURAL GARDEN TO THE SPIRITUAL GARDEN

1.   The SEED planted in both gardens must grow up and bear FRUIT or they have no purpose for being planted.

2.   The trees planted in both gardens may grow and look healthy and have lots of leaves as many Christians today. If they do NOT BEAR FRUIT, what was the purpose of them being planted in the Lord?

3.   If NOAH did not GO and find the TREE to make the BOARDS, he could not have built the ARK! *Likewise, if we do not GO and find the SOULS, we cannot BUILD THE CHURCH of Jesus Christ!*

JESUS GIVES US UNDERSTANDING - THAT THERE IS WORK TO DO

1.   **FATHER**

Jn 5:17   **"...My Father worketh hitherto, AND I WORK."**

Comment: *AND I WORK* - The Father's work was finished, and now Jesus was **working** to bring about the ***GREATEST AND MOST IMPORTANT EVENT IN HISTORY, THE SACRIFICE OF HIMSELF,*** to redeem mankind from Satan's grip. We are His workmanship, created in CHRIST JESUS to carry this message to the world through the Baptism of the Holy Ghost and POWER!

2.   **JESUS FINISHED HIS WORK**

Jn 17:4   **"I have glorified the FATHER on the earth:"** ***"I HAVE FINISHED THE WORK WHICH THOU GAVEST ME TO DO."***

3.   **TO US TODAY**

Matt 4:19   **"...Follow me, and I will make you fishers of men."** *The first words they heard when they met Jesus on the shores of Galilee.*

NOW WE MUST FINISH OUR WORK WITH HIM

2 Corinth 6:1-2   **"We then, as workers together with HIM, beseech you also** *that ye receive NOT THE GRACE OF GOD IN VAIN."*

"(For he saith, I have heard thee in a time accepted, and in the day of salvation have I succoured thee: behold, now *is* the accepted time; behold, now *is* the day of salvation.)"

REMEMBER:

2 Corinth 5:19   "...__THAT GOD WAS IN CHRIST__, reconciling the WORLD UNTO HIMSELF,... and hath COMMITTED UNTO US THE *WORD OF RECONCILIATION.*" (Now, we know our calling.)

TRUE WITNESSES

Comment: The RESPONSIBILITY of **RECONCILING THE WORLD UNTO GOD** became evident on **THE DAY OF PENTECOST** when the HOLY GHOST was poured out from HEAVEN, revealed in the following scripture:

Acts 1:8   "But ye shall **RECEIVE POWER, __AFTER__** (the day of Pentecost) **that the HOLY GHOST is come upon you: AND YE SHALL BE WITNESSES UNTO ME, both in Jerusalem, and in all Judaea, and in Samaria, and unto the UTTERMOST PART OF THE EARTH.**"

Acts 5:32   "**AND WE ARE HIS WITNESSES of these things; __AND SO IS ALSO THE HOLY GHOST__, whom GOD HATH GIVEN TO THEM THAT __OBEY HIM__.**" (That follow us in the faith of Jesus Christ.)

Comment: The disciples that walked with HIM on the earth were present at HIS CRUCIFIXION, BURIAL AND RESURRECTION, and were **positively HIS WITNESSES!**

Question: *"How then do we at <u>this time</u> be a WITNESS?"*

Answer: ***"<u>AND SO IS THE HOLY GHOST</u>, WHOM GOD has given to them that OBEY HIM*** *(or are walking in all the truth that they know of!)"*

ABRAHAM GIVES THE EXAMPLE WHEN TESTED

Gen 14:21-24 READ: (Abraham's decision for SOULS instead of this world's goods and riches!)

"And the king of Sodom said unto Abram, Give me the persons, and take the goods to thyself.

And Abram said to the king of Sodom, I have lift up mine hand unto the LORD, the most high God, the possessor of heaven and earth,

That I will not *take* from a thread even to a shoelatchet, and that I will not take any thing that *is* thine, lest thou shouldest say, I have made Abram rich:

Save only that which the young men have eaten, and the portion of the men which went with me, Aner, Eshcol, and Mamre; let them take their portion."

JESUS SPEAKS OF THE IMPORTANCE OF BEARING FRUIT

Jn 15:1-18 READ: **"You have not chosen ME, but I have chosen you, and ordained you, that you should GO and bring forth FRUIT, and that your fruit should remain: that whatsoever ye shall ask of the FATHER in MY NAME, HE may give it you."**

The above scripture is a way to have our prayers answered!

Jn 15:26 **"But when the Comforter is come, whom I will send unto you from the Father, *even* the Spirit of truth, which proceedeth from the Father, he shall testify of me: "**

JESUS SPEAKS TO THOSE THAT DENY HIM

Matt 10:32-39 READ: **"Whosoever therefore shall confess ME before men, him will I confess also before MY FATHER which is in heaven. But whosoever shall deny ME before men, him will I also deny before MY FATHER which is in heaven."**

JESUS SPEAKS TO THOSE THAT DENY HIM (cont.)

If we don't witness WE ARE DENYING HIM.

Lk 9:23-26   "And he said to *them* all, If any *man* will come
                    after me, let him deny himself, and take up his
                    cross daily, and follow me. For whosoever will
                    save his life shall lose it: but whosoever will lose
                    his life for my sake, the same shall save it. For
                    what is a man advantaged, if he gain the whole
                    world, and lose himself, or be cast away? <u>For
                    whosoever shall be ashamed of me and of my
                    words, of him shall the Son of man be ashamed</u>,
                    when he shall come in his own glory, and *in his*
                    Father's, and of the holy angels."

Lk 6:46   "And why call ye ME, LORD, LORD, and do
                    not the things which I say?"

Matt 15:7-9   "Ye hypocrites, well did Esaias prophesy of you,
                    saying, This people draweth nigh unto ME with
                    their mouth, and honoureth ME with their lips;
                    but their heart is far from ME."

Matt 7:15-29 READ: "Not every one that saith unto ME, LORD,
                    LORD, shall enter into the kingdom of heaven;
                    *but he that doeth the will of MY FATHER which
                    is in heaven.*"

Matt 12:30   "He that is not with ME is against ME; and he
                    that gathereth not with ME scattereth abroad."

STRONG SCRIPTURES REGARDING WITNESSING.

TITHING

Lk 16:11,12 READ: *THE TEST* (If ye have not been faithful in the
                    <u>unrighteous mammon</u> who will put to your trust
                    the <u>TRUE RICHES</u>?)

If we don't TITHE, we have THE ROOT of all evil in us, THE **LOVE** OF MONEY, and THE LORD cannot trust us with THE TRUE RICHES; THE SOULS of mankind.

2 Corinth 4:3-4   **"But if our gospel be hid, it is hid to them that are lost: in whom the god of this world hath blinded the minds of them which believe not,** *lest the light of the glorious gospel of Christ, who is the image of GOD,* **should shine in unto them."**

ENCOURAGEMENT TO GO, THE DECISION IS OURS

Is 6:1-8   *(Then said I, Here am I; SEND ME.)*

"In the year that king Uzziah died I saw also the Lord sitting upon a throne, high and lifted up, and his train filled the temple.

Above it stood the seraphims: each one had six wings; with twain he covered his face, and with twain he covered his feet, and with twain he did fly.

And one cried unto another, and said, HOLY, HOLY, HOLY, *is* the LORD of hosts: the whole earth *is* full of his glory.

And the posts of the door moved at the voice of him that cried, and the house was filled with smoke.

Then said I, Woe *is* me! For I am undone; because I *am* a man of unclean lips, and I dwell in the midst of a people of unclean lips: for mine eyes have seen the King, the LORD of hosts.

Then flew one of the seraphims unto me, having a live coal in his hand, *which* he had taken with the tongs from off the altar:

And he laid *it* upon my mouth, and said, Lo, this hath touched thy lips; and thine iniquity is taken away, and thy sin purged."

"Also I heard the voice of the Lord, saying, **WHOM SHALL I SEND, AND WHO WILL GO FOR US? THEN SAID I, HERE *AM* I; SEND ME.**"

Ps 2:8   "Ask of ME, and I shall give thee the heathen for thine inheritance, and the uttermost parts of the earth for thy possession."

CHALLENGE TO EVERY CHRISTIAN

Is 53:1-12 READ: (Who hath believed our report? And to whom is the arm of THE LORD revealed? AND WHO SHALL DECLARE HIS GENERATION?)

OUR RESPONSIBILITY BEFORE OUR LORD
TIME IS RUNNING OUT!!

Matt 9:37, 38 READ: "Then said He unto His disciples, The harvest truly is plenteous, but the labourers are few;"

Jms 5:7   "...Behold, the husbandman <u>waiteth</u> for the precious fruit of the earth, and hath long patience for it, until he receive the early and the latter rain."

WE MUST NOT DELAY OUR DECISION

Jn 4:35   "Say not ye, There are yet four months, and *then* cometh Harvest? Behold, I say unto you, lift up your eyes, and look on the fields; for they are white already to harvest."

RESPONSIBILITY IS UPON US TODAY

Rom 8:18-23 "For I reckon that the sufferings of this present time *are* not worthy *to be compared* with the glory which shall be revealed in us.

For the earnest expectation of the creature waiteth for the manifestation of the SONS OF GOD.

For the creature was made subject to vanity, not willingly, but by reason of him who hath subjected *the same* in hope,

Because the creature itself also shall be delivered from the bondage of corruption into the glorious liberty of the children of God.

For we know that the whole creation groaneth and travaileth in pain together until now.

And not only *they*, but ourselves also, which have the firstfruits of the Spirit, even we ourselves groan within ourselves, waiting for the adoption, *to wit*, the redemption of our body."

FINALLY - JESUS SAID:

Matt 28:18-19 "And Jesus came and spake unto them, saying, ALL POWER IS GIVEN UNTO ME IN HEAVEN AND IN EARTH. GO YE THEREFORE, AND TEACH ALL NATIONS, BAPTIZING THEM IN THE NAME OF THE FATHER, AND OF THE SON, AND OF THE HOLY GHOST:" (Which is Jesus)

AND THAT POWER IS THE BAPTISM OF THE HOLY GHOST!

EARLY CHURCH:

Acts 17:6	"...These that have turned the world upside down..."
Lk 19:13	"...OCCUPY TILL I COME"
Rev 12:11	"And they overcame him by the blood of the LAMB, and by the WORD OF THEIR TESTIMONY; and they loved not their lives unto the death."
2 Corinth 5:10	"For we must ALL APPEAR before the JUDGMENT SEAT OF CHRIST; that every one may receive the things *done* in *his* body, according to that he hath done, whether *it be* good or bad."
Heb 11:1-40 READ:	*A GOOD EXAMPLE FOR US TODAY!*
Heb 12:1-2	"WHEREFORE SEEING WE ALSO ARE COMPASSED ABOUT WITH SO GREAT A CLOUD OF WITNESSES, LET US LAY ASIDE EVERY WEIGHT, AND THE SIN WHICH DOTH SO EASILY BESET *US*, AND LET US RUN WITH PATIENCE THE RACE THAT IS SET BEFORE US,
	LOOKING UNTO JESUS THE AUTHOR AND FINISHER OF *OUR* FAITH; WHO FOR THE JOY THAT WAS SET BEFORE HIM ENDURED THE CROSS, DESPISING THE SHAME, AND IS SET DOWN AT THE RIGHT HAND OF THE THRONE OF GOD."

A SONG TO STIR OUR HEARTS

HAVE YOUR EYES CAUGHT THE VISION:

Have your eyes caught the vision? Has your heart felt the thrill?

To the call of the MASTER, Have you answered "I WILL"?

Through the conflict of the ages, Told by Prophets and by Sages

Its FURY is upon us, is upon us today!

Chapter Nineteen

The True Worshippers

WORSHIP IS ONE OF THE MOST IMPORTANT TRUTHS FOLLOWING THE SPIRIT BIRTH INTO THE KINGDOM OF GOD.

Without the TRUE SPIRITUAL WORSHIP, we will not experience THE BAPTISM OF THE HOLY GHOST for they complement one another!

Jn 4:23-24   **(JESUS SAID,) "...THE TRUE WORSHIP-PERS, shall worship the FATHER in SPIRIT and in TRUTH:"**

This scripture reveals that it is not man's worship, but a SPIRITUAL WORSHIP, "TRUTH" that our WORSHIP shall be according to THE WORD OF THE LORD.

PAUL'S SPIRITUAL REVELATION ON HOW TO WORSHIP

Acts 24:14-16   **"THIS I CONFESS UNTO THEE, THAT AFTER THE WAY WHICH THEY CALL HERESY, SO WORSHIP I THE GOD OF MY FATHERS, BELIEVING ALL THINGS WHICH ARE WRITTEN IN THE LAW AND THE PROPHETS:"**

Paul was questioned by the religious leaders of his day on how to WORSHIP and gave the above answer.

LET US NOW LOOK TO THE LAW AND THE PROPHETS FOR TRUE WORSHIP

This prophetic truth was forecast by the prophets.

Ps 102:16-20 READ: **"This shall be written for the GENERATION TO COME: The people that shall be CREATED, SHALL PRAISE THE LORD."**

Is 42:5-12 READ: **(New things do I declare before they spring forth, I tell you of them.)**

Is 43:18-21 READ:	**"This people have I FORMED FOR MYSELF; they shall SHEW FORTH MY PRAISE."**
Is 61:11 READ:	**(The Lord will cause RIGHTEOUSNESS AND PRAISE to SPRING FORTH before ALL NATIONS.)**
Note:	Praise will lead us into worship and worship will lead us into praise. They are two different aspects of our approach to God.

THE IMPORTANCE OF PRAISE AND WORSHIP FOR OUR LIVES

Many praise the Lord without learning the true Spiritual worship of the Lord, which is a separate act of reverence through a relationship with the Father.

Ps 22:3 READ:	**(God INHABITS the PRAISES OF ISRAEL, or HIS PEOPLE.)**
Ps 24:7-10	**"Lift up your heads, O ye gates; and be ye lift up, ye everlasting doors; and the King of glory shall come in.**
	Who *is* this King of glory? The LORD strong and mighty, the LORD mighty in battle.
	LIFT UP YOUR HEADS, O ye gates; even lift *them* up, ye everlasting doors; and the KING OF GLORY SHALL COME IN.
	Who is this King of glory? The LORD of hosts, he *is* the King of glory. Selah."

Our mouths are the gates, and as we worship and praise HIM, THE LORD makes HIS entry and comes in with His presence and anointing!

Prov 27:21	**"As a fining pot for silver, and a furnace for gold; SO IS A MAN TO HIS PRAISE."**

THE IMPORTANCE OF PRAISE AND WORSHIP FOR OUR LIVES (cont.)

As silver and gold are placed in the furnace, all the impurities come to the surface, so with us, as THE HOLY GHOST AND FIRE through PRAISE AND WORSHIP: pass through our lives in HIS HOLY PRESENCE, there is a cleansing of our souls, and the ground around us becomes HOLY GROUND.

Ps 100:1-5	(**PASSWORD** into His courts, or presence.)
	"A Psalm of praise. Make a joyful noise unto the LORD, all ye lands.
	Serve the LORD with gladness: come before his presence with singing.
	Know ye that the LORD he *is* **God:** *it is* **he** *that* **hath made us, and not we ourselves;** *we are* **his people, and the sheep of his pasture. Enter into his gates with thanksgiving,** *and* **into his courts with praise: be thankful unto him,** *and* **bless his name.**
	For the LORD *is* **good; his mercy** *is* **everlasting; and his truth** *endureth* **to all generations."**
Is 61:3 READ:	(**GARMENT** - of praise for the spirit of heaviness.)
Heb 13:15 READ:	(**SACRIFICE** - of praise for the spirit of heaviness.)
Ps 67:1-7 READ:	(**INCREASE - THEN THE EARTH WILL YIELD HER INCREASE!**)
	"To the chief Musician on Neginoth, A Psalm *or* **Song. God be merciful unto us, and bless us;** *and* **cause his face to shine upon us; Selah. That thy way may be known upon earth, thy saving health among all nations. Let the people praise thee, O God; let all the people praise thee."**

> "O let the nations be glad and sing for joy: for thou shalt judge the people righteously, and govern the nations upon earth. Selah. Let the people praise thee, O God; let all the people praise thee.
> *Then* shall the earth yield her increase; *and* God, *even* our own God, shall bless us.
> God shall bless us; and all the ends of the earth shall fear him."

Ps 40:3

(NEW SONG)

"And he hath put a new song in my mouth, *even* praise unto our God: many shall see *it*, and fear, and shall trust in the LORD."

PRAISE AND WORSHIP IS THE ANSWER FOR VICTORY IN EVERY CHRISTIAN LIFE!

WHAT IS PRAISE?

Hebrew:			
YADA	-	To revere or worship with extended hands.
TOWDA	-	Extension of the hands - sacrifice of PRAISE - confession and thanksgiving.
ZAMAR	-	To make MUSIC - accompanied by the VOICE - celebrate in SONG.
SHABACH	-	To address in a LOUD TONE - GLORY - PRAISE - TRIUMPH.
HALAL	-	Make a SHOW, BOAST - clamorously foolish - sing - praise celebrate.

HOW TO PRAISE THE LORD
READ:

Ps 22:22	(I will declare THY NAME unto my brethren. In the midst of the CONGREGATION WILL I PRAISE THEE.)
Ps 34:1	(Praise shall be continually in my mouth.)
Ps 63:3	(My lips shall praise THEE.)
Ps 66:8	(Make the VOICE OF HIS PRAISE TO BE HEARD.)
Ps 109:30	(Praise the Lord with thy MOUTH.)
Ps 47:7	(Sing praises with UNDERSTANDING.)
Ps 109:30	(I will greatly praise the LORD with my mouth; yea, I will praise him among the multitude.)
Ps 150:1-6	(Praising the LORD in music.)

"Praise ye the LORD. Praise God in his sanctuary: praise him in the firmament of his power.
Praise him for his mighty acts: praise him according to his excellent greatness.
Praise him with the sound of the trumpet: praise him with the psaltery and harp.
Praise him with the timbrel and dance: praise him with stringed instruments and organs.
Praise him upon the loud cymbals: praise him upon the high sounding cymbals.
Let every thing that hath breath praise the LORD. Praise ye the LORD."

LET US NOW LOOK AT THE WAY TO WORSHIP THE LORD
(ACCORDING TO PAUL'S REVELATION IN THE LAW AND THE
PROPHETS)

Reference: Acts 24:14

THE LIFTING UP OF OUR HANDS

Ps 134:2	"LIFT UP your hands in the sanctuary, and BLESS THE LORD."
1 Tim 2:8	"I will therefore that men PRAY EVERY WHERE, (How?)...Lifting up HOLY HANDS..."
Ps 141:2	"Let my prayer be set forth before thee as incense; and the lifting up of my hands as the evening sacrifice."
Ps 113:3 READ:	(Praise HIM from the RISING OF THE SUN to the GOING DOWN.)
Neh 8:5-6 READ:	(As Ezra read the WORD - and the people answered AMEN - AMEN, with the LIFTING UP OF THEIR HANDS.)
Heb 12:11-14	"Wherefore LIFT UP THE HANDS THAT HANG DOWN, and STRENGTHEN THE FEEBLE KNEES; and MAKE STRAIGHT PATHS FOR YOUR FEET, lest that which is lame be turned out of the way;"

LIFT UP THE HANDS TOWARD HIS DWELLING PLACE

Ps 28:2	"Hear the voice of my supplications,...<u>when</u> I lift up my hands toward thy holy oracle."

BLESSING THE LORD

Ps 63:4	"Thus will I bless thee while I live: I will lift up my hands in thy name."

LIFT UP THE HANDS TOWARD HIS DWELLING PLACE (cont.)

Ps 119:48   "My hands will I lift up unto thy
                          commandments, which I have loved;..."

FOR THE YOUNG CHILDREN

Lament 2:19 READ: (Lift up your hands toward Him for the life of
                          thy young children.)

LIFT UP OUR HEARTS

Lament 3:40-41 READ: (Let us lift up our hearts with our hands.)

MOSES GIVES EXAMPLES FOR VICTORY
THE POWER OF THE LIFTING UP OF OUR HANDS

Ex 17:8-12   (As Moses lifted up his hands - ENEMY
                          DEFEATED!)

                          "Then came Amalek, and fought with Israel
                          in Rephidim.

                          And Moses said unto Joshua, Choose us out
                          men, and go out, fight with Amalek: tomorrow
                          I will stand on the top of the hill with the rod of
                          God in mine hand.

                          So Joshua did as Moses had said to him, and
                          fought with Amalek: and Moses, Aaron, and
                          Hur went up to the top of the hill.

                          And it came to pass, when Moses held up his
                          hand, that Israel prevailed: and when he let
                          down his hand, Amalek prevailed.

                          But Moses' hands *were* heavy; and they took a
                          stone, and put *it* under him, and he sat thereon;
                          and Aaron and Hur stayed up his hands, the

one on the one side, and the other on the other side; and his hands were steady until the going down of the sun."

DEDICATION OF SOLOMON'S TEMPLE

1 Kings 8:22-30　　　　　(SOLOMON'S DEDICATION BY LIFTING UP OF HIS HANDS!)

"And Solomon stood before the altar of the LORD in the presence of all the congregation of Israel, and spread forth his hands toward heaven:

And he said, LORD God of Israel, *there is* no God like thee, in heaven above, or on earth beneath, who keepest covenant and mercy with thy servants that walk before thee with all their heart:

Who hast kept with thy servant David my father that thou promisedst him: thou spakest also with thy mouth, and hast fulfilled *it* with thine hand, as *it is* this day.

Therefore now, LORD God of Israel, keep with thy servant David my father that thou promisedst him, saying, There shall not fail thee a man in my sight to sit on the throne of Israel; so that thy children take heed to their way, that they walk before me as thou hast walked before me.

And now, O God of Israel, let thy word, I pray thee, be verified, which thou spakest unto thy servant David my father."

"But will God indeed dwell on the earth? Behold, the heaven and heaven of heavens cannot contain thee; how much less this house that I have builded?

Yet have thou respect unto the prayer of thy servant, and to his supplication, O LORD my God, to hearken unto the cry and to the prayer, which thy servant prayeth before thee to day:

That thine eyes may be open toward this house night and day, *even* toward the place of which thou hast said, My name shall be there: that thou mayest hearken unto the prayer which thy servant shall make toward this place.

And hearken thou to the supplication of thy servant, and of thy people Israel, when they shall pray toward this place: and hear thou in heaven thy dwelling place: and when thou hearest, forgive."

1 Kings 8:54   (Solomon ends his prayer from kneeling on his knees with his hands spread toward Heaven!)

"And it was *so*, that when Solomon had made an end of praying all this prayer and supplication unto the LORD, he arose from before the altar of the LORD, from kneeling on his knees with his hands spread up to heaven."

OUR LORD'S FINAL BLESSING ON EARTH

Lk 24:50-53   "And Jesus lifted up his hands and blessed them

And he led them out as far as to Bethany, and he lifted up his hands, and blessed them."

"And it came to pass, while he blessed them, he was parted from them, and carried up into heaven.

And they worshipped him, and returned to Jerusalem with great joy:

And were continually in the temple, praising and blessing God. Amen."

CLAPPING OF HANDS

Ps 47:1   "O clap your hands, all ye people; shout unto God with the voice of triumph."

Ps 98:1-9 READ: (Let the floods clap their hands.)

Is 55:12 READ: (For ye shall go out with joy, and be led forth with peace: the mountains and hills shall break forth before thee, all the trees of the field shall clap their hands!)

DANCING BEFORE THE LORD

CHALLENGE TO MINISTRY IN THIS HOUR

Jer 50:6   My people have been lost sheep: their shepherds have caused them to go astray,..."(mountain to the hill.)

Lament 5:14-18   "The elders have ceased from the gate, young men from their music. The joy of our heart is ceased; our dance is turned into mourning. For this our heart is faint and our eyes dim."

PRAISING GOD IN THE DANCE

Ps 150:4 READ: (Praise God with timbrel and dance.)

YOUNG MEN AND OLD

Jer 31:12-14 READ: (Young men and old will dance.)

WOMEN LEAD THE DANCE OF VICTORY

Ex 15:20-21 READ: (After Israel's deliverance from slavery in
                             Egypt, Miriam and all the women - danced and
                             sang with timbrels.)

Judges 11:34 READ: (Jephthah's daughter came out to meet King
                             David after his victory with timbrel and dances.)

1 Samuel 18:6-7 READ: (After King David's victory over the Philistines,
                             women came out of all the cities with timbrels
                             and dances.)

DAVID PRAISES GOD FOR DELIVERANCE

Ps 30:11-12 READ: (David declares his mourning turned
                             into dancing.)

OPPOSITION TO PRAISE AND DANCING

2 Samuel 6:14-16 READ:(David brings the ark (spirit) back with danc-
                             ing - trumpets - shouting, but Michal, Saul's
                             daughter, David's wife, looked through a
                             window and saw David leaping and dancing
                             before the Lord. *AND SHE DESPISED HIM
                             IN HER HEART.)*

Note: I hope we are not a MICHAL and despise these
                             writings, I suppose that in many other churches,
                             if King David were alive today they would despise
                             him and ask him to leave, *(something to
                             think about).*

LAME MAN LEAPS AND DANCES

Acts 3:8	(Peter and John see lame man leap and dance after healing.)
	(Something greater than healing has happened!)
	"And he leaping up stood, and walked, and entered with them into the temple, walking, and leaping, and praising God."

RETURN OF THE PRODIGAL SON

Lk 15:25 READ:	(As the Prodigal Son is found, there is a feast and rejoicing with music and dances.)

THE BALANCE

Eccl 3:1-8 READ:	(A time to weep - time mourn - time to laugh - time to dance.)

MESSAGE TO THE CHURCH

1 Pet 2:9	"But ye *are* a chosen generation, a royal priesthood, an holy nation, a peculiar people; that ye should shew forth the praises of HIM who hath called you out of darkness into HIS marvellous light:"

EARLY CHURCH

Acts 2:47	(They were praising God - Lord added to the church daily.)
	"Praising God, and having favour with all the people. And the Lord added to the church daily such as should be saved. "

This must take place in THE CHURCH today, if we are going to have an increase from the Lord.

Lk 24:49-53 READ: They were continually in the temple, praising
                         and blessing God.

THE VOICE OF THE LAST DAY CHURCH

Jer 33:11 READ: (1)   The voice of gladness
                         (2)   The voice of the bridegroom
                         (3)   The voice of the bride
                         (4)   The voice of them that shall say <u>praise
                                  ye the Lord</u>!

Ps 149:6   "Let the high praises of God be in their mouth,
                         and the two edged sword in their hand;..."

Ps 150:1-6 READ: (Let everything that hath breath praise the
                         Lord!)

THE FOUNDATIONS OF THE TRUE CHURCH

Eph 2:20 READ: (We are founded upon the foundations of
                         apostles and prophets Jesus Christ the chief
                         corner stone.)
Question:
Ps 11:3   "If the foundations be destroyed, what can the
                         righteous do?"
Answer:
Is 61:4 READ: (They shall build again the foundations the
                         desolations of many generations)

ADDITIONAL SCRIPTURES ON PRAISE
READ:
Ps 104:33   (I will sing praise to my God while I have
                         my being.)
Ps 106:12   (They that believe His words - will praise him.
Ps 106:47   We will triumph in His Praise!)
Ps 113:3   (Praise Him from the rising of the sun unto the
                         going down of the same.)
Ps 118:21   (I will praise thee: because thou hast heard me.)

Chapter Twenty

Who Is
The Holy Ghost

I want to settle THIS QUESTION once and for ALL, turning to THE HOLY WORD OF GOD FOR THE ANSWERS!

Some have even been close to BLASPHEMING THE HOLY GHOST in their SPIRITUAL BLINDNESS, in speaking against THE WORD that reveals THE BAPTISM OF THE HOLY GHOST, WHEN THE FATHER AND THE SON ARE THE HOLY GHOST!

WARNING FROM THE PROPHETS

Is 8:20   **"TO THE LAW AND TO THE TESTIMONY: IF THEY SPEAK NOT ACCORDING TO THIS WORD, *IT IS* BECAUSE *THERE IS* NO LIGHT IN THEM."**

This question we should ask ourselves, "DO I SPEAK AGAINST THIS WORD?" Something to think about!

THE HOLY GHOST is the MOST MISUNDERSTOOD person of the GODHEAD!

I WONDER IF WE WOULD STILL REJECT THE HOLY GHOST, IF WE UNDERSTOOD THAT THE FATHER AND THE SON ARE THE HOLY GHOST, AND THEIR PLAN FROM THE BEGINNING WAS TO LIVE IN THE MANY MEMBERED BODY OF CHRIST THE CHURCH, THAT WE MAY BE ONE AS THEY ARE ONE.

These questions and answers will be revealed by THE WORD OF GOD as we continue, AND NOT BY MAN'S OPINIONS!

The CHURCH IS THE FINAL DWELLING PLACE, FOR THE **FATHER and THE SON**, THROUGH THE BAPTISM OF THE HOLY GHOST!

THE FOUNDATIONS FOR THE HOLY GHOST BAPTISM

Again, for our UNDERSTANDING, let us start at the BEGINNING.

Gen 1:16   **"AND GOD <u>MADE TWO GREAT LIGHTS</u>; THE GREATER LIGHT TO RULE THE DAY, AND THE LESSER LIGHT TO RULE THE NIGHT: *HE MADE* THE STARS ALSO."**

This is the beginning of the SPIRITUAL REVELATION OF THE GODHEAD in the HEAVENS, **THE FATHER, THE SON, AND THE CHURCH. THE TWO GREAT LIGHTS are THE FATHER AND THE SON.** THE STARS we will mention later as we proceed, for THE STARS are THE MANY MEMBERED BODY OF CHRIST, THE CHURCH.

Romans 1:20   "For the invisible things of him from the creation of the world are clearly seen, being understood by the things that are made, *even* his eternal power and Godhead; so that they are without excuse:"

1 Jn 5:7   (The Apostle John confirms the above scripture,) **"THERE ARE THREE THAT BEAR RECORD IN HEAVEN, THE FATHER, THE WORD** (SON) **AND THE HOLY GHOST; AND THESE THREE ARE ONE."**

By this scripture alone we can understand that, if we reject THE HOLY GHOST, we reject **THE FATHER AND THE SON, "BECAUSE THESE THREE ARE ONE."**

This is the beginning of the REVELATION OF **THE FATHER AND THE SON** who are also THE HOLY GHOST, **"BECAUSE THESE THREE ARE ONE".**

The CHURCH IS THE FINAL DWELLING PLACE, FOR THE **FATHER and THE SON**, THROUGH THE BAPTISM OF THE HOLY GHOST!

THE FATHER AND THE SON MAKE THEIR FUTURE DWELLING PLACE

Gen 1:26-27   **"AND GOD SAID, LET US (FATHER AND SON) MAKE MAN IN OUR IMAGE, AFTER OUR LIKENESS: and let them have dominion over the fish of the sea, and over the fowl of the air, and over the cattle, and over all the earth, and over every creeping thing that creepeth upon the earth."**

        "So God created man in HIS *OWN* IMAGE, in the IMAGE OF GOD created he him; male and female created HE THEM."

Question: Why did **THEY** make man in **THEIR** IMAGE after **THEIR** LIKENESS?

Answer: Because **THE FATHER AND THE SON** would live in THEIR TEMPLE, through THE BAPTISM OF THE HOLY GHOST on the DAY OF PENTECOST! BECAUSE, THE FATHER AND THE SON ARE THE HOLY GHOST!

Jn 14:23   Confirms THE ANSWER, **"JESUS ANSWERED AND SAID UNTO HIM, IF A MAN LOVE ME, HE WILL KEEP MY WORDS:** (NOT CHANGE THEM) **AND MY FATHER WILL LOVE HIM, AND WE WILL COME UNTO HIM, AND MAKE OUR ABODE WITH HIM."**

We can again see, that, <u>**THE FATHER AND THE SON**</u>, ARE THE HOLY GHOST, and will come and live in us through THE BAPTISM OF THE HOLY GHOST.

Paul said, **"KNOW YE NOT, YOUR BODY IS THE TEMPLE OF THE HOLY GHOST?"** (Which is <u>**THE FATHER AND THE SON?**</u>)

THE FOUNDATIONS FOR THE HOLY GHOST BAPTISM

Jesus said, "MY FATHER WORKETH HITHERTO AND I WORK." (Again THE FATHER AND THE SON.)

THE FATHER'S WORK

The FATHER laid ALL THE FOUNDATION OF TRUTH to give us understanding of that which was to come.

THE FOUNDATIONS FOR THE HOLY GHOST BAPTISM

1 Jn 5:7   **"THERE ARE THREE THAT BEAR RECORD IN HEAVEN, THE FATHER, THE WORD, (JESUS), AND THE HOLY GHOST: <u>AND THESE THREE ARE ONE.</u>"**

GOD is a SPIRIT and chose to reveal HIMSELF as THREE PERSONS. FATHER, SON and HOLY GHOST, therefore revealing THE GODHEAD. Without perfect understanding of the FATHER, SON and HOLY GHOST and THEIR WORK OF REDEMPTION for us, we will never understand our great salvation!

Many through their lack of SPIRITUAL UNDERSTANDING, refer to THE GODHEAD as FATHER, SON AND HOLY SPIRIT, and have eliminated the THIRD PERSON OF THE GODHEAD, THE HOLY GHOST, when we should know that the FATHER, SON AND HOLY GHOST are all SPIRIT, but still THREE PERSONS.

Would we then say, THERE ARE THREE THAT BEAR RECORD IN HEAVEN, THE SPIRIT, THE SON AND THE HOLY GHOST? We would immediately say, YOU HAVE ELIMINATED THE FATHER! Likewise if we say, FATHER, SPIRIT AND HOLY GHOST, WE HAVE ELIMINATED THE SON our Saviour! The same applies when we refer to THE GODHEAD as FATHER SON AND HOLY SPIRIT and ELIMINATE THE HOLY GHOST.

Remember, THAT IF WE ELIMINATE THE HOLY GHOST, referring to Him as "HOLY SPIRIT", total confusion will result because we have ELIMINATED THE FATHER AND THE SON also, **"BECAUSE THESE THREE, FATHER, SON AND HOLY GHOST ARE ONE!"**

THE FOUNDATIONS FOR THE HOLY GHOST BAPTISM (cont.)

Gen 1:26 **"AND GOD SAID, <u>LET US</u> (FATHER AND SON) MAKE MAN <u>IN OUR</u> IMAGE, AFTER <u>OUR LIKENESS</u>:..."**

This human body, numbering, one hundred and twenty, was waiting in the upper room for the BAPTISM OF THE HOLY GHOST ON THE DAY OF PENTECOST, obeying the COMMANDMENT OF OUR LORD JESUS, which was, **"WAIT FOR THE PROMISE OF THE FATHER."** — THIS WAS A COMMANDMENT, THE SPIRIT BIRTH WAS, **"WHOSOEVER WILL MAY COME."**

Paul said, **"Know ye not, that your body is THE TEMPLE OF THE HOLY GHOST?"** (THE FATHER AND THE SON.)

(The Lord said,)
2 Corinth 6:18 **"And will be a Father unto you, and ye shall be my sons and daughters, saith the Lord Almighty."** (Revealing the beautiful RELATIONSHIP as THE FATHER AND THE SON make THEIR ABODE IN US, following the BAPTISM OF THE HOLY GHOST.)

SHADOW OF THE HOLY GHOST SEEKING A BRIDE FOR JESUS

Gen 24:1-67 READ: (ABRAHAM'S SERVANT, SEEKING A BRIDE FOR ISAAC.)

This is a shadow of the Holy Ghost (Servant) on the day of Pentecost seeking a Bride for Jesus (Isaac), and **ALL** THE GIFTS were in the Servant's hand (Gifts of the Spirit).

ANNOUNCING THE HOLY GHOST TO COME

Is 28:9 **"WHOM SHALL HE TEACH KNOWLEDGE? AND WHOM SHALL HE MAKE TO UNDERSTAND DOCTRINE? *THEM THAT ARE* WEANED FROM THE MILK, *AND* DRAWN FROM THE BREASTS."**

In plain words, THE LORD WANTS TO KNOW WHO HE CAN TEACH KNOWLEDGE, AND UNDERSTAND DOCTRINE.

The Lord GIVES THE ANSWER, "THEM THAT ARE WEANED FROM THE MILK AND DRAWN FROM THE BREASTS," in other words, those that have gone beyond THE SPIRIT BIRTH in TRUTH because HE has more to say to us.

THE FOUNDATIONS FOR THE HOLY GHOST BAPTISM (cont.)

Is 28:11-12   **"FOR WITH STAMMERING LIPS AND ANOTHER TONGUE WILL <u>HE SPEAK</u> to this people."**

                   "To whom he said, This *is* **the rest** *wherewith* **ye may cause the weary to rest; and this** *is* **the refreshing: YET THEY WOULD NOT HEAR."**

JOHN THE BAPTIST INTRODUCES JESUS TO THE WORLD AS THE BAPTIZER WITH THE HOLY GHOST

Matt 3:11   **"I INDEED BAPTIZE YOU WITH WATER UNTO REPENTANCE: BUT HE THAT COMETH AFTER ME IS MIGHTIER THAN I, WHOSE SHOES I AM NOT WORTHY TO BEAR: HE SHALL BAPTIZE YOU WITH THE HOLY GHOST, AND** *WITH* **FIRE:"**

This scripture plainly reveals, THAT JESUS IS THE BAPTIZER WITH THE HOLY GHOST, AND AS JESUS SAID, **"<u>I AND THE FATHER ARE ONE</u>,"** REVEALING AGAIN THAT THEY ARE THE HOLY GHOST.

Jn 1:33   **"AND I KNEW HIM NOT: BUT HE** (THE FATHER) **THAT SENT ME TO BAPTIZE WITH WATER, THE SAME SAID UNTO ME, UPON WHOM THOU SHALT SEE THE SPIRIT DESCENDING, AND REMAINING ON HIM, THE SAME IS HE WHICH BAPTIZETH WITH THE HOLY GHOST."**

Many preach and say, "BAPTIZED IN THE SPIRIT" and eliminate THE HOLY GHOST, when the scripture says, "BAPTIZED IN THE HOLY GHOST." It is not good that we eliminate "THE HOLY GHOST," for this will cause confusion over "THE SPIRIT BIRTH" and many will say, I am Baptized IN THE SPIRIT when they are only BORN AGAIN OF THE SPIRIT, for they are separate experiences, and when we are BAPTIZED WITH THE HOLY GHOST, we will SPEAK IN OTHER TONGUES.

THE WORK OF THE SON

JESUS BEGINS TO LAY THE FOUNDATIONS FOR THE HOLY GHOST BAPTISM TO COME ON THE DAY OF PENTECOST.

THE FOUNDATIONS FOR THE HOLY GHOST BAPTISM (cont.)

Jn 7:37-39   "In the last day, that great *day* of the feast, Jesus stood and cried, saying, If any man thirst, let him come unto me, and drink.

He that believeth on me, as the scripture hath said, out of his belly shall flow rivers of living water.

(BUT THIS SPAKE HE OF THE SPIRIT, WHICH THEY THAT BELIEVE ON HIM SHOULD RECEIVE: FOR <u>THE HOLY GHOST WAS NOT YET *GIVEN*</u>; BECAUSE THAT JESUS WAS NOT YET GLORIFIED.)"

This scripture reveals that THE BAPTISM OF THE HOLY GHOST was coming, and that it was separate from THE SPIRIT BIRTH.

JESUS REVEALS THAT THE HOLY GHOST IS A PERSON AND AS JESUS AND THE FATHER ARE ONE, THEY <u>*ARE*</u> THAT PERSON.

Jn 14:15-18   "If <u>YE LOVE</u> me, keep my commandments.

And I will pray the Father, and he shall give you another Comforter, that <u>HE</u> may abide with you for ever;

Even the Spirit of truth; whom the world cannot receive, because it seeth <u>HIM</u> not, neither knoweth <u>HIM</u>: but ye know <u>HIM</u>; for <u>HE</u> dwelleth with you, and shall be in you.

I will not leave you comfortless: I will come to you." (Because I and the Father are one.)

Jn 14:23   "Jesus answered and said unto him, If a man love me, he will keep my words: and my Father will love him, and <u>WE</u> will come unto him, and make our abode with him. (Positively revealing that the <u>FATHER AND THE SON</u> are the Holy Ghost.)"

Jn 14:26   "But the Comforter, *which is* the Holy Ghost, whom the Father will send in my name, <u>HE</u> shall teach you all things, and bring all things to your remembrance, whatsoever I have said unto you."

JESUS REVEALS THAT THE HOLY GHOST IS A PERSON

Jn 16:13-14   "Howbeit when <u>HE</u>, the Spirit of truth, is come, <u>HE</u> will guide
                 you into all truth: for <u>HE</u> shall not speak of HIMSELF; but
                 whatsoever <u>HE</u> shall hear, *that* shall <u>HE</u> speak: and <u>HE</u> will
                 shew you things to come."

                 "<u>HE</u> shall glorify me: for <u>HE</u> shall receive of mine, and shall
                 shew *it* unto you."

The reason for showing THE HOLY GHOST IS A PERSON, IS because THE
HOLY GHOST IS THE FATHER and THE SON, that would return on THE DAY OF
PENTECOST to BAPTIZE US IN THE HOLY GHOST.

Acts 2:4   **"And they were all filled with the Holy Ghost, and began to
                 speak with other tongues, as the Spirit gave them utterance."**

Note: To be filled with THE HOLY GHOST, who is the FATHER AND
                 THE SON, is to be filled with ALL THE WORK OF THE
                 FATHER AND THE SON and that OUR BODIES BECOME
                 LIVING EPISTLES, OR LIVING WORD, AS "THE SPIRIT
                 OF TRUTH" which IS THE HOLY GHOST fills us with
                 "ALL TRUTH."

THE FATHER AND THE SON ARE THE HOLY GHOST

FOR OUR UNDERSTANDING:

Jn 10:30   **"I AND MY FATHER ARE ONE."**

Jn 14:9 READ: (HE THAT HAS SEEN ME, HAS SEEN THE FATHER.)

Note: Every time THE HOLY GHOST was mentioned in THE
                 PROPHETS; it was referring to **THE FATHER and THE SON,
                 WHO ARE ONE.**

Let us now prove by THE WORDS OF JESUS, that **THE FATHER AND THE
SON ARE** THE HOLY GHOST.

Jn 14:23   **"Jesus answered and said unto him, <u>IF A MAN LOVE ME,
                 HE WILL KEEP MY WORDS</u>: AND MY FATHER WILL
                 LOVE HIM, AND <u>WE</u> WILL COME UNTO HIM, AND
                 MAKE OUR ABODE WITH HIM."**

THE FATHER AND THE SON ARE THE HOLY GHOST (cont.)

Positively revealing, THAT **THE FATHER AND THE SON** ARE THE HOLY GHOST, and will come and live in us (HIS TEMPLE) that THEY MADE in Genesis 1:26 in the beginning, with the above conditions!

Jn 14:18	**"I WILL NOT LEAVE YOU COMFORTLESS: I WILL COME TO YOU."**

Comment :	As Jesus and the Father are one, they would come again to us by the Baptism of the Holy Ghost, and live in us.

Again: **Jn 10:30**   **"I AND THE FATHER ARE ONE."**

Again revealing that the **FATHER AND THE SON** ARE THE HOLY GHOST.

Jn 14:28   **"... I GO AWAY, AND COME AGAIN UNTO YOU..."**

Again: **Jn 10:30**   **"I AND THE FATHER ARE ONE."**

JESUS AND THE FATHER would return on THE DAY OF PENTECOST as THE HOLY GHOST, revealing that they are the HOLY GHOST.

Jn 16:7	**NEVERTHELESS, I TELL YOU THE TRUTH, IT IS EXPEDIENT FOR YOU THAT I GO AWAY, FOR IF I GO NOT AWAY, THE COMFORTER** (which IS The Holy Ghost) **WILL NOT COME UNTO YOU, BUT IF I DEPART, I WILL SEND HIM UNTO YOU."**

Jesus went away to heaven in his human body that was glorified, and returned on THE DAY OF PENTECOST IN THE PERSON OF THE HOLY GHOST, THE FATHER AND THE SON. And will return again in HIS GLORIFIED BODY to take THE CHURCH to our home in Heaven which THE FATHER has prepared for them that LOVE HIM AND KEEP HIS COMMANDMENTS!

WHAT HAPPENED WHEN WE WERE BAPTIZED IN THE HOLY GHOST?

Jn 14:20	**"AT THAT DAY,** (Day of Pentecost) **YE SHALL KNOW THAT I AM IN MY FATHER, AND YE IN ME, AND I IN YOU."** **(Revealing once more that the Father and the Son are positively the Holy Ghost.)**

THE FATHER AND THE SON ARE THE HOLY GHOST (cont.)

The above scripture is the fulfillment of <u>THE FATHER AND THE SON</u> and their plan that was revealed in the BEGINNING, accomplished through THE BAPTISM OF THE HOLY GHOST, **BECAUSE THESE THREE ARE ONE.**

IN THE BEGINNING

1 Jn 5:7   **"AND THERE ARE THREE THAT BEAR RECORD IN HEAVEN, THE FATHER, THE WORD AND THE HOLY GHOST; <u>AND THESE THREE ARE ONE.</u>"** <u>(The Father and the Son</u> are revealed in the beginning because they are one.)

IN THE END

1 Jn 5:7   **"AND THERE ARE THREE THAT BEAR RECORD IN HEAVEN, THE FATHER, THE WORD AND THE HOLY GHOST; <u>AND THESE THREE ARE ONE.</u>"** <u>(The Father and the Son</u> are revealed in the end because they are one.)

Jn 14:20   **"AT THAT DAY,** (Day of Pentecost) **YE SHALL KNOW THAT I AM IN MY FATHER, AND YE IN ME, AND I IN YOU."** (Revealing again that the) **<u>FATHER AND THE SON</u>** (are the Holy Ghost.)

OUR LORD'S FINAL PRAYER

Jn 17:11   **"And now I am no more in the world, but these are in the world, and I come to thee. Holy Father, keep through thine own name** (JESUS) **those whom thou hast given me, THAT THEY MAY BE ONE, AS WE *ARE*."** (One as we are through the Baptism of the Holy Ghost.)

Jn 17:26   **"And I have declared unto them thy name, and will declare *it*: that the love wherewith thou hast loved me may be IN them, and I in them."**

To all the children of the Lord,

"GRACE BE UNTO YOU AND PEACE, FROM GOD THE FATHER AND OUR LORD JESUS CHRIST WHO IS BLESSED FOREVER!" AMEN.

<u>ONE MIGHT ASK, HOW WILL SATAN DECEIVE THE CHILD OF GOD?</u>

Answer: By a MINISTER of the GOSPEL OF JESUS CHRIST WHO MINISTERS THE FOLLOWING:

1)   CHANGING THE WORD OF GOD, ADDING OR TAKING AWAY FROM THE WORD OF GOD.
2)   BY APPEALING TO THE NATURAL MAN, THAT RECEIVES NOT THE THINGS OF THE SPIRIT FOR THEY ARE FOOLISHNESS UNTO HIM.
3)   BY PRINTING NEW BIBLES, AND MIXING LIES WITH THE TRUTH, THAT IF IT WERE POSSIBLE, WOULD FOOL THE VERY ELECT IN CHRIST, **ESPECIALLY WHEN THE AMERICAN STANDARD VERSION AND THE NEW INTERNATIONAL VERSIONS OF THE BIBLE ELIMINATE <u>THE VIRGIN BIRTH AND THE PRECIOUS BLOOD OF CHRIST</u>!**

As I proceed, I WILL CHALLENGE THE SUBLETY OF SATAN **BY** THE HOLY WORD OF GOD. Certain men, deceived by Satan, crept in unawares to CHANGE THE WORD OF GOD through the BLINDNESS OF THEIR HEART. The most important message from THE LORD in this hour **IS** THE BAPTISM OF THE HOLY GHOST!

THE FOLLOWING SCRIPTURES REVEAL THE SUBTLETY OF SATAN AND THE REASON FOR THIS WRITING - TO WAKE UP THE CHURCH. (AUTHORIZED KING JAMES BIBLE.)

Acts 19:1   **"And it came to pass, that Apollos was at Corinth, and Paul having passed through the upper coast, came to Ephesus, and FINDING CERTAIN DISCIPLES,** (who were Christian believers).

Acts 19:2   And Paul said, unto these Christian believers, **"HAVE YE RECEIVED THE HOLY GHOST <u>SINCE</u> YE BELEIVED?"**

The above scripture reveals that THE HOLY GHOST BAPTISM IS A SEPARATE EXPERIENCE that **follows** the BORN AGAIN experience.

THE HOLY WORD OF GOD WAS CHANGED TO READ:

"The Living Bible" reads in Acts19:2, and I quote; "DID YOU RECEIVE THE HOLY SPIRIT, **WHEN** YOU BELIEVED." It was changed by individuals who crept in unawares and who, through the BLINDNESS of their HEARTS, resisted THE HOLY WORD OF GOD regarding THE BAPTISM OF THE HOLY GHOST, when CHRIST **IS** THE HOLY GHOST, **AS THE FATHER - THE SON** and **THE HOLY GHOST** are **ONE,** AND ALSO THAT JESUS IS THE ONE THAT BAPTIZES WITH THE HOLY GHOST.

Matt 3:11	"I INDEED BAPTIZE YOU WITH WATER UNTO REPENTANCE: BUT HE THAT COMETH AFTER ME IS MIGHTIER THAN I, WHOSE SHOES I AM NOT WORTHY TO BEAR: HE SHALL BAPTIZE YOU WITH THE HOLY GHOST AND FIRE."
Jn 1:33	"AND I KNEW HIM NOT: BUT HE THAT SENT ME TO BAPTIZE WITH WATER, THE SAME SAID UNTO ME, UPON WHOM THOU SHALT SEE THE SPIRIT DESCENDING, AND REMAINING ON HIM, THE SAME IS HE WHICH BAPTIZETH WTH THE HOLY GHOST."

I say, **WAKE UP CHURCH** to the TRUTH OF GOD'S WORD and be not blinded by man's traditions and opinions that are attempting to divide and destroy THE CHURCH - when JESUS prayed that we may BE ONE!

Moreover, Jesus said in John 10:27, "MY SHEEP HEAR MY VOICE, I KNOW THEM, THEY FOLLOW ME."

My dear children of THE LORD, if there was ever a time to listen to HIS VOICE in these last days before HIS COMING, it is today, for HIS VOICE WILL NEVER DECEIVE YOU!

THE GREATEST QUESTION THAT IS ASKED TODAY

Matt 24:3-5	(This question was asked by HIS disciples,) "**...WHAT SHALL BE THE SIGNS OF THY COMING AND OF THE END OF THE WORLD?**"
	"**AND JESUS ANSWERED AND SAID UNTO THEM, TAKE HEED THAT NO MAN DECEIVE YOU.**"
	"**FOR MANY SHALL COME IN MY NAME SAYING "I AM CHRIST" AND SHALL DECEIVE MANY.**"
2 Pet 2:1	"**But there were false prophets also among the people, even as there shall be false teachers among you, who privily shall bring in damnable heresies, even denying the Lord that bought them, and bring upon themselves swift destruction.**"

2 Cor 11:14   **"And no marvel; for Satan himself is TRANSFORMED INTO AN ANGEL OF LIGHT.** Therefore it is no great thing if his ministers also be transformed as the ministers of RIGHTEOUSNESS; who's end shall be according to their works."

There is no greater way to DECEIVE the CHRISTIAN CHURCH in this hour than to CHANGE THE HOLY WORD OF GOD, in which we trust, and to print new Bibles in an attempt to do away with THE BAPTISM OF THE HOLY GHOST!!

Satan in the beginning, through his subtlety by adding and changing the Word, caused Adam through DISOBEDIENCE to THE WORD, to lose his fellowship with the Lord and caused SIN to come on the human race, BECAUSE HE LISTENED TO THE WRONG VOICE!!

That same voice, through subtlety is speaking today as he goes about like a roaring lion, seeking whom he may devour or destroy, and many Christians once more are listening to his voice as he CHALLENGES THE HOLY WORD OF GOD by distorting THE TRUTH and ADDING and TAKING AWAY FROM THE WORD OF GOD. By CHANGING the WORD, and printing many NEW BIBLES, he attempts to subvert THE PRECIOUS CHURCH OF JESUS CHRIST. The irony of it all, is that he found many who call themselves Christians to carry out his PLAN OF DECEPTION to DIVIDE THE CHURCH, when Jesus said take heed that no man (Christian) deceive you, as we can see today, when there is ONLY ONE CHURCH, and JESUS prayed to THE FATHER that we be ONE AS THEY ARE ONE.

THE PURPOSE OF THIS WRITING is to expose THE ERRORS written in "THESE **DIFFERENT** BIBLES", once and FOR ALL, and it will amaze you how they have attempted to DISTORT and remove THE PRECIOUS TRUTHS that our HEAVENLY FATHER gave us in THE AUTHORIZED KING JAMES BIBLE, which has endured its critics for hundreds of years!

WE MUST ASK OURSELVES THIS QUESTION:

Why should these individuals CHANGE THE WORD OF GOD and print NEW BIBLES, when, THE AUTHORIZED KING JAMES BIBLE reveals the POWER AND THE ANOINTING, that has been operating through THE BAPTISM OF THE HOLY GHOST, by great men of GOD, like C.T. STUD, DAVID LIVINGSTON and many others as they healed the sick, opened the deaf ears and made the lame to walk and THE BLIND to see?

"YE SHALL KNOW THE TRUTH AND THE TRUTH SHALL SET YOU FREE."

I'd like to mention in particular two versions of the Bible, "The New International Version and The New American Standard Version."

One might ask, "What is their purpose for being written in the first place?"

1)   To do away with the Baptism of the Holy Ghost.
2)   To change the Godhead where all understanding begins.
3)   To distort the truth and give a fleshly interpretation by adding to the Word and taking away from the Word the commandments of the Lord, that the children of the Lord become confused, and ask themselves, "Is it the Word of man?" Or Is it the Word of God, whose commandments we must obey?"

They do this, knowing the judgement of God for committing such ungodly acts in changing the Word and adding to it, when the Lord warned,

Deut 4:1-2   **"NOW THEREFORE HEARKEN, O ISRAEL, UNTO THE STATUTES AND UNTO THE JUDGMENTS, WHICH I TEACH YOU, FOR TO DO *THEM*, THAT YE MAY LIVE, AND GO IN AND POSSESS THE LAND WHICH THE LORD GOD OF YOUR FATHERS GIVETH YOU.**

YE SHALL NOT ADD UNTO THE WORD WHICH I COMMAND YOU, NEITHER SHALL YE DIMINISH *OUGHT* FROM IT, THAT YE MAY KEEP THE COMMANDMENTS OF THE LORD YOUR GOD WHICH I COMMAND YOU."

Rev 22:18-19   **"FOR I TESTIFY UNTO EVERY MAN THAT HEARETH THE WORDS OF THE PROPHECY OF THIS BOOK, IF ANY MAN SHALL ADD UNTO THESE THINGS, GOD SHALL ADD UNTO HIM THE PLAGUES THAT ARE WRITTEN IN THIS BOOK:**

AND IF ANY MAN SHALL TAKE AWAY FROM THE WORDS OF THE BOOK OF THIS PROPHECY, GOD SHALL TAKE AWAY HIS PART OUT OF THE BOOK OF LIFE, AND OUT OF THE HOLY CITY, AND *FROM* THE THINGS WHICH ARE WRITTEN IN THIS BOOK."

We should ask ourselves this question as Christians, **"DOES THE LORD DIVIDE HIS CHURCH THROUGH HIS HOLY WORD THAT HE HAS WRITTEN, WHEN THE SPIRIT AND THE WORD AGREE?** When each Christian is born of that Spirit?

Did the Lord in these last days change his mind and bring confusion into the body of Christ? When He said, **I AM THE LORD AND I CHANGE NOT!**

Will the changes in these Bibles regarding the Holy Word give you **POWER** over all the works of the enemy?

In the deceitfulness of their act to introduce their ungodly thoughts, they mixed the True Word of God, with their spirit of error.

As we proceed, I will endeavor to reveal to those with a true heart, the truth by exposing the falseness of their interpretation of the Word and their "speaking against it," When our Lord said, **"TO THE LAW AND THE TESTIMONY IF ANY MAN SHALL SPEAK AGAINST THIS WORD, IT IS BECAUSE THERE IS NO LIGHT IN THEM."**

As I proceed you will well understand what I meant when I said, "Put your trust in the Authorized King James Bible, for their are no ungodly lies in its pages."

THE BLOOD:

THE TRUTH:

THE AUTHORIZED KING JAMES BIBLE states in Colossians 1:14: "In whom we have redemption through His blood, even the forgiveness of sins."

THE NEW VERSIONS DO AWAY WITH THE BLOOD

THE LIE:

The New American Standard version reads and I quote Colossians 1:14:
*   "In whom we have redemption _____ **(THE BLOOD OMITTED!)** the forgiveness of sins.
The New International version reads and I quote Colossians 1:14:
*   "In whom we have redemption _____ **(THE BLOOD OMITTED!)** the forgiveness of sins.

Comment: My dear brothers and sisters in Christ, the subtlety of taking away from the Word, the most precious of all; **THE BLOOD OF JESUS CHRIST GOD'S HOLY SON,** takes away our salvation for without the shedding of blood revealed in the Father's writings, that **ALL LIFE OF THE FLESH IS IN THE BLOOD.**

Lev 17:11	**"For the life of the flesh *is* in THE BLOOD: and I have given it to you upon the altar to make an atonement for your souls: for it *is* THE BLOOD *that* maketh an atonement for the soul."**

For where there is no **SHEDDING OF BLOOD**, there shall be **NO** forgiveness of sins. If we delete from the Word, the PRECIOUS BLOOD OF CHRIST, we have done away with the crucifixion of OUR LAMB, and we are still in our sins.

THE VIRGIN BIRTH

THE TRUTH:

THE AUTHORIZED KING JAMES BIBLE states in Luke 2:33: "And Joseph and his mother marvelled at those things which were spoken of him."

THE NEW VERSIONS DO AWAY WITH THE VIRGIN BIRTH

THE LIE:

The New American Standard version reads and I quote Luke 2:33:
* "And **HIS** FATHER AND MOTHER were amazed at the things that were being said about him."

The New International Version reads and I quote Luke 2:33:
* "The CHILD'S FATHER AND MOTHER marvelled at what was said about him."

Comment:	Let us concentrate for the present time on **FATHER AND MOTHER.**

JESUS was child of the **HOLY GHOST** and Joseph was **NOT HIS FATHER!**

If they say that Joseph is his father, then they have done away with the sinless virgin birth and we have no hope.

Remember that we have only revealed two of the most important truths, that are really, the foundation of our faith.

THE VIRGIN BIRTH and the PRECIOUS BLOOD OF CHRIST. I don't think it is important to reveal all the other lies, that are written in these books, for they are too numerous to mention. For if they say there is no VIRGIN BIRTH, and omit the BLOOD OF CHRIST, we are still in our sins. As a brother and a father in Christ, I exhort you to get rid of these new Bibles mentioned, before they vex your righteous souls.

QUESTION: Where are THE FATHERS and PILLARS of THE CHURCH, that they have not cried out against THE CHANGING OF THE WORD in **Acts 19:2**? Are they DECEIVED BY SATAN as well? Are they in darkness that they cannot see where they are leading THE CHURCH OF JESUS CHRIST?

Is 8:20   (The Prophet said,) **"To the law and to the testimony: If they speak not according to this word it is because THERE IS NO LIGHT IN THEM."**

CHALLENGING SCRIPTURES REGARDING CHANGE

Gen 2:7   **"And the Lord God formed man of the dust of the ground, and breathed into his nostrils the breath of life: and man became a living soul."**

Shall THE SOUL that was CREATED BY THE WORD, now CHANGE THE WORD that created him?

One might ask, "WHAT PORTION OF THE HOLY WORD OF GOD WILL THESE MEN ATTEMPT TO CHANGE NEXT?" When our Lord Jesus IS the WORD.

Mal 3:6   *(When THE LORD SAID:)* **"FOR I AM THE LORD,** (THE WORD) **I CHANGE NOT."**

                       TO CHANGE THE WORD IS TO CHANGE JESUS WHO IS THE WORD!

I see the subtlety of Satan at work here!

IT IS TIME TO SEARCH THE HOLY SCRIPTURES IN THE AUTHORIZED KING JAMES BIBLE FOR OURSELVES, BECAUSE WE MAY BE TRUSTING IN A BIBLE LIKE THE TWO MENTIONED ABOVE THAT HAVE ELIMINATED **THE BLOOD AND THE VIRGIN BIRTH**, EVEN THOUGH THEY CONFIRM SOME TRUTH, TO THROW US OFF GUARD! FOR WITHOUT THE **VIRGIN BIRTH OF WHICH JESUS IS CHILD OF THE HOLY GHOST (AND NOT THE SON OF JOSEPH),** AND ALSO THE **PRECIOUS BLOOD OF JESUS CHRIST, GOD'S SON,** WE WOULD HAVE NO SALVATION AND WE WOULD STILL BE IN OUR SINS.

"FOR WITHOUT THE SHEDDING OF BLOOD THERE IS NO REMISSION OF SINS!"

Summary

To all the faithful ministry and my dear brothers and sisters in THE FAITH of our LORD JESUS CHRIST,

"Grace be unto you and peace from GOD THE FATHER and our LORD JESUS CHRIST."

I now conclude this message on THE TRUTH of THE BAPTISM OF THE HOLY GHOST, which has revealed THE SPIRITUAL REVELATION in the HOLY SCRIPTURES from Genesis to THE DAY OF PENTECOST when THE HOLY GHOST was poured out on the disciples of our Lord Jesus.

THIS IS THE MESSAGE the LORD laid on my heart for this hour, though I have encountered MUCH OPPOSITION, I have been faithful to all of GOD'S children in writing it, for I am your brother in CHRIST and I ask for your prayers.

My heartfelt prayer is that this message by THE WORD OF THE LORD may reach the hearts of many, and by acknowledging THE TRUTH and not man's opinions, they will preach it with POWER in every nation of the world!

THE TIME HAS COME THAT JUDGEMENT MUST BEGIN AT THE HOUSE OF GOD and we <u>ARE</u> THAT HOUSE! If our ears are closed to THE MESSAGE ON THE BAPTISM OF THE HOLY GHOST spoken of by our HEAVENLY FATHER through THE PROPHETS, and revealed unto us by HIS SON who <u>IS</u> THE WORD, I can only say what JESUS said, "THE WORDS THAT I SPEAK SHALL JUDGE THEM IN THE LAST DAY."

Finally, I leave you to make your own decision on the Truth of God's Word, to us in this writing. For the time is at hand in this Last Call to the church, that we would once and for all understand who the Holy Ghost is.

If there are dear brothers and sisters or pastors who the Word of the Lord has touched your hearts, and have any sincere questions regarding the Baptism of the Holy Ghost and the speaking in other tongues, I would be so pleased to hear from you either by mail, fax or E-mail at the addresses following the information **"ABOUT OUR CHURCH IN VANCOUVER, BRITISH COLUMBIA, CANADA."**

Finally, our love to you in our Lord Jesus Christ, who **IS** the Baptizer with the Holy Ghost.

AMEN, AND AMEN!

Pastor Ross F. Norris

About The Church

ABOUT OUR CHURCH IN VANCOUVER, BRITISH COLUMBIA, CANADA

REGISTERED WITH THE GOVERNMENT IN VICTORIA, BRITISH COLUMBIA.

THE MOTHER CHURCH IS THE NORTH SHORE CHRISTIAN CENTRE.

OUR VISION:

According to the COMMANDMENT OF OUR LORD JESUS, to go into ALL the world and preach THE GOSPEL, and to attain this end, our vision is to train and raise up young men and women that will move in THE POWER OF THE HOLY GHOST to fulfill the GREAT COMMISSION THE LORD HAS GIVEN US.

At present our vision is centered on Europe, particularly the land of Germany with many young people that are being trained to fulfill the Lord's commission. At present we also have fellowship churches in India that are catching the excitement of what the Lord is doing in this FINAL HOUR.

We warmly welcome you to contact us with all sincerity for we are members with you in THE BODY OF CHRIST.

ADDRESS:

Write to: **"THE LORD'S LAST CALL"**

Box #250-1531 Lonsdale Avenue
British Columbia, Canada
V7M 3L6

E-Mail: mail@thelordslastcall.com

Facsimile: 604-988-2970

Or contact our Website: www.thelordslastcall.com

Order Form

QTY.	Title	Price	Can. Price	Total
	THE LORD'S LAST CALL **Pastor Ross Norris**	**$12.95**	**$12.95 CN**	
	Shipping and Handling Add $3.50 for orders in the US/Add $7.50 for Global Priority			
	Sales tax (WA state residents only, add 8.6%)			
	Total enclosed			

Telephone Orders:
Call **1-800-461-1931**
Have your VISA or
MasterCard ready.

INTL. Telephone Orders:
Toll free **1-877-250-5500**
Have your credit card ready.

Fax Orders:
425-672-8597
Fill out this order form and fax.

Postal Orders:
Hara Publishing
P.O. Box 19732
Seattle, WA 98109

E-mail Orders:
harapub@foxinternet.net

Method of Payment:

☐ Check or Money Order

☐ VISA

☐ MasterCard

Expiration Date: _____
Card #: _____
Signature: _____

Name _____
Address _____
City _____ **State** ____ **Zip** _____
Phone ( ) _____ **Fax (**) _____

Quantity discounts are available.
Call (425) 776-3390 for more information.
Thank you for your order!